Learn Azure Administration

Explore cloud administration concepts with networking, computing, storage, and identity management

Kamil Mrzygłód

BIRMINGHAM—MUMBAI

Learn Azure Administration

Group Product Manager: Pavan Ramchandani
Publishing Product Manager: Neha Sharma
Book Project Manager: Ashwini Gowda
Senior Editor: Mohd Hammad
Technical Editor: Rajat Sharma
Copy Editor: Safis Editing
Proofreader: Safis Editing
Indexer: Rekha Nair
Production Designer: Shankar Kalbhor
DevRel Marketing Coordinator: MaryLou De Mello

First published: September 2020
Second edition: December 2023

Production reference: 1061223

Published by
Packt Publishing Ltd.
Grosvenor House
11 St Paul's Square
Birmingham
B3 1RB, UK

ISBN 978-1-83763-611-2

www.packtpub.com

To Klaudia, for being my soulmate for so many years

Contributors

About the author

Kamil Mrzygłód is a technical lead and technology advisor, working with multiple companies on designing and implementing Azure-based systems and platforms. He's a former Microsoft Azure **Microsoft Most Valuable Professional** (**MVP**) and certified trainer, who shares his knowledge via various channels, including conference speeches and open source projects and contributions. Kamil lives in Poland with his two cats and one dog, dedicating some of his time to video games, cooking, and traveling.

About the reviewers

Sasha Kranjac is a Microsoft **Regional Director (RD)**, Microsoft MVP in two categories (the Azure and Security categories), a **Microsoft Certified Trainer (MCT)**, an MCT Regional Lead, **Certified EC-Council Instructor (CEI)**, a CompTIA Instructor, a frequent speaker at various international conferences, user groups, and events, and a book author on cloud security, Microsoft Azure, Microsoft 365, and Windows Server. Sasha is the CEO of Kloudatech, an IT training and consulting company, a Microsoft Partner, an AWS Partner, and a CompTIA Authorized Delivery Partner, as well as the CEO of Kranjac Consulting and Training, a consulting and engineering company, which specializes in cloud security architecture, civil engineering, and CAD design.

Mustafa Toroman is a technology professional and the **Chief Technology Officer (CTO)** at run.events, a company that provides a platform to organize and manage events. He has over 20 years of experience in the IT industry and has held various technical and leadership positions in companies around the world. Mustafa has a deep understanding of software development, cloud computing, and IT infrastructure management. Mustafa is a Microsoft MVP, a frequent speaker at technology conferences and events, and a community leader, organizing meetups and events. He is also a published author and has written several books on Microsoft technologies and cloud computing.

Table of Contents

Part 2: Networking for Azure Administrator

3

Understanding Azure Virtual Networks 53

4

Exploring Azure Load Balancer 85

Part 3: Administration of Azure Virtual Machines

5

6

7

8

Configuring and Managing Disks   171

Part 4: Azure Storage for Administrators

9

Configuring Blob Storage   189

10

Azure Files and Azure File Sync   211

11

Azure Storage Security and Additional Tooling   227

Part 5: Governance and Monitoring

12

Using Azure Policy   247

13

Azure Monitor and Alerts   263

14

Azure Log Analytics   283

15

Exploring Network Watcher   299

Index   309

Other Books You May Enjoy   322

Preface

Cloud computing is one of the cornerstones of today's IT infrastructure. With platforms such as Amazon Web Services, Microsoft Azure, and Google Cloud Platform, you're able to build complex computer systems with ease and without any cumbersome management of hardware installation and supplies. Managing cloud platforms, though, is not the same as managing on-premises installations. It is a challenge, which this book intends to help you with.

In this book, you'll learn about the topics and tasks required by Azure administrators in their day-to-day activities. You can also think about it as a good introduction to the skills required to obtain Azure certifications as the book provides detailed explanations of Azure services and features, knowledge of which is necessary to become a certified Azure specialist.

During the process of writing this book, Microsoft decided to rename *Azure Active Directory* to *Microsoft Entra ID*. However, this change doesn't affect the value of the information contained within the book, so you'll be able to leverage the concepts described in exactly the same way as you'd have been able to before the rebranding process.

Who this book is for

This book is intended for everyone wanting to understand topics related to managing and configuring infrastructure in Microsoft Azure. As it focuses more on the operational aspects of cloud infrastructure, the main audience is people with experience in infrastructure management (IT administrators, SysOps, and infrastructure support engineers), though it'll be beneficial to everyone responsible for infrastructure provisioning in Microsoft Azure.

What this book covers

Chapter 1, *Azure Fundamentals*, offers an introduction to basic Microsoft Azure concepts including core Azure services such as Microsoft Entra ID and Azure Resource Manager.

Chapter 2, *Basics of Infrastructure as Code*, discusses automated deployments of infrastructure in Azure using ARM templates, Azure Bicep, and Terraform.

Chapter 3, *Understanding Azure Virtual Networks*, introduces networking in Microsoft Azure, starting with general virtual network concepts, best practices, and configuration options.

Chapter 4, *Exploring Azure Load Balancer*, sees us implement load balancing in Microsoft Azure using Azure Load Balancer in connection with Azure Virtual Machines.

Chapter 5, Provisioning Azure Virtual Machines, discusses the fundamentals of virtual machines in Microsoft Azure, including concepts such as provisioning, automation, and storage.

Chapter 6, Configuring Virtual Machine Extensions, examines how to configure extensions for virtual machines in Azure to allow you to enhance the configuration and service provisioning process.

Chapter 7, Configuring Backups, shows you how to configure backups for virtual machines using Azure Backup.

Chapter 8, Configuring and Managing Disks, discusses working with managed disks in Microsoft Azure, including different disk types, performance options, and cost optimizations.

Chapter 9, Configuring Blob Storage, examines how to store files in Azure Storage using Blob Storage for future integrations and services.

Chapter 10, Azure Files and Azure File Sync, looks at working with file shares in Microsoft Azure as an alternative to file shares configured on-premises.

Chapter 11, Azure Storage Security and Additional Tooling, uncovers some advanced topics related to storage in Microsoft Azure including replication, security, and automation.

Chapter 12, Using Azure Policy, looks at how to set up automated governance of infrastructure in Microsoft Azure using both built-in and native policies.

Chapter 13, Azure Monitor and Alerts, introduces monitoring in Microsoft Azure with Azure Monitor, including configuring alerts.

Chapter 14, Log Analytics, examines how to aggregate logs in Microsoft Azure with Kusto queries run within a Log Analytics workspace.

Chapter 15, Exploring Network Watcher, shows how to validate and debug network flows in Microsoft Azure using Network Watcher and its capabilities.

To get the most out of this book

To get started with the book, make sure you have access to a Microsoft Azure subscription, and that you are the owner of that subscription. If you don't have such a subscription, take a look at a free account for Microsoft Azure at `https://azure.microsoft.com/en-us/free`.

Software/hardware covered in the book	Operating system requirements
Azure PowerShell	Windows, macOS, or Linux
Azure CLI	Windows, macOS, or Linux
cURL	Windows, macOS, or Linux
PuTTY	Windows, macOS, or Linux
AzCopy	Windows, macOS, or Linux

If you are using the digital version of this book, we advise you to type the code yourself.

Code in Action

The Code in Action videos for this book can be viewed at `https://packt.link/GTX9F`.

Conventions used

There are a number of text conventions used throughout this book.

`Code in text`: Indicates code words in text, database table names, folder names, filenames, file extensions, pathnames, dummy URLs, user input, and Twitter handles. Here is an example: "Look at one of the returned fields called `primaryEndpoints`:"

A block of code is set as follows:

```
{
    "creationTime": "2023-07-29T20:44:48.299346+00:00",
    "keyName": "key1",
    "permissions": "FULL",
    "value": "K4gPP5UuDwl2/…+AStZ6ODSw=="
},
```

Any command-line input or output is written as follows:

```
az policy definition list --query "[].{Name:name,
DisplayName:displayName}" -o table
```

Bold: Indicates a new term, an important word, or words that you see onscreen. For instance, words in menus or dialog boxes appear in **bold**. Here is an example: "To simplify things for now, we'll use the basic configuration by clicking on the **Create storage** button."

> **Tips or important notes**
> Appear like this.

Get in touch

Feedback from our readers is always welcome.

General feedback: If you have questions about any aspect of this book, email us at `customercare@packtpub.com` and mention the book title in the subject of your message.

Errata: Although we have taken every care to ensure the accuracy of our content, mistakes do happen. If you have found a mistake in this book, we would be grateful if you would report this to us. Please visit `www.packtpub.com/support/errata` and fill in the form.

Piracy: If you come across any illegal copies of our works in any form on the internet, we would be grateful if you would provide us with the location address or website name. Please contact us at copyright@packt.com with a link to the material.

If you are interested in becoming an author: If there is a topic that you have expertise in and you are interested in either writing or contributing to a book, please visit authors.packtpub.com.

Share Your Thoughts

Once you've read *Learn Azure Administration – Second Edition*, we'd love to hear your thoughts! Scan the QR code below to go straight to the Amazon review page for this book and share your feedback.

https://packt.link/r/1837636117

Your review is important to us and the tech community and will help us make sure we're delivering excellent quality content.

Download a free PDF copy of this book

Thanks for purchasing this book!

Do you like to read on the go but are unable to carry your print books everywhere?

Is your eBook purchase not compatible with the device of your choice?

Don't worry, now with every Packt book you get a DRM-free PDF version of that book at no cost.

Read anywhere, any place, on any device. Search, copy, and paste code from your favorite technical books directly into your application.

The perks don't stop there, you can get exclusive access to discounts, newsletters, and great free content in your inbox daily.

Follow these simple steps to get the benefits:

1. Scan the QR code or visit the link below

https://packt.link/free-ebook/9781837636112

2. Submit your proof of purchase
3. That's it! We'll send your free PDF and other benefits to your email directly

Part 1:
Introduction to Azure for Azure Administrators

In this part, you'll learn about the fundamentals of Microsoft Azure, including topics such as basic resource structure, deployment models, identity management, and authorization. You'll also read about automated deployments of infrastructure, using tools such as ARM templates, Azure Bicep, and Terraform.

This part has the following chapters:

1

Azure Fundamentals

Getting started with Microsoft Azure is not an easy task. It's a dynamic, robust, and cross-disciplinary environment that requires lots of knowledge and attention to get things done as per best practices. We'll start our journey with a detailed explanation of the most fundamental topics that are important from the Azure administrator's point of view.

In this chapter, we're going to cover the following main topics:

- Azure Resource Manager, including main components in relation to Azure resources
- Entra ID for basic understanding of identity concepts in Azure
- Authorization using RBAC and ABAC with a focus on role definitions and assignments
- Basic toolset – the Azure CLI, Azure PowerShell, and Cloud Shell

Technical requirements

For the exercises from this chapter, you'll need the following:

- The Azure CLI (`https://learn.microsoft.com/en-us/cli/azure/install-azure-cli`)
- Azure PowerShell (`https://learn.microsoft.com/en-us/powershell/azure/install-az-ps?view=azps-9.4.0`)
- Command line of any kind (either the one available in your operating system or your favorite one)

The Code in Action video for this book can be viewed at: `https://packt.link/GTX9F`

Exploring Azure Resource Manager

We cannot start talking about Microsoft Azure without describing one of the most important available parts of its ecosystem, which is **Azure Resource Manager** (or its much simpler abbreviation, **ARM**). It's a foundation of all services in Azure, which allows for provisioning new instances of resources and interacting with existing ones. It's impossible to create a database, disk, or virtual machine without calling one of the available endpoints of this API.

> **Important note**
>
> Don't confuse ARM being Azure's management layer with the ARM processor architecture. For the sake of this book, if we at any point talk about both the API and the availability of ARM processors in Azure, we'll make a clear distinction in that section.

Let's take a deeper dive into the topic to see what benefits ARM grants and what kinds of functionalities we can leverage for our needs.

Architecture and terminology of ARM

Although ARM is one of the most important elements where Azure is concerned, it's not as difficult to understand as many people suppose. Let's look at the following architecture diagram:

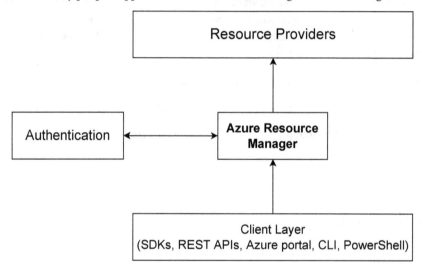

Figure 1.1 – High-level architecture diagram of Azure Resource Manager

To get a better understanding, we need to explain all the presented components a little bit:

- **Client layer** – A layer that is available for each client using Azure. It consists of various SDKs, the Azure CLI, Azure PowerShell, REST API, and, of course, the Azure portal. It's basically an access layer for anybody who wants to interact with cloud resources.

- **Authentication** – Components responsible for authenticating and authorizing requests coming to ARM. It involves Entra ID and RBAC/ABAC authorization. We'll cover that topic a little later in the chapter.

- **Resource providers** – APIs responsible for provisioning, configuring, and managing resources in Azure. It's a collection of REST operations that can be called and are given the responsibility to interact with a connected resource type.

For now, that's all you need to know – of course, there's still more to uncover, but we'll get there later in the book. To complete the introduction, let's briefly cover one more concept called **Infrastructure as Code** (**IaC**), which is connected to ARM.

There are lots of different methods when it comes to deploying resources in Azure. You can do it manually in the Azure portal, use the CLI (both the Azure CLI and Azure PowerShell), or download the SDK and write a simple application in your favorite language to provision something in the cloud. This list is already quite impressive, but it's not yet complete.

The general idea of IaC is to use a text file(s) to automate and unify a way of creating and managing resources in the cloud. ARM natively supports two different tools:

- ARM templates (`https://learn.microsoft.com/en-us/azure/azure-resource-manager/templates/overview`)

- Azure Bicep (`https://learn.microsoft.com/en-us/azure/azure-resource-manager/bicep/`)

Both tools are officially supported by Microsoft and enable you to even work with not-yet-released features (which include private preview services and functionalities, for example). Using an SDK to define your infrastructure and manage it that way could also be considered IaC, but in this book, we'll simplify that definition. We'll talk more about IaC in *Chapter 2*.

Scopes

The second topic that is important to understand when talking about ARM is scopes. Scopes are crucial because they're related to resources, policies, and role assignments. In other words, they define multiple layers of your cloud infrastructure and can be used for separating applications and security segmentation.

In Azure, there are five different scopes available:

- Tenant
- Management group
- Subscription
- Resource group
- Resource

All these scopes have the following dependencies on each other:

- Tenants can be deployed separately without an Azure subscription assigned
- Tenants can have multiple subscriptions assigned
- Management groups are optional and may contain zero or multiple Azure subscriptions

- Subscriptions are the main layer of separation for other resources and can be assigned to both tenants and management groups

- Resource groups are required for the deployment of resources that are scoped to resource groups

- Resources require a higher scope to be deployed

We can also visualize these dependencies with the following diagram:

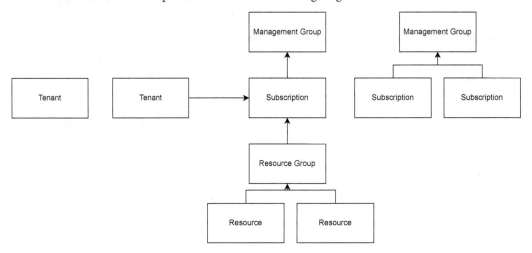

Figure 1.2 – Dependencies between different ARM scopes

Let's now talk a little bit about smaller details where scopes are concerned.

Target scope

Multiple resources can be scoped to a given parent scope. For instance, to deploy a subscription, you need a tenant. To deploy a resource group, you need a subscription. When talking about resources in general, you need to understand their scope before deployment.

> **Important note**
>
> In Azure, there are resources that can be deployed on multiple scopes, so there's no exact target scope to select. These are called **extension resources**. An example would be role assignment – it can be deployed on the subscription, resource group, or resource level and works as an extension to the parent resource.

Most of the time, you don't need to worry about the target scope as it'll be automatically selected, or you'll be given hints about the correct decision.

Extension resources

Some resources in Azure can extend other resources. This means that they don't provide a typical child-to-parent relation and instead can be used as a form of adding functionality to other resources.

The simplest example of an extension resource is a resource lock. Once added to a resource level, it can prevent it from deletion or set it as read-only.

Tenants and subscriptions

A tenant can have zero, one, or multiple subscriptions assigned. You can move subscriptions between tenants. This works well if you want to limit access to a subscription to a limited number of people (it can be done via RBAC/ABAC, but there are scenarios in which separation must be much stricter). It can also be used to transfer ownership of a subscription to another company or client. The only thing to remember is that doing this doesn't always transfer the financial details related to a subscription. In such cases, you may need to contact Azure Support.

Resource groups

While we'll talk about tenants, subscriptions, management groups, and other concepts very often in this book, there's one thing that is basically the bread and butter of Azure administration. That thing is a resource group.

Resource groups are the main deployment scope for most Azure services, though, from the perspective of administration, they become even more important because they're also a target of various policies defining allowed resource types and configurations. Resource groups can be treated as metadata storage for resources and are often referred to as resource containers.

> **Important note**
>
> When a resource group is deployed, one needs to select its location. While it may be unintuitive in the beginning, you'll quickly get used to it. Selecting a proper location may be important from the compliance point of view when you need to ensure that all the infrastructure-related data is stored within compliant locations.

As mentioned before, while lots of resources require a resource group to be deployed, being an Azure administrator requires a wider perspective, as lots of resources you'll be interested in can be deployed on higher scopes. Still, most of the development of cloud infrastructure in Azure happens on the resource group level.

Resource groups are free and provide logical separation of resources in Azure. This means that resources from one resource group can connect to another without additional configuration. If you want to limit connectivity and apply network policies, you'll need to use dedicated resources such as virtual networks, network security groups, and firewalls.

Tags

Many resources in Azure can be tagged. A tag is a simple label consisting of a key and a value, which can be applied on the resource level for grouping, metadata, or compliance reasons. Normally, resources don't inherit tags from their parents, though there are exceptions (including managed resource groups created for resources such as Azure Kubernetes Service or Azure Databricks) that automatically get tags applied to a parent resource.

Remember that tags are stored as plain text. Don't attempt to store any sensitive or secret value there.

Quotas and limits

In Azure, you cannot deploy resources without limits. This means that there are certain quotas, depending on the resource type, which will block deployment exceeding a limit. For example, you may initially have a quota of 10 vCores per virtual machine family, which is considered a soft limit. If you feel that you need more, you can manually increase it on your subscription level.

Besides soft limits, there are also hard limits. While soft limits can be increased, a hard limit is something you normally cannot exceed. Individual agreements, consulted on a per-scenario basis, are possible after reaching out to Azure Support.

With some basics of ARM covered, let's now proceed to Entra ID – a service that is very closely related to ARM but serves a different purpose and can be used without having an Azure subscription.

Microsoft Entra ID

Microsoft Entra ID (previously referred to as **Entra ID** or **AAD**) is a cloud service that is responsible for managing cloud-based identities. In other words, it's a directory of users, applications, and devices that are *centralized* and managed within defined boundaries (tenant). As mentioned earlier, it can be used with or without other Azure resources (such as subscriptions, resource groups, or cloud services).

> **Important note**
>
> Don't confuse Microsoft Entra ID with Active Directory. Although they are quite similar in their functionalities and general purposes, Entra ID is not a direct replacement for its on-premises counterpart. It's rather a service that addresses gaps in common on-premises environments by enabling an organization to provide hybrid identities for its principals.

To get started, we'll discuss a little bit of terminology regarding the service.

Terminology

As Entra ID is quite a huge cloud component, it'll be difficult in the beginning to understand all the concepts. We'll focus on the most important ones and try to introduce advanced features a little bit later.

Here are the most popular concepts used when talking about Entra ID:

- **Tenant** – Simply put, a tenant is an Entra ID directory that contains users, applications, devices, and all the configuration related to the service.

- **Identity** – This is an object that can be anything that can be authenticated. Depending on the context, it could be a user, application, or external service.

- **Entra ID roles** – These are groups of permissions that allow a given object to perform a set of operations. Note that Entra ID roles are different than the roles that you'll use in ARM.

- **Entra ID licenses** – There are multiple tiers of Entra ID that offer different sets of functionalities. Depending on the chosen tier, there's either no charge or a charge per license.

There are also things such as service principals, app registrations, and enterprise applications, which we'll describe later in the chapter.

Users and groups

In Entra ID, the most basic principal types are users and groups. A user is a person who got their account created in an Entra ID tenant. A group is a collection of users who were put in the same container.

User and their username

When a user is created, they get their username and password that are assigned by the Entra ID tenant administrator. A username is an equivalent of an email address, though it doesn't mean that the user can automatically use it in their email client (in fact, it depends on the organization's setup – a username in an Entra ID tenant may not reflect an email address used by a user).

To get things a little bit clearer, let's imagine your company is named ITMasters and owns the `itmasters.com` domain. If there's somebody in your company named John Doe, they most probably have an email address like `john.doe@itmasters.com`.

This email address is used for both internal and external communication. Now, your boss has asked you to create an Entra ID tenant. Once the tenant is created, it automatically assigns the `<yourcompany>.onmicrosoft.com` domain to it. If you decide to create a user now, they'll get the following username:

```
john.doe@itmasters.onmicrosoft.com
```

As you can see, the same person will have the following setup:

- Email address: `john.doe@itmasters.com`

- Entra ID username: `john.doe@itmasters.onmicrosoft.com`

Even though the Entra ID username looks like an email address, it's not usable out of the box unless you introduce a change in the DNS zone, mapping this domain to your mail server. Fortunately, it's possible to map a custom domain to an Entra ID tenant. We'll describe that shortly.

Creating a user

The simplest way to create a user is to use either the Azure CLI or Azure PowerShell. Let's see the syntax:

```
// Remember to run `az login` or `Connect-AzAccount` as the first step

// Azure CLI
az ad user create --display-name <display-name> \
  --password <password> \
  --user-principal-name <username>@<domain>

// Azure PowerShell
$PasswordProfile = New-Object -TypeName Microsoft.Open.AzureAD.Model.
PasswordProfile
$PasswordProfile.Password = "<Password>"
New-AzureADUser -DisplayName "<display-name>" -PasswordProfile
$PasswordProfile -UserPrincipalName "<username>@<domain>"
-AccountEnabled $true
```

Let's clarify those commands a little bit. As you can see, both the Azure CLI and Azure PowerShell require the same parameters (there are many other optional parameters available, but we're not going to cover them here):

- Display name
- Password
- Username + domain

Display name and password are common parameters that are used to define the name of a user, which will be displayed (display name) with their password. There's also a username and domain, which have the following requirement: the value of the domain parameter must reflect one of the validated domains.

For example, if you created an Entra ID tenant and assigned a custom domain (itmasters.com), you'll have two validated domains available:

- itmasters.onmicrosoft.com
- itmasters.com

Now, when creating a user and defining their username, the following values would be accepted:

- john.doe@itmasters.onmicrosoft.com
- john.doe@itmasters.com

Assigning `john.doe@itheroes.com` couldn't work unless you validate that you are the owner of that domain and then assign it to your Entra ID tenant.

Group types

In Entra ID, a group can be one of the following two types:

- **Security** – Used for simplifying the management of roles and permissions
- **Microsoft 365** – Used for extending the capabilities of a group with a shared mailbox, calendar, and files

As Microsoft 365 groups are a concept that works mostly with Microsoft 365 tools, we won't use them in this book. However, if your organization is working on integration with that platform, it will become helpful to you at some point.

Membership types

In Entra ID, you can select one of the available membership types. Each type defines a slightly different way of assigning members to a group:

- **Assigned** – You manually decide who is a member of a group and what their permissions are.
- **Dynamic user** – You can use the dynamic membership rule for the automated process of assigning and removing a user from a group. This feature is based on the user's attributes and monitors them for possible changes.
- **Dynamic device** – This works in the same way as the dynamic user membership type, but in this case, it refers to devices.

> **Important note**
> The use of dynamic groups in Entra ID requires a paid license – Entra ID Premium P1 or Intune for Education.

Most Entra ID groups you'll work with will be groups with the membership type set to **Assigned**. Still, the use of dynamic assignments and removals may be helpful in cases where you're looking for optimizations in the process of group management.

Creating a group

Creating a group in Entra ID is even simpler than creating a user, as the only thing you need is to provide a name for a group and its members. There is, however, one *gotcha* – neither the CLI nor PowerShell, by default, enable you to provide advanced configuration of a group. That means that you cannot create an Entra ID group with a dynamic membership type out of the box, and you need to either install an appropriate extension or leverage the Azure portal or Entra ID admin center.

For the sake of our exercise, we'll go for a simple example with a standard group using the assigned membership type:

```
// Remember to run `az login` or `Connect-AzAccount` as the first step

// Azure CLI
az ad group create --display-name <display-name> --mail-nickname
<display-name>
// Azure PowerShell
New-AzureADGroup -DisplayName "<display-name>" -MailEnabled $false
-SecurityEnabled $true -MailNickName "<display-name>"
```

As you can see, there's a small difference between running the same command using the Azure CLI and Azure PowerShell. In the Azure CLI, you need to provide both a display name and a mail alias for that group (though, as we're not using Microsoft 365 groups, it won't matter). Azure PowerShell requires providing two additional parameters:

- `MailEnabled` – indicating whether mail is enabled for that group
- `SecurityEnabled` – indicating whether this group is a security group

Besides some differences in syntax, those two commands will create a group with the same configuration.

Applications and service principals

Users and groups are not the only concept when it comes to creating objects in Entra ID for managing access. Sometimes, you want to run a service or an application and give users or groups access to cloud resources. In those scenarios, Entra ID comes with a concept of applications and service principals, which work as an artificial user that can be assigned to an object outside the Entra ID directory.

Let's consider the following situation. Somebody deployed an application to Azure; it's a basic web application that connects to a database for obtaining data. Normally, that application can access the database using a connection string. An alternative would be to give it *personality*, so we can treat it as any other object inside Entra ID.

Another scenario would be an automation script that reads the metadata of Azure resources and builds a report indicating the current inventory of your cloud environment. As ARM integrates with Entra ID, that script must obtain a token that will be validated. To avoid passing our own username and password (which would be a serious security flaw), we could think about giving it an identity and receive a token based on that.

All these challenges can be solved by using applications and service principals in Entra ID. We'll describe them in detail.

Service principals

Any entity trying to access a resource secured by Entra ID needs to have some kind of representation. If we're talking about users or groups, things are simple – they are represented by appropriate objects in the directory. If that entity is an abstract concept, such as an application, script, or virtual machine, things require more advanced configuration.

In Entra ID, objects that are not users or groups will be represented by service principals. There are three different kinds available:

- **Application** – When you want to give access to Azure resources to an application or script, you can create an application object in Entra ID. Once that object is created, you may create a corresponding service principal object assigned to it. Service principal creation will also happen if the application is given consent to configured permissions (in scenarios where it can act on behalf of the user).

- **Managed identity** – This is a very specific kind of service principal as it's closely connected to the development of applications and systems in Azure. The purpose of managed identity is to eliminate a need to programmatically obtain credentials for accessing Azure resources. It is assigned on a resource level and can be used from within the application's code. We'll talk more about it later in *Chapter 11*.

- **Legacy** – This is an old concept existing for backward compatibility. Before applications were added to Entra ID, service principals worked in a very similar way to the current app registration feature, which we'll discuss in a moment. As this is a legacy feature, we'll not use it throughout this book.

Let's now talk a little bit more about a layer above service principals, which is the application layer.

Application

When talking about applications in Entra ID, we need to make a distinction between two related concepts:

- Application registration
- Application object

We already know that under the hood, each application consists of a service principal. However, a service principal is used to represent an application object on the authentication/authorization level. Before that happens, we need to delegate identity and access management to Entra ID. This is what application registration is for.

When we create application registration, we configure the way it's going to be used. We can decide whether it's a single or multi-tenant application. If we plan to use it to interact with user authentication flows, we'll configure how authentication will be performed and how users will be redirected.

Once registration is completed, each application obtains a unique identifier (named `ApplicationId` or `ClientId`). This identifier will come in handy when connecting an application to other resources or creating role assignments.

Creating an application

To discuss applications in detail, let's create one using the command line. Conceptually, this exercise isn't much more difficult than creating a user or a group. However, we'll split our demonstration between the Azure CLI and Azure PowerShell as they require slightly different approaches.

In the Azure CLI, you can simply use the following command:

```
// Remember to run `az login` or `Connect-AzAccount` as the first step
az ad app create --display-name <display-name>
```

This will create an application with the provided display name and default parameters. Note that we're not passing additional configurations such as key type, optional claims, or delegated permissions (though it's, of course, possible in more advanced scenarios).

In Azure PowerShell, you'll need to install an additional Entra ID module:

```
Install-Module AzureAD
```

Then, we can create an application in the same way as in the Azure CLI:

```
// Remember to run `az login` or `Connect-AzAccount` as the first step
New-AzureADApplication -DisplayName "<display-name>"
```

The output of running these commands depends on the environment (the CLI versus PowerShell), but the result will be the same. Assuming I named my application `AzureAdministrator01`, I should be able to find its details using one of the available commands (`az ad app show` or `Get-AzureADApplication`). Unfortunately, it's not as straightforward as we'd like it to be. Let's see how to obtain that information.

Finding application details

As mentioned previously, we can use one of the two available commands for fetching information about an application:

- `az ad app show`
- `Get-AzureADApplication`

These two commands serve the same purpose but are used differently. The easiest way to get an application is to use its `ApplicationId`. `ApplicationId` is a unique identifier that is assigned to each application in Azure. If we know what value our application has, the whole thing will be a piece of cake. If we don't, we need to approach it using available alternatives.

`Get-AzureADApplication` has a parameter called `-Filter`. Inside such a filter, we can provide the field and value we're looking for. For example, for the aforementioned `AzureAdministrator01`, we could use the following command:

```
Get-AzureADApplication -Filter "DisplayName eq 'AzureAdministrator01'"
```

We'll get a result with three columns – `ObjectId`, `ApplicationId`, and `DisplayName`. We'll describe the difference between `ObjectId` and `ApplicationId` in a second.

In the Azure CLI, we could use a similar command, but the problem is that it accepts only one parameter. That parameter is `-id` and can be either `ObjectId`, `ApplicationId`, or the URI of the application. Not very helpful, is it? Fortunately, we could use a workaround with the following command:

```
az ad app list --display-name "AzureAdministrator01"
```

Alternatively, we could also leverage the `-filter` parameter like so:

```
az ad app list --filter "DisplayName eq 'AzureAdministrator01'"
```

All these commands can be used in the same context (though, obviously, the returned object will be slightly different for the CLI and PowerShell).

ObjectId versus ApplicationId

There's always a little confusion when people realize that an application in Entra ID has two separate identifiers. When it comes to passing the correct identifier, there's a moment of hesitation – should I use `ObjectId` or `ApplicationId`? Fortunately, the answer is quite simple.

We mentioned previously that when an application is registered in Entra ID, there's a possibility to create a service principal so that the application can be authenticated and security policies can be applied to it. While the service principal itself is a separate being (at least conceptually), it's attached to each application registration.

You can create a service principal for an application using the Azure CLI:

```
az ad sp create --id "<application-id>"
```

Once this command completes, it'll create a new service principal object in Entra ID, which will be linked to your application. You can confirm that the service principal is created by running the following command:

```
az ad sp show --id "<application-id>"
```

The result will be a JSON object, which will contain an `appId` field containing the value of the `ApplicationId` field of your application. So, there's even more confusion – now we have three separate identifiers (`appId` being the same for both objects, and two separate `objectId` identifiers):

- **Application**:
  - `appId` – 87be43fc-f329-4f1b-a6ad-9f70499e4e1d
  - `objectId` – f2b23bfe-53be-4ed4-8ba5-366b1f2fd06f

- **Service principal**:
  - `appId` – 87be43fc-f329-4f1b-a6ad-9f70499e4e1d
  - `objectId` – eed243a8-356e-4d5c-96bf-c603895a9645

> **Important note**
>
> The values of the fields presented previously will be different for each application and service principal you create. Don't expect that they'll be the same as in the examples from this book.

As you can see, the field that links both objects is `appId`. On the other hand, `objectId` is different for each of them. It's important to remember how these fields are interpreted:

- `appId` is an identifier of an application
- `objectId` of an application is an identifier of that application within the Entra ID directory
- `objectId` from a service principal is an identifier of a service principal within the Entra ID directory

This distinction will become very important, for instance, when assigning a role to an Azure resource for an application. As a service principal is used for all the features related to security, you will need to use its `objectId` to create the proper assignment. `appId`, on the other hand, will be used when referring to an application itself.

Authenticating as a service principal

When using the Azure CLI or Azure PowerShell, you can use the following commands to authenticate:

```
Az login // CLI
Connect-AzAccount // PowerShell
```

They allow you to log in as a user and get access to resources within your Azure subscriptions.

> **Important note**
>
> The prior commands can be used even when there's no subscription linked to an account. In such a scenario, you may need to use the `--allow-no-subscriptions` option in the Azure CLI to ignore the default mechanism of selecting a default subscription.

A scenario when you log in as a user is not always something you want – in fact, you will face many situations when you want to avoid providing your own credentials (e.g., when running an automation script). We talked a little bit about creating application registration and service principals. Let's see how to use them to authenticate.

Each application in Entra ID can have credentials generated, which could be either a password or a certificate. You can list them using the Azure CLI, for instance, like so:

```
az ad app credential list --id "<application-id>"
```

As you can see, for this command, we are using the value of the `appId` field we saw earlier. For now, as this is probably an application we just created, there are credentials generated. We'll change that with the following command:

```
az ad app credential reset --id "<application-id>"
```

As a result, you should receive output like mine:

```
{
  "appId": "87be43fc-f329-4f1b-a6ad-9f70499e4e1d",
  "password": "TaInm~…",
  "tenant": "c2d4fe14-…-5a65748fd6c9"
}
```

Note the value of the `password` field – we'll use it in a moment.

Once we have generated credentials, let's see whether we can authenticate as an application. Use one of the following commands:

```
// Azure CLI
az login --service-principal --username "87be43fc-f329-4f1b-a6ad-
9f70499e4e1d" --password "TaInm~…" --tenant "c2d4fe14-…-5a65748fd6c9"
--allow-no-subscriptions

// Azure PowerShell
$Credential = New-Object -TypeName System.Management.Automation.
PSCredential -ArgumentList "87be43fc-f329-4f1b-a6ad-9f70499e4e1d",
"TaInm~…"
Connect-AzAccount -ServicePrincipal -TenantId "c2d4fe14-…-
5a65748fd6c9" -Credential $Credential
```

Here's a short clarification – to authenticate as an application, we must use three parameters:

- `ApplicationId`
- `TenantId`
- `Password`

In the Azure CLI, we're also passing `--allow-no-subscriptions` as our application hasn't been added to any Azure resources yet. Once authenticated, you will act as a non-user – the policies and roles normally applied to you as a user are no longer there because you're not using your own account.

This scenario is very common in all the cases where you need to delegate running a script or an application to an object, which can be controlled by other members of your team or organization. Throughout the book, you will see that using an application (or service principal) will become one of the most common actions you do in Azure.

Let's extend our knowledge of Entra ID with the next section of this chapter, where we discuss authorization using RBAC and ABAC.

Authorization using RBAC and ABAC

So far, we've talked mostly about objects in Entra ID, which can be authenticated. Before we take a step forward, let's quickly recap what authentication and authorization are. Understanding this distinction is important to fully understand the concepts we're about to cover:

- **Authentication** – This answers the question of *Who/what wants to access a resource?* It's a process that tells you what object is behind a request.

- **Authorization** – This answers the question of *Is that object allowed to access that resource?* This process is responsible for making sure that an authenticated object has the necessary permissions to make a request.

As you can see, most of the time, authorization cannot exist without authentication. Alternative scenarios are possible (mostly in cases where we don't care who or what makes a request and base the authorization mechanism on a key or certificate passed along). However, in this book, all the scenarios we're going to cover will follow the authentication and authorization process.

We know the difference between key concepts related to authorization, so let's now talk a little bit about RBAC and ABAC. These abbreviations (or concepts) are not unique to Azure – in fact, you can find them in other cloud providers and even on-premises environments. If you don't know what they mean, here's a short introduction:

- **Role-based access control** (**RBAC**): This is an authorization mechanism that is based on roles assigned to an object. Each role consists of one or many permissions that define granular access to multiple operations.

- **Attribute-based access control** (**ABAC**): This concept is like RBAC, but instead of explicitly assigned roles, it works based on attributes, which can be assigned to resources and objects. Then, authorization is based on checking whether an object and resource have the same attribute.

While initially, both RBAC and ABAC will look similar, you'll quickly realize that though they serve the same purpose, they allow different security models.

RBAC

In Azure, RBAC works by combining a role definition, a role assignment, and a security principal, which gets a role assigned to it. Each role is assigned on a specific level (a scope, as we discussed when talking about ARM). This can be visualized with the following diagram:

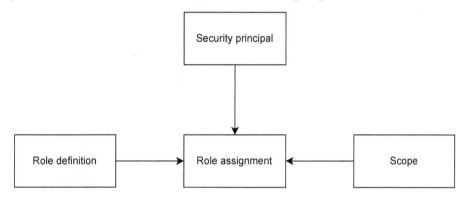

Figure 1.3 – Diagram of RBAC in Azure

Let's discuss these concepts in detail now.

Role definition

Each role has its own definition. A definition is represented as a JSON document containing allowed actions that can (or cannot) be performed when the role is assigned to a security principal. An example definition of a Reader role (one of many in-built roles available) looks like this:

```
{
    "assignableScopes": [
    "/"
    ],
    "description": "View all resources, but does not allow you to make
any changes.",
    "id": "/subscriptions/cf70b558…-9048-ebcefb926adf/providers/
Microsoft.Authorization/roleDefinitions/acdd72a7-3385-48ef-bd42-
f606fba81ae7",
    "name": "acdd72a7-3385-48ef-bd42-f606fba81ae7",
```

```
    "permissions": [
      {
        "actions": [
          "*/read"
        ],
        "dataActions": [],
        "notActions": [],
        "notDataActions": []
      }
    ],
    "roleName": "Reader",
    "roleType": "BuiltInRole",
    "type": "Microsoft.Authorization/roleDefinitions"
}
```

As you can see, each definition has a couple of fields, which define how the role is interpreted:

- `assignableScopes` – tells us what scope a role can be assigned

- `description` – human-friendly description of a role

- `id` – unique identifier of a role (role definitions, like many other Azure concepts, are resources themselves)

- `name` – unique name of a role definition (do not confuse it with `roleName`, which is a human-friendly name of a role)

- `permissions` – an array of available permissions that define allowed/disallowed operations

- `roleName` – human-friendly name of a role

- `roleType` – information about the origin of a role (whether it's an in-built/custom role)

- `type` – resource type (the same for each role definition)

It may be a little bit overwhelming for now, but you'll quickly learn how to handle definitions and even build custom ones. For now, the only clarification needed is on permissions. As you probably realized, there are four different fields defining them:

- `actions` – operations allowed on the Azure control plane

- `dataActions` – operations allowed on the Azure data plane

- `notActions` – operations disallowed on the Azure control plane

- `notDataActions` – operations disallowed on the Azure data plane

Before we proceed, we need to define what the control and data planes are.

Control and data planes

In Azure, when performing operations on a resource level, you can interact with one of the available planes:

- Control plane
- Data plane

The control plane consists of operations that work on the ARM level. As each operation performed against it ends up sending a request to the REST endpoint, you can easily find it by investigating the underlying URL. If it starts with `https://management.azure.com`, you know that it's a control plane you're working with.

> **Important note**
> The ARM URL may be different depending on your Azure environment. Azure Government, Azure Germany, and Azure China have different endpoints available. While we're not going to describe alternative environments in this book, most of the examples will be relevant no matter which one you're using on a daily basis.

On the other hand, when the data plane is in play, it's not limited to REST API requests. While many operations performed on the data plane in Azure will be standard HTTP calls (such as managing secrets in Azure Key Vault or many operations in Azure Cognitive Services), there will still be some actions that don't use a typical REST endpoint. That includes logging in to Azure Virtual Machines and managing Azure SQL Database via SQL queries.

You may wonder how control and data plane operations affect your work. Well, depending on the plane type, you may need to implement different means to manage, control, and secure Azure resources. As many data plane operations may skip policies configured in your cloud environment, additional tools and processes will be needed to keep everything in control.

Creating a custom role

Azure has lots of built-in roles such as Reader, Contributor, and Owner. Many services also provide their own roles, which can be used to limit granted permissions. When talking about role definition, we used the Reader role as an example. Let's compare it with another role that is also built in but much more specialized. Here's a definition of the Storage Blob Data Reader role:

```
{
    "assignableScopes": [
      "/"
    ],
    "description": "Allows for read access to Azure Storage blob
```

```
containers and data",
    "id": "/subscriptions/cf70b558-...-9048-ebcefb926adf/providers/
Microsoft.Authorization/roleDefinitions/2a2b9908-6ea1-4ae2-8e65-
a410df84e7d1",
    "name": "2a2b9908-6ea1-4ae2-8e65-a410df84e7d1",
    "permissions": [
      {
        "actions": [
          "Microsoft.Storage/storageAccounts/blobServices/containers/
read",
          "Microsoft.Storage/storageAccounts/blobServices/
generateUserDelegationKey/action"
        ],
        "dataActions": [
          "Microsoft.Storage/storageAccounts/blobServices/containers/
blobs/read"
        ],
        "notActions": [],
        "notDataActions": []
      }
    ],
    "roleName": "Storage Blob Data Reader",
    "roleType": "BuiltInRole",
    "type": "Microsoft.Authorization/roleDefinitions"
}
```

As you can see, when compared to the Reader role, it offers a much more narrowed set of assigned permissions. While Reader defines actions as `*/read`, Storage Blob Data Reader is designed mostly to allow the reading of data stored in blob containers. However, sometimes, even specialized built-in roles are not enough. In that case, we need to create our own definition and then assign it to desired security principals.

Roles in Azure can be created in a variety of ways. We can use the Azure portal; alternatively, we can create them using ARM templates/Azure Bicep (as we mentioned previously, each role definition is also a resource). We can also create them using the Azure CLI or Azure PowerShell. We'll go for the latter as it will be the simplest approach.

To create a role, we need to construct its definition. The easiest way to do that is to fetch it using an already existing role and use it as a template. You can obtain the role definition with the following command:

```
az role definition list --name <role-name>
```

It'll return a JSON object, which you can copy to your favorite editor and modify. For this exercise, let's create a role that allows the reading of all resource data except the storage account:

```
{
    "assignableScopes": [
        "/subscriptions/<subscription-id>"
    ],
    "description": "Allows reading all data except storage account",
    "actions": [
        "*/read"
    ],
    "dataActions": [],
    "notActions": [
        "Microsoft.Storage/storageAccounts/*/read"
    ],
    "notDataActions": [],
    "name": "Custom Resource Reader"
}
```

As you can see, the role definition to be created differs slightly when compared to an existing one. We're missing `id` and `type`, and the name is equivalent to `roleName`. The whole structure is also flattened. I defined this role in a way that will forbid performing a read action on any storage account within the used scope.

> **Important note**
>
> The prior definition blocks read operations only. This means that with that role assigned, it's not possible to create/delete/modify any Azure resources. It's caused by the fact that our `actions` block specifies only read operations. If we ever decide to change the definition, once changes are applied, they will immediately affect all the security principals.

To create a role definition, you can use one of the following commands:

```
// Azure CLI
az role definition create --role-definition @<file-name>.json

// Azure PowerShell
New-AzRoleDefinition -InputFile "<file-name>.json"
```

The preceding commands assume that you're running them in the same directory where you placed your JSON with the role definition.

Assigning a role

We've learned about custom and built-in roles. We've also talked about security principals and scopes. To complete the RBAC picture, we need to create a role assignment. Once a role is assigned to a chosen security principal on the selected scope, Azure will start to evaluate it, meaning the role will become active.

Creating an assignment is actually a very simple process. It can be quickly done with one of the following commands:

```
// Azure CLI
az role assignment create --assignee "<assignee-name>" --role "<role-
name>"

// Azure PowerShell
New-AzRoleAssignment -ObjectId <object-id>
-RoleDefinitionName <role-name>
```

These are the simplest versions of commands you can use. Optionally, you can pass the --scope (-Scope in PowerShell) parameter, so you can define which scope should be used for that assignment.

ABAC

When using RBAC, you can easily control who or what can access resources by assigning a role with linked permissions. This security model is enough for most scenarios but can become a little bit cumbersome when you need to manage many assignments or provide more granular access. This is where ABAC comes in handy, as it combines RBAC with additional means of security by adding an additional layer.

As of now, ABAC works only with Azure Blob Storage and Azure Queue Storage data actions. This list will expand in the future.

Assignment with conditions

Assigning proper roles can be a lengthy process, especially if you have hundreds of resources to browse. The more resources, the more time it'll take to create assignments, and the easier it is to make a mistake. In Azure, it's possible to create a role assignment that is based on conditions, making it easier to manage and configure access.

> **Important note**
> Some of the features used in conditions (such as security principal attributes) are currently in preview. They might still change until they reach general availability in the future.

When using ABAC, we need to use an additional parameter when creating an assignment, such as in the following example:

```
az role assignment create --role "Custom Resource Reader" --assignee
"<assignee-name>" --condition
"@Resource[Microsoft.Storage/storageAccounts/blobServices/
containers:Name] stringEquals '<container-name>'"
```

As you can see, here we have a `--condition` parameter used, where we're passing a string containing a condition. A condition is a special syntax that provides logic used for checking whether that role assignment should be respected.

Conditions can be combined by using AND/OR operators, like so:

```
(@Resource[Microsoft.Storage/storageAccounts/blobServices/
containers:Name] stringEquals '<container-name>')
OR | AND
(@Resource[Microsoft.Storage/storageAccounts/blobServices/containers/
blobs/tags:Project StringEquals 'AzureAdministratorBook')
```

In fact, conditions are based on properties that are exposed to ARM (and are accessible for other tools, such as filtering in the Azure CLI/Azure PowerShell or expressions in ARM templates/Azure Bicep). You can also access other sources:

- `@Resource` is for accessing given resource properties
- `@Request` is for obtaining information from the request performed on a resource level (so it'll be evaluated for each GET/POST/PUT/DELETE operation)
- `@Principal` is for accessing the properties available for a security principal performing an operation

As you can see, this functionality allows for building a much more advanced security mechanism than RBAC alone. Even though there are still many limitations in place, it can be used to extend security for Azure Storage if needed.

Let's focus now on the last topic of this chapter – a detailed introduction to the Azure CLI, Azure PowerShell, and Cloud Shell.

Basic toolset – the Azure CLI, Azure PowerShell, and Cloud Shell

Many operations in Azure can be performed using various tools. People starting with the cloud favor using the Azure portal. When you are working as a more advanced user, the Azure CLI and Azure PowerShell will become much more useful, especially when building automation scripts. For infrastructure deployments, ARM templates and Azure Bicep will be tools used on a daily basis. This section aims to discuss them in detail and show the various tips and tricks available.

Azure CLI

The Azure CLI is a tool that was written in Python and can be used on any machine that has that runtime installed. It's a cross-platform solution that can be used in many places – from your local machine to remote machines and CI/CD agents. Making yourself familiar with it will not only improve your knowledge of Azure but will also help when reading the documentation, as many examples are based on the Azure CLI.

Logging in

When the Azure CLI is installed, you can immediately get started working with it by running the `az login` command in your terminal. Depending on the scenario (authenticating as a user/service principal/managed identity), you'll see a slightly different path for obtaining credentials:

- When authenticating as a user, most of the time a browser window will appear where you can enter your username and password. If MFA is enabled for the account, you'll be asked to confirm your identity.

- For authenticating as a service principal, you'll need a password/certificate.

- To use managed identity, you need to have that feature enabled on a machine/service where the command is being executed. That scenario is meant for Azure resources, and we'll discuss it later in the book.

No matter which scenario we cover, `az login` will be the first command we need to execute when using the Azure CLI for the first time.

Checking the current account

To see what account was used to authenticate in the Azure CLI, you can use the `az account show` command. When run, it'll display a result like this:

```
{
    "environmentName": "AzureCloud",
    "homeTenantId": "c2d4fe14-…-5a65748fd6c9",
    "id": "cf70b558-…-ebcefb926adf",
    "isDefault": true,
    "managedByTenants": [],
    "name": "PAUG",
    "state": "Enabled",
    "tenantId": "c2d4fe14-…-5a65748fd6c9",
    "user": {
      "name": "kamil@...com",
      "type": "user"
    }
}
```

The result contains the currently used account with the selected subscription. Note that it also describes the context that will be used for most of the Azure CLI commands. While it's not always applicable (as there are commands that work no matter which context is chosen), it's important to always double-check which subscription was selected. It'll prevent you from making accidental changes to resources that shouldn't be modified.

Logging in to another tenant

Sometimes, you may need to switch tenants when performing the Azure CLI commands. We have already discussed the fact that most operations are performed using a currently selected context. As context selection is an implicit thing (i.e., you don't choose it directly – it's evaluated based on the account you used for signing in), you need to remember to not only choose a subscription, but also a tenant if needed.

> **Important note**
>
> When logging in to your default tenant, you don't need to pass `tenantId` as a parameter. It's required only if there are additional tenants where you have the same username as in your default one.

To log in with a non-default tenant, we will use the same command we used previously, but with an additional parameter:

```
az login --tenant <tenant-id>
```

Once this has been run, the login process will run as usual, but the request will be forwarded to the correct Entra ID tenant. The same parameter is used no matter whether you want to log in as a user, service principal, or managed identity (though for principals other than user, there will rarely be a valid scenario).

Azure PowerShell

An alternative to the Azure CLI is Azure PowerShell, which will be useful for anybody who's already worked with PowerShell. A few years ago, the main advantage of the Azure CLI over Azure PowerShell was the ability to run it on multiple platforms. Nowadays, with PowerShell Core, that benefit is no longer valid.

You may find Azure PowerShell useful in all the places where you need more structured language and capabilities for scripting when compared to shell scripts using the Azure CLI. What's more, as PowerShell allows you to use .NET libraries, it opens many interesting, advanced scenarios for authentication, and interacting with the operating system or external services.

Logging in

Like the Azure CLI, to start working with Azure PowerShell, you need to authenticate. The easiest way is to use the following command:

```
Connect-AzAccount
```

This is the equivalent of `az login` as described previously. It'll log you in to the default tenant and subscription of the account you selected.

An alternative authentication mode is to use device code authentication as follows:

```
Connect-AzAccount -UseDeviceAuthentication
```

This will ask you to provide a one-time code displayed in your terminal instead of authenticating using the provided credentials. It's also possible to authenticate using the service principal:

```
$credential = Get-Credential -UserName <application-id>
Connect-AzAccount -ServicePrincipal -Credential $credential
```

As you can see, in Azure PowerShell, it's a little bit more complicated when compared to the Azure CLI, as we need to create a `PSCredential` object first. Still, there's a downside to that approach – it'll ask us for a username and password (which, in our case, will be `applicationId` and a secret generated for that service principal). Such functionality will be difficult to handle in automated scenarios, so we'd need to change the code a little bit:

```
$sp = Get-AzureADServicePrincipal -ObjectId <object-id>
$password = $sp.PasswordCredentials.SecretText | ConvertTo-
SecureString -AsPlainText -Force
$credential = New-Object -TypeName System.Management.Automation.
PSCredential -ArgumentList $sp.AppId, $password
Connect-AzAccount -ServicePrincipal -Credential $credential
```

This will ensure that we're not using a plain text password while preserving the desired functionality. The last option for authentication would be using managed identity:

```
Connect-AzAccount -Identity
```

Depending on the configuration (system-assigned or user-assigned identity), it's possible that you'd need to pass an additional parameter, `-AccountId`, with a value of `clientId` assigned to the underlying security principal. Don't worry, we'll cover that later in the book.

Checking the current account

To identify what context will be used for Azure PowerShell commands, use the following command:

```
Get-AzContext
```

It'll display information about the subscription, your username, the environment, and the tenant. If you want to switch the selected context, you'll need the name or identifier of a subscription and these commands:

```
// List all the subscriptions your principal has access to
Get-AzSubscription

// Select a subscription
Select-AzContext -Subscription <subscription-id-or-name>
```

This will switch the current context to the selected subscription. Remember that for using subscriptions from different tenants, you may need to re-authenticate.

Logging in to another tenant

In Azure PowerShell, you can easily select a tenant to sign into by using the -Tenant parameter:

```
Connect-AzAccount -Tenant <tenant-id>
```

This functionality works in the same way as the one in the Azure CLI – without passing that identifier, you'll log in to your default tenant. If there's any other tenant where you can use the same username, use the presented parameter to redirect the authentication request.

Cloud Shell

As of now, we've mostly talked about using the Azure CLI or Azure PowerShell on your local computer (or, at least, that was our assumption). To complete the picture, we'll discuss a functionality called Cloud Shell. Let's characterize its main features:

- It's a built-in shell available in the Azure portal, the Azure mobile app, and at https://shell.azure.com

- It's a managed service, so you don't need to worry about maintaining its infrastructure

- It automatically authenticates you in Azure (though it's possible to change the context if needed)

- It's offered with a simple graphical editor and mounted storage for persistence

- It's free of charge – the only cost is the storage account deployed in your subscription

In this section, you'll learn how to use the basic and advanced features of this component.

Getting started with Cloud Shell

For the exercises in this section, we'll use https://shell.azure.com, though, in fact, it won't matter which environment is used. Once Cloud Shell is set up, its capabilities are the same in each place it's available.

The first time you use Cloud Shell, you will be asked to set up a storage account for it. However, in some scenarios (such as when Cloud Shell is used for the very first time), you may need to register its resource provider like so:

```
az account set --subscription <subscription-name-or-id>
az provider register --namespace Microsoft.CloudShell
```

Note that you need to do it once for each subscription you want to work with. What's more, those commands need to be run in your terminal as without a registered resource provider, Cloud Shell won't start.

The next step is to set up a storage account:

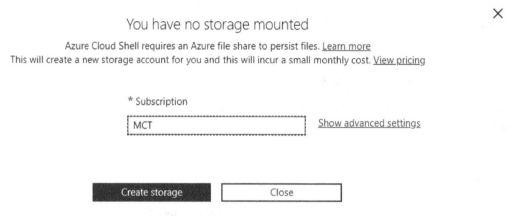

Figure 1.4 – Mounting storage for Cloud Shell

For configuration, there are two methods – you either go for a basic configuration (and select only a subscription where a storage account should be created) or use advanced settings. To simplify things for now, we'll use the basic configuration by clicking on the **Create storage** button. After several seconds, a storage account will be provisioned for you and Cloud Shell will be ready to use.

Selecting the command-line tool

Cloud Shell allows you to work with either the Azure CLI or Azure PowerShell. It's up to you which tool will be used – what's more, you can change it at any time. A selection is made by choosing the Azure CLI or Azure PowerShell from the dropdown:

Figure 1.5 – Selecting a tool in Cloud Shell

PowerShell will allow you to use Azure PowerShell, while **Bash** will be a standard bash environment with the Azure CLI installed. The main difference between these two modes is the ability to use different tools compatible with the one you selected.

Working with Cloud Shell

When you're using Cloud Shell, you should treat it as any other command-line environment where you can use different tools and commands. The availability of commands will differ depending on the selected mode (PowerShell or Bash). Still, for many scenarios, the user experience while working with Cloud Shell will stay the same, as you can use many commands no matter which mode is selected:

- You can list files in the directory with both `dir` and `ls`

- To read the contents of a file, you can use both `type` and `cat`

- You can easily use `chmod` in both PowerShell and Bash modes

What's more, Cloud Shell comes with preinstalled tools and libraries that you can use out of the box. These include, but are not limited to, the following:

- Terraform

- Git

- .Net

- Java

- Python

- Node.js

This gives you a robust and useful sandbox environment for day-to-day work.

Persisting files in Cloud Shell

Once the storage account is mounted in Cloud Shell, you can use the underlying storage for file persistence. It works as your personal disk that can be used for storing the output of your work.

> **Important note**
> In general, sharing the same storage account among various users is a bad security practice. However, you need to remember that if a user has appropriate access to one of the higher scopes (resource group/subscription/management group), they will be able to read the contents of each storage account within that scope.

The mechanism of file persistence is based on the following functionalities:

- Your file share includes a disk image that is automatically synced whenever a change is persisted to the filesystem

- File shares are automatically mounted and mapped to the underlying Azure storage

You can check that very easily by running `ls -la` in Cloud Shell in your user's directory. It'll give you a list of files, directories, and mounts, where one of the elements should look like this:

```
lrwxrwxrwx 1 john john     22 Mar  8 14:14 clouddrive -> /usr/csuser/
clouddrive
```

Additionally, we could check the contents of our file share:

```
az storage file list --share-name <file-share-name> --account-name
<cloud-shell-storage-account-name>  --path .cloudconsole
```

The result of the preceding command will be a JSON object, which should look like this:

```
[
  {
    "metadata": null,
    "name": "acc_john.img",
    "properties": {
      "contentLength": 5368709120,
      "contentRange": null,
      "contentSettings": {
        ...
      },
      "copy": {
        ...
      },
      "etag": null,
      "lastModified": null,
      "serverEncrypted": null
    },
    "type": "file"
  }
]
```

As you can see, it contains a file named `acc_<user>.img`, which is the image we talked about.

That's all for now! Let's summarize what you've learned in the very first chapter.

Summary

In this chapter, we covered the fundamentals of Azure by looking at Azure Resource Manager, Microsoft Entra ID, the authorization mechanism, and the basic toolset. By now, you should be familiar with topics such as security principals, RBAC, and ABAC. What's more, you started building skills related to the Azure CLI and Azure PowerShell. Those come in very handy in the next chapters, where we'll cover various Azure services in detail.

In the next chapter, we'll talk a little bit about IaC. While that topic is a very wide area linked to various roles (development, operations, and security), getting a basic understanding of how Azure resources can be deployed will improve your skillset and simplify many tasks.

2

Basics of Infrastructure as Code

Even though this book is mostly related to administrative tasks in Azure, some other topics are worth knowing. One of those is **Infrastructure as Code** – often abbreviated as **IaC**. You might be wondering why this topic is so important. Is the Azure administrator somebody who deploys infrastructure? Well, while an administrator may be loosely related to infrastructure deployment and configuration, in Azure, you cannot just ignore various ways for provisioning. What's more, in an advanced Azure environment containing multiple resources, policies, and rules, it's much easier to leverage infrastructure automation and management using an IaC approach.

In this chapter, we'll focus on the basics of IaC, which will help you learn topics that will be covered in the next few chapters:

- What is IaC?
- ARM templates
- Migrating to Azure Bicep
- Using **Azure Container Registry** (**ACR**) as a repository of modules

Let's see what areas wait for us on the next pages!

Technical requirements

To get the most from this chapter, you'll need the following components:

- The Azure CLI (https://learn.microsoft.com/en-us/cli/azure/install-azure-cli)
- Any kind of IDE that allows you to work with text files

The Code in Action video for this book can be viewed at: https://packt.link/GTX9F

What is IaC?

In the previous chapter, we talked about using the Azure CLI and Azure Powershell for managing and deploying Azure resources. We also mentioned that you can use the Azure portal for manual provisioning and configuration. Unfortunately, those methods are not always solutions that allow automation.

Imagine the following scenario – you need to deploy a cluster of **virtual machines** (**VMs**) that will be used by some teams for their projects. You could do everything step by step using the Azure portal (the easiest option for beginners as it'll show you all the necessary resources), use the command line to deploy components one by one, or even prepare a simple shell script that contains all the commands:

```
az vm create \
    --resource-group <resource-group-name> \
    --name <vm-name> \
    --image Win2022AzureEditionCore \
    --public-ip-sku Standard \
    --admin-username <username>

az vm create \
    --resource-group <resource-group-name> \
    --name <vm-name2> \
    --image Win2022AzureEditionCore \
    --public-ip-sku Standard \
    --admin-username <username>
```

This script could contain any number of VMs with various parameters passed. There's also one trick here – we're using an Azure CLI command, which will implicitly create most of the resources for us. To have full control over the creation process, you'd need to create not only a VM, but also a disk, virtual network, IP address, and other required components.

Now, imagine that teams are asking you to create the same cluster but with slightly different parameters. At the same time, you realize that you may need another subscription for it, a different resource group, and so on. If you created the first cluster by hand in the Azure portal, you'd need to do everything from scratch. The same applies to running CLI commands one by one. Only using a custom script would save you from redoing the same steps.

This is where we're approaching the IaC pattern. It's a way of working where your infrastructure is coded in such a way that it can be parameterized and run automatically; it is also possible to version it using a version control system, such as `git`. While the aforementioned script with Azure CLI commands fulfills all those requirements, there are some problems with it:

- It's not a structured approach, meaning everyone can introduce conventions, making maintaining and understanding the code more difficult

- It doesn't support any kind of testing, error validation, or syntax highlighting

- Even though it supports basic building blocks such as parameters, variables, conditional blocks, or loops, they may not be the best fit in complex scripts

- It lacks more advanced constructs, such as helper functions or dependencies

In simple cases, this script would be just fine when IaC is considered. However, in day-to-day work, you'll need more robust tools, which will simplify your work. This is why we'll focus on native IaC solutions for Azure, which are ARM templates and Azure Bicep. Note that there are other tools available in the market (such as Terraform or Pulumi), but they would require a much more detailed introduction, which this book is not intended for.

Exploring ARM templates

ARM templates are the oldest IaC solution for Azure and the most popular (we're still talking about native solutions). They are based on JSON documents, which can be sent to ARM as deployments. Once a deployment is received by ARM, it parses the document and orchestrates the required changes to our Azure infrastructure.

Template schema

The high-level structure of each template looks like this:

```
{
  "$schema": "https://schema.management.azure.com/schemas/2019-04-01/
deploymentTemplate.json#",
  "contentVersion": "",
  "apiProfile": "",
  "parameters": {  },
  "variables": {  },
  "functions": [  ],
  "resources": [  ],
  "outputs": {  }
}
```

As you can see, it contains a couple of blocks that can be used for defining the overall structure of your deployment. The preceding schema contains all the main blocks that are available, but it can be simplified to the following one:

```
{
  "$schema": "https://schema.management.azure.com/schemas/2019-04-01/
deploymentTemplate.json#",
  "contentVersion": "",
  "resources": []
}
```

Let's compare them. It seems that the required fields are as follows:

- `$schema`: Defines the schema that's used for the JSON document
- `contentVersion`: This is used for assigning a version to the template on your end (it has a purely decorative purpose; ARM isn't using it)
- `resources`: This is an array of resources that should be provisioned by ARM

The important thing when working with ARM templates (or most IaC tools in general) is that they don't imply what should be added, removed, or changed. You just prepare a definition and deploy it. Then, you can change it at any moment and deploy it once again. In the case of ARM templates, it's the responsibility of ARM to understand the current and desired state. This is one of the biggest differences between the declarative approach (where you describe the desired state) and the imperative approach (such as using the Azure CLI or Azure PowerShell commands to tell an API what to do step by step).

> **Important note**
>
> When working with other IaC tools (such as Terraform), don't make assumptions that they're designed in the same way as ARM templates. They may require a different approach to handling the state of your infrastructure and follow different patterns.

Now, let's talk about creating a deployment.

Creating a deployment

Each ARM template can be deployed using the following Azure CLI command:

```
az deployment group create \
    --name <deployment-name> \
    --resource-group <resource-group-name> \
    --template-file <template-file-path>
```

Here, we're telling the Azure CLI to take our template and create a deployment based on it. This command deploys our template in the provided resource group, but other options are possible:

- `az deployment group create`
- `az deployment sub create`
- `az deployment mg create`
- `az deployment tenant create`

Each of these commands accepts the `--template-file` parameter, where we point to the location of our ARM template. The only difference is the scope, which we discussed in *Chapter 1*. Some resources support multiple scopes, so you need to use a different command to deploy them. For example, you may want to deploy a role assignment for a management group. If you use the first command, it won't work – the deployment is executed at the resource group level, which doesn't have access to upper scopes.

Deployment modes

Previously, we mentioned that once a template is sent to ARM, it'll infer what to do with our resources. Unfortunately, by default, ARM is unable to determine what needs to be removed. This is caused by the default deployment mode called **Incremental**. There are two deployment modes you can select:

- Incremental
- Complete

The difference between them is that Complete mode treats your template as the desired state within the given scope. For instance, if you deployed your template initially with a VM and then removed it from the template, the next Incremental deployment would ignore that change (that is, the deployed VM would stay the same). But if you choose Complete mode, the VM will be deleted as it's no longer your deployment state.

You can select a deployment mode like so:

```
az deployment group create \
   --name <deployment-name> \
   --resource-group <resource-group-name> \
   --template-file <template-file-path>
   --mode Incremental | Complete
```

Be cautious when using Complete mode, though – you may easily remove important resources such as disks or databases if you're not careful!

Creating and deploying a simple template

Now that we've learned some basic information about ARM templates, it's time to try them out:

1. First, create a resource group using the following command:

   ```
   az group create --name <resource-group-name> --location
   <location>
   ```

   We'll use it when we create our deployment.

2. The next step is to use an empty template and populate it with an example resource. For this exercise, we'll use an Azure storage account, which doesn't require additional resources to be deployed:

```
{
  "$schema": "https://schema.management.azure.com/schemas/2019-
04-01/deploymentTemplate.json#",
  "contentVersion": "1.0.0.0",
  "resources": [
    {
      "type": "Microsoft.Storage/storageAccounts",
      "apiVersion": "2021-09-01",
      "name": "<storage-account-name>",
      "location": "[resourceGroup().location]",
      "sku": {
        "name": "Standard_LRS"
      },
      "kind": "StorageV2",
      "properties": {}
    }
  ]
}
```

Note that we need to provide a value for the storage account we want to create using the `"name"` field. It can be any value between 3 to 24 characters, which contains letters or numbers only. You also need to provide a location for that resource, which is ideally the same location as the one you used for the resource group.

3. When you're ready, save the template as `my-first-template.json` and use the following command to create a deployment. Remember to run it from the same directory where you saved the template:

```
az deployment group create \
  --name myfirsttemplate \
  --resource-group <resource-group-name> \
  --template-file my-first-template.json
```

After several seconds, you should receive a result of running a deployment, which will be a JSON object containing data related to it.

4. Look for the `"provisioningState"` field – if it contains `"Succeeded"`, you can go to the Azure portal to see your created resource. If you see any other value, check for deployment errors. Sometimes, deployment can fail due to transient errors – try to rerun it if that's the case.

Let's talk about listing deployments now.

Listing deployments

If everything went well in the previous exercise, you should be able to list any deployment you made. Deployments, such as VMs, databases, or even roles, are a standard resource from an Azure point of view. This means you can query, delete, and manage them as any other component provisioned in Azure.

To obtain a list of deployments for a given scope, you'll need to learn a couple of new commands. Let's see what's needed for that:

1. To list deployments, we can use the `az deployment list` command, which has slightly different syntax depending on the deployment scope:

    ```
    // List resource group deployments
    az deployment group list --resource-group <resource-group-name>

    // List subscription deployments
    az deployment list

    // List management group deployments
    az deployment mg list --management-group-id <management-group-
    name>

    // List tenant deployments
    az deployment tenant list
    ```

    Commands that you need to use will always depend on the scope of a deployment you created. In the previous section, we created a simple ARM template with a single Azure storage account. As we used the `az deployment group create` command, that deployment used the resource group scope as a baseline.

2. Now, we can use the `az deployment group list` command to see if that deployment can be found:

    ```
    az deployment group list --resource-group-name <resource-group-
    name> -o table
    ```

3. Let's use the `-o` parameter, which is equivalent to using the `--output` parameter to get prettier output. Once completed, you should get a similar result to mine:

    ```
    Name                 State        Timestamp
    Mode                 ResourceGroup
    --------------------------------------------------------------------
    myfirstdeployment    Succeeded    2023-03-19T11:29:24.440914+00:00
    Incremental          aach02
    ```

4. The number of results will depend on the number of deployments you performed at that scope. Over time, as the list grows, it'll be much easier to find what you need by using the `az deployment show` command, like so:

```
az deployment group show --name <deployment-name> --resource-
group <resource-group-name>
az deployment sub show -name <deployment-name>
az deployment mg show --management-group-id <management-
group-id> --name <deployment-name>
az deployment tenant show --name <deployment-name>
```

As in the previous examples, you may use different syntax depending on the deployment scope you used.

Let's continue our exploration of IaC concepts with Azure Bicep, which is a fantastic successor of ARM templates and is quickly becoming a state-of-the-art solution for managing Azure infrastructure natively.

Migrating to Azure Bicep

Even though ARM templates have become very popular among people and companies working with Microsoft Azure, they're hardly an ideal solution. As templates are simply JSON documents, they tend to become too verbose and difficult to maintain over time. It's also difficult to develop a good ecosystem around such a tool because of the characteristics of JSON being a data format, not a real **domain-specific language (DSL)**.

This is why Microsoft decided to take a step forward and proposed a new tool called Bicep. It is 100% compatible with ARM templates but provides a much smoother DevEx experience, better tooling, and IDE support with clean and easy-to-learn syntax. In this section, we'll try to learn the main Bicep concepts and compare them to the template we created using ARM templates.

Bicep language

Bicep is a **DSL**, which is somewhat like the **Hashicorp Configuration Language** (**HCL**) language used by Terraform (which is another IaC tool developed by another company, *HashiCorp*). Let's look at a very basic template written in it:

```
resource storageAccount 'Microsoft.Storage/storageAccounts@2021-06-01'
= {
  name: <storage-account-name>
  location: resourceGroup().location
  sku: {
    name: 'Standard_LRS'
  }
  kind: 'StorageV2'
  properties: {
```

```
        accessTier: 'Hot'
    }
}
```

If you compare this Bicep file with the ARM template from the previous section, you'll find many similarities:

- The `Microsoft.Storage/storageAccounts` type is used in both files
- JSON fields (such as `name`, `location`, and `sku`) are the same in ARM templates and Bicep
- The SKU has the same value in both files (`Standard_LRS`); the same applies to `kind`
- In both files, we can use the `resourceGroup().location` function

The main difference is the syntax. Bicep is no longer a JSON document – it's a special-purpose language, which is aimed at easier and faster development of infrastructure automation. We won't do a deep dive into Bicep syntax in this book, but don't worry – all the concepts we'll use will be described and explained to you in the next few exercises.

ARM templates and Bicep compatibility

Previously, I mentioned that ARM templates and Bicep are 100% compatible. This statement comes from the fact that when a deployment is created using a Bicep file, it's transformed into an ARM template before being sent to Azure Resource Manager. Normally, this operation is performed on your behalf when using tools such as the Azure CLI, but we can also do it manually.

Note that the Azure CLI doesn't have Bicep implemented. In the previous versions, you needed to either install the Bicep CLI by yourself or make sure your version of the Azure CLI had Bicep embedded. At the time of writing, neither of those two things should be needed, but let's confirm that. Run the following command in your terminal to see the result:

```
az bicep version
```

The result should look as follows:

```
Bicep CLI version 0.16.1 (d77dcc750a)
```

If you see nothing or the Azure CLI says Bicep is not installed, run the installer:

```
az bicep install
```

After a few minutes, Bicep should be installed and available on your computer.

> **Important note**
>
> If you have a very old version of the Azure CLI, you won't have the `az bicep` command available. To fix that, run `az upgrade` and wait a couple of minutes for it to complete.

Once the Bicep is ready, we can use it to transform the Bicep file into an ARM template. To do that, save the template from the beginning of this section as `deployment.bicep` and run the following command in the same directory where you saved the file:

```
az bicep build --file deployment.bicep
```

After a moment, compilation should be completed (most probably with some warning, which you can safely ignore) and the ARM template file should be created. The name of the ARM template file will be the same as the Bicep file – the only difference will be the extension (`.bicep` versus `.json`). Open the `deployment.json` file – the content will be like the ARM template from the beginning of this chapter. However, when you examine it, you'll notice that an additional section has been added:

```
"metadata": {
    "_generator": {
      "name": "bicep",
      "version": "0.16.1.55165",
      "templateHash": "9330809271120159779"
    }
},
```

The values of the fields may vary, depending on your Bicep version and template content, but your template should contain it, nonetheless. The `metadata` section presented here is an optional section of a template that contains descriptive information that's useful to different tools working with ARM templates. It's automatically added to each file generated by the Bicep CLI to denote that it was generated automatically.

Performing deployments

As Azure Bicep is 100% compatible with ARM templates, you can use the same toolset to perform deployments. In the previous sections, we discussed using the Azure CLI with the `az deployment create` command – when working with Bicep, it's still a valid option:

```
az deployment group create \
   --name myfirsttemplate \
   --resource-group <resource-group-name> \
   --template-file my-first-template.bicep
```

Note that the only change here is using a file with the `.bicep` extension instead of a `.json` file. This gives you more flexibility when migrating ARM templates to Bicep as you can have both types of templates in one place and incrementally rewrite the old ones.

Decompiling an ARM template to Bicep

If you have lots of ARM templates and want to migrate to Bicep, you may need to look for a tool that will automatically transform the former into the latter. The Azure CLI (or rather the Bicep CLI underneath) has such functionality built in:

```
az bicep decompile --file <your-template>.json
```

Once run, the Azure CLI will attempt to transform the template you provided into a Bicep file. The conversion is not guaranteed to be 100% accurate – bugs or quirks may be introduced in the process. However, it can work as a boilerplate for the Bicep file you're going to work on.

You can also use that command to quickly transform the exported resource group template into Bicep:

```
az group export --name "<resource-group-name>" > <resource-group-
name>.json
az bicep decompile --file <resource-group-name>.json
```

This could be useful in scenarios where you have resources for Azure but no template available. Those two commands will quickly give you a basic Bicep module to work on. Then, you'll need to refine it by fixing the naming conventions of, for example, the variables used in it.

With that, we've covered the basics of Azure Bicep and the migration process from ARM templates to the newer solution. Now, let's learn how to use **Azure Container Registry** (**ACR**) as storage for Azure Bicep modules so that they can be shared across the organization.

Using ACR as a repository of modules

One of the important topics when talking about IaC in a company is building a central registry of modules that can be reused by other teams. Such a registry satisfies a couple of requirements:

- An authorization mechanism
- Integration with the chosen IaC tool
- Easy to use and manage

There are lots of different tools on the market that can act as such solutions, but in this chapter, we'll focus on using one of the Azure services for that.

What is ACR?

ACR is a managed service in Azure that was originally meant to be a private container repository. You could prepare a container image (for example, Docker) and push it to your instance of ACR. Then, you could set up access policies and allow other users or applications to pull images from your registry.

Throughout ACR's development, it has gained additional features and functionalities. You can use it to run jobs, store Helm charts, or act as a registry for Bicep modules.

Creating an ACR instance

Before we can push anything to our ACR instance, we need to create it. We'll use the Azure CLI for this:

```
az acr create --resource-group <resource-group-name> --name <acr-name>
--sku Basic
```

This command will create an empty instance of ACR with a Basic tier. We're using it because we don't need features available in higher tiers – however, if you already have ACR in the Standard or Premium tier, you can safely use it for exercises from that section.

With ACR created, we need a Bicep module that we can push. Let's prepare one.

Creating a module

ACR can store any Bicep module – it doesn't matter what resource type is used or how many resources are defined within it. A Bicep module is a standard Bicep file – the only difference is how it's referenced. For simplicity, we'll create a module that can be used to provision new instances of ACR:

```
param name string
param location string = resourceGroup().location

@allowed([
  'Basic'
  'Standard'
  'Premium'
])
param sku string

resource acr 'Microsoft.ContainerRegistry/registries@2022-12-01' = {
  name: name
  location: location
  sku: {
    name: sku
  }
  properties: {
  }
}
```

Let's quickly summarize our code:

- It defines a single resource – ACR
- It requires three parameters – `name`, `location`, and `sku`:
  - `location` is an optional parameter that has a default value that's inferred from a resource group
  - `sku` allows three predefined values to be used
- Once the registry has been created, it will have default values for all the fields that we didn't define

Save that Bicep code as `acr.bicep` on your computer. Now, it's time to push it as a module to the ACR instance we created in the previous step.

Publishing a Bicep module

To publish our file as a Bicep module, we can use either Azure PowerShell or the Azure CLI, as follows:

```
// Azure PowerShell
Publish-AzBicepModule -FilePath ./acr.bicep -Target br:<acr-name>.
azurecr.io/bicep/modules/acr:v1


// Azure CLI
az bicep publish --file acr.bicep --target br:<acr-name>.azurecr.io/
bicep/modules/acr:v1
```

Note the value of the `--target` parameter – it's prefixed with an indicator that states that we're publishing the file as a Bicep module and pushing it to ACR. Once the command has run, wait a couple of seconds until publishing is completed. To confirm that the module is available, run the following command:

```
az acr repository list -n <acr-name>
```

You should see an array of repositories containing the module we published:

```
[
    "bicep/modules/acr"
]
```

Now that most of our setup is complete, let's proceed to the last step – using the published module in our code.

Using the published Bicep module

Using a module in Bicep is an easy task – it's just a matter of pointing to the right source. In many cases, Bicep modules are developed as local files and references using a local path. Since we created a remote module, we need to introduce some modifications to that approach. Let's create a local file named `acr-from-module.bicep` and put the following code in it:

```
module acr 'br:<acr-name>.azurecr.io/bicep/modules/acr:v1' = {
  name: 'acr-module'
  params: {
    name: '<new-acr-name>'
    sku: ,<sku-name>'
  }
}
```

As you can see, the preceding definition is slightly different from the one we mentioned earlier. We no longer use the `resource` keyword – it's replaced with `module`. We also don't provide a full resource type – instead, we define a reference to the repository created in ACR. The last change is related to the `name` parameter – it defines the name of the nested deployment rather than the name of a resource to be created. We won't go into details of modules in Bicep, but let's quickly describe how this works.

When you work with Bicep without modules (that is, you put all the resources in the same Bicep file), the whole code you created will be transformed into an ARM template without additional work. However, when modules are used, more complex transformation occurs. This is caused by the fact that ARM templates don't have a typical concept of modules. As Bicep is compatible with them, a workaround was needed to overcome that limitation. This is why, under the hood, Bicep modules are transformed into nested deployments – you can think about them as *templates within templates*. Because a nested deployment works as a standard deployment, it needs a name. Standard deployments also need a name, but it's often inferred from the name of the deployment file. In the case of nested deployments, you must provide it explicitly.

To complete our exercise, you can try to create a deployment based on the code we created:

```
az deployment group create -g <resource-group-name> --template-file
acr-from-module.bicep
```

If you want, you can add other resources to the file. Once the deployment has been completed, you should be able to find a new instance of ACR that's been created with the name you selected and the SKU of your choice.

> **Important note**
>
> If you are working with Bicep using an IDE that supports its syntax (for example, VS Code with the Bicep plugin), you'll also notice that when providing the `sku` parameter, there's an automatic suggestion of possible values. We defined this when we created our module.

You can also verify that your deployment triggered another deployment named `acr-module` using the following command:

```
az deployment group list -g <resource-group-name> -o table
```

This command will return a list of deployments from the resource group – note that it contains both deployments – that is, `acr-from-module` and `acr-module`:

```
Name                 State
----------------     ----------
acr-module           Succeeded
acr-from-module      Succeeded
```

That's it! You can play around with different names and settings to check how they affect both the resource that's been provisioned and the names of deployments. If you want to publish a new version of the ACR module, you can use the same command we used – it will overwrite the previous version and replace it with a new one. If you'd like to have multiple versions, make sure that you change the tag:

```
// V1
br:<acr-name>.azurecr.io/bicep/modules/acr:v1

// V2
br:<acr-name>.azurecr.io/bicep/modules/acr:v2
```

This will introduce a second version of the module while keeping the first one.

With that, we've covered everything we need to know about IaC. Now, let's quickly summarize what we've learned and what we can find in the next few chapters.

Summary

In this chapter, you learned the basics of IaC. We talked about the use of ARM templates and Azure Bicep, their use cases, and the differences between them. You also had a chance to practice not only deployments but also using remote modules. The last topic is especially important from the point of Azure administration since, in many scenarios, you may need to set up and manage a central repository of modules. Such modules are then used by development teams, so it's important to set up proper access policies (using RBAC) and think about the proper architecture of such a repository (including networking setup).

In the next chapter, we'll be starting *Part 2* of this book and taking a deep dive into Azure Virtual Networks. This topic will be extremely important to you as networks are part of most Azure solutions and act as one of the core infrastructure components that are used to secure and segment services.

Part 2: Networking for Azure Administrator

Part 2 is an introduction to networking topics in Microsoft Azure, including load balancing using Azure Load Balancer. In this part, you'll learn about designing networks in Azure, the security of networks using network security groups, and the implications of invalid network designs on your cloud infrastructure.

This part has the following chapters:

- *Chapter 3, Understanding Azure Virtual Networks*
- *Chapter 4, Exploring Azure Load Balancer*

3

Understanding
Azure Virtual Networks

Networks are one of the most important topics when talking about infrastructure, as they provide basic security mechanisms for our services and allow us to segment them. In Azure, networking is quite an extensive subject – networks integrate not only with **Infrastructure-as-a-Service** (**IaaS**) components such as **Azure Virtual Machines** but can also be found in **Platform-as-a-Service** (**PaaS**) scenarios. This chapter is going to give you a thorough overview of Azure virtual networks and accompanying services.

Topics from this chapter will help you better understand networks in Azure and what capabilities they offer in terms of integration, security, and network segmentation.

In this chapter, we're going to cover the following main topics:

- Planning and deploying virtual networks
- Understanding **network security groups** (**NSGs**)
- Working with virtual network peerings
- Network routing and endpoints

Technical requirements

To perform the exercises from this chapter, you'll need the following tools:

- The Azure CLI (`https://learn.microsoft.com/en-us/cli/azure/installazure-cli`)
- A favorite **IDE** (I recommend VS Code)
- **cURL** or similar tool allowing you to perform HTTP requests
- A tool supporting **SSH connections** (you can use the built-in capabilities of your terminal or download PuTTY or something similar)

The Code in Action video for this book can be viewed at: `https://packt.link/GTX9F`

Planning and deploying virtual networks

Before we start designing and building networks in Azure, let's define what a **virtual network** actually is. When working with physical infrastructure (for example, on-premises), most of the elements of the system infrastructure are physically available and installed in a data center. Networks of such systems consist of multiple switches, routers, and firewalls that need to be managed by administrators and IT engineers locally.

In a cloud environment, you don't have access to physical infrastructure. Instead, you're given access to a virtualized environment where you can decide which service you'd like to deploy. The **physical networks** are still there – the only difference is that it's not your responsibility to administer them.

This is why we're going to talk about virtual networks instead – an abstract software layer over physical components that emulates capabilities of existing hardware and enables you to do the following:

- Define address spaces and prefixes
- Configure communication over given ports and protocols
- Describe security rules
- Segment resources over subnets
- Isolate services from each other
- Connect applications via network peering

As you can see, there are a lot of things that can be done using virtual networks in Azure. You should have a basic understanding of that concept now – let's start building something!

Planning a network in Azure

To correctly plan a network in Azure, we need to understand four important concepts that will affect our decisions later:

- **Address space**: Each network has a fixed number of IP addresses that can be assigned to resources residing within it. Those addresses are collectively known as an address space.
- **Subnets**: Each virtual network is a huge container for resources. If you like, you can put all of them into it and work with such a setup. However, if you're looking for segmentation, better address allocation methods, and improved security, you should take subnets into consideration. Subnets in Azure are almost identical to traditional subnets, so if you're familiar with that concept, you'll be able to reuse your knowledge.
- **Regions**: In general, Azure virtual networks are limited to a single region only. To enable multiple networks to connect with each other, we'll use **peerings**, presented in the second half of this chapter.

- **Subscription**: The concept of an Azure subscription is now familiar to you. In the context of virtual networks, a subscription will act as a boundary that cannot be crossed.

Let's now see what the baseline is for building an efficient network in Azure. It's important to understand concepts such as non-overlapping address space and the resizing of a subnet structure in order to improve the quality of configured infrastructure. We'll cover those topics in the upcoming sections.

Non-overlapping address spaces

We'll start with a simple problem that often gets overlooked when getting started with Microsoft Azure. In many scenarios, organizations already have their own network that they plan to extend using a cloud environment. As each network has its own address space, it's extremely important to keep that in mind when starting to build networks in Azure.

Why is that? Well, even though virtual networks may be easier to provision and configure, they will still introduce challenges if we need to redesign them with services inside. It's possible to both resize existing address space in an Azure virtual network and add/remove an address range. Should you ever perform such an operation, it's important to consider possible outcomes.

Let's review the following scenario:

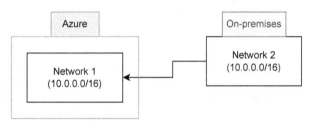

Figure 3.1 – Overlapping address spaces

As you can see in *Figure 3.1*, we have an overlapping address space in both networks. Obviously, such a configuration won't work – resources within the network won't be able to properly resolve the IP address as it'd exist in both networks simultaneously.

> **Important note**
>
> In this section, we're making the assumption that we'd like to connect both networks at some point in the future. If you want to keep networks isolated, it's perfectly fine to have overlapping address space.

If *Network 1* is empty, a fix will be quick and easy – you'll just need to redeploy that virtual network. However, if that network already contains resources, you'll need to reconfigure them. Reconfiguration will depend on the complexity of your setup and used services – it can be much more difficult in IaaS scenarios with lots of VMs and will become much simpler when working with PaaS components. Let's see now how to approach the problem of overlapping address spaces by resizing existing networks.

Resizing an empty Azure virtual network

When approaching the problem of overlapping address space, we need to check whether networks contain resources already. If they don't, the resizing process for a network will be quite easy.

Let's see how to resize a virtual network using Azure CLI commands. To perform this exercise, we'll need an existing network. Proceed as follows:

1. Create a virtual network using the following command:

```
az group create --name <resource-group-name> --location
<location>
az network vnet create --name <vnet-name> --resource-group
<resource-group-name>
```

2. Once the command completes, you should get a **JSON** result containing the configuration of the created virtual network. We'll confirm everything worked correctly using one more command:

```
az network vnet show --name <vnet-name> --resource-group
<resource-group-name> -o table
```

3. It will give you a result like mine:

```
EnableDdosProtection       Location       Name        ProvisioningState
--------------------       --------       --------    -----------------
False                      westeurope     aach03-01   Succeeded
```

Figure 3.2 – Virtual network information obtained using an Azure CLI command

We have an empty network created. You may wonder how we could provide additional information – address space, subnets, or even location. The command we used uses default values for a virtual network – for instance, it's created without subnets, with a `10.0.0.0/16` address space. It's possible to use optional parameters to provision a resource, which is much more aligned with our needs. Check the following link to learn more: `https://learn.microsoft.com/en-us/cli/azure/network/vnet?view=azure-cli-latest#az-network-vnet-create`.

As our network is empty, we shouldn't have many problems resizing it. To perform that operation, we could use the **Azure portal**, **Infrastructure as Code (IaC)**, or even **Azure PowerShell**. To keep the context, we'll continue using the Azure CLI. Use the following command to update your network:

```
az network vnet update --address-prefixes 10.0.0.0/24 --name <vnet-
name> --resource-group <resource-group-name>
```

If the operation succeeds, you'll get a standard JSON response as the result. Unless there are some transient issues, resizing an empty virtual network in Azure should always end successfully. However, if your network has resources within it, you may need to perform additional steps to complete the operation. Let's check that scenario in the next section.

Resizing an Azure virtual network with resources

Let's try to perform a more difficult exercise – we'll try to resize a virtual network with existing subnets in it. To do that, we need to create them. Use the following commands to get started:

```
az group create --name <resource-group-name> --location <location>
az network vnet create --name <vnet-name> --resource-group <resource-
group-name>
az network vnet subnet create --resource-group <resource-group-name>
--vnet-name <vnet-name> --address-prefixes 10.0.0.0/24 --name subnet1
az network vnet subnet create --resource-group <resource-group-name>
--vnet-name <vnet-name> --address-prefixes 10.0.1.0/24 --name subnet2
```

Those commands will create a new resource group, a virtual network, and two subnets inside it. As our virtual network was created with default values, it has a 10.0.0.0/16 address space defined, giving us $2^16 = 65536$ IP addresses available. Each of the subnets uses the same range defined as /24, which gives us $2^8 = 256$ IP addresses. As you can see, we still have plenty of space available – but what would happen if we ever decide that we need to resize that virtual network to reclaim some of the addresses?

Let's update our network in the same way as we did in the previous exercise:

```
az network vnet update --address-prefixes 10.0.0.0/24 --name <vnet-
name> --resource-group <resource-group-name>
```

This time, this command won't succeed – instead, you'll receive the following error:

```
(NetcfgInvalidSubnet) Subnet 'subnet2' is not valid in virtual network
<vnet-name>.
Code: NetcfgInvalidSubnet
Message: Subnet 'subnet2' is not valid in virtual network '<vnet-
name>.'.
```

It seems that we have a problem with the second subnet. While the error message may be a little bit misleading, it tells us that the virtual network cannot be updated as it'd render subnet2 invalid. Why is that?

To answer that question, we need to clarify the available addresses for the /16 and /24 ranges:

- /16 – from 10.0.0.0 to 10.0.255.255
- /24 – from 10.0.0.0 to 10.0.0.255

Now it becomes much easier to understand – if we resize our virtual network, the subnet defined with the `10.0.1.0/24` range won't fit. In fact, all the address space would be taken by `subnet1`. To complete our operation, we'd need to first resize `subnet1` to a smaller subnet, then update `subnet2` to have IP addresses within the allowed range, and finally, resize the virtual network. This is why it's always better to plan your networks (including virtual networks) upfront – while resizing is possible, it may become cumbersome at some point, especially if our networks are peered; that is, connected with each other (because after resizing, they would need to be synchronized to exchange updated IP address ranges).

Great! We were able to learn how to resize networks if overlapping happens and we cannot redeploy whole networks. Let's now cover the next challenge when working with networks in Azure – dealing with excessively large subnets.

Avoiding subnets that are like virtual networks

When designing networks in Azure, you may be tempted to create **super-subnets** – subnets that are as big or almost as big as the virtual network containing them. While such a concept has benefits (the most obvious one being you'll probably never need to resize them), it also comes with a bunch of pitfalls.

Having a huge subnet will limit your ability to segment virtual networks. Take a look at *Figure 3.3* to see what such an infrastructure setup would look like:

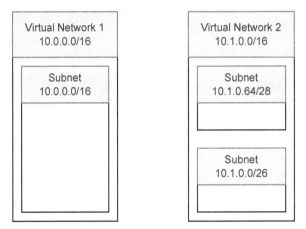

Figure 3.3 – Different designs for virtual network subnet ranges

As you can see, we have two virtual networks with the same range (`/16`, meaning 65,536 IP addresses) but with different concepts for subnets inside them. The first network consists of a single subnet that is spread across the whole network. The second one introduces two separate subnets with much smaller address ranges (59 (`/26`) and 11 (`/28`) available addresses respectively).

> **Important note**
>
> Remember that Azure reserves five IP addresses for each subnet for internal services. This is why subnets from *Virtual Network 2* in *Figure 3.3* are described as having 59 and 11 IP addresses available. In normal circumstances, the /28 subnet would have 16 addresses available, while the /26 subnet would have 64.

The main difference between presented networks is their ability to host more resources. *Virtual Network 1* is already occupied – the only way to add more resources to it is to place them inside the existing subnet. *Virtual Network 2*, however, is much more flexible – as existing subnets occupy only the range needed, you can easily provision more resources inside that network by creating a new subnet. A rule of thumb in this case is that it's always better to reserve some ranges for the future and make sure that the virtual network is not overprovisioned.

As you can see, working with networks in Azure in terms of fundamental topics is not a difficult task – it just requires some initial considerations regarding their desired shape and structure. As you've gained some fundamental knowledge about networks and their concepts, let's now learn about the deployment of a virtual network resource.

Deploying a virtual network

We've covered most of the basic concepts and considerations for Azure virtual networks. We also did a couple of exercises that required the deployment of that resource. In this section, we'll focus on deploying networks in multiple scenarios – including additional concepts such as **naming resolution** and **network throughput**.

Planning a network

Besides the concepts covered in the previous section, such as using correct address space, avoiding too-big subnets, and avoiding overlapping addresses, there are additional things to consider before you deploy a network:

- **Region**: Remember that networks are regional resources, meaning resources provisioned within a virtual network must be deployed to the same region as the network. What's more, in most cases you'll search for a region that guarantees you the lowest latency.

- **Segmentation**: Depending on your requirements, you may need a different approach to network segmentation. Some scenarios require different networks as that architecture will allow for more granular access via **role-based access control** (RBAC). Networks also have limitations when it comes to the number of network interfaces and private addresses available – take that into account when designing your solution.

- **Connectivity**: Remember that by default, subnets within the same virtual network can communicate with each other. This can be mitigated using NSGs, which will be covered later in this chapter.

- **Peerings**: If you plan to implement peerings for your networks, make sure you understand different requirements and constraints depending on the characteristics of your virtual networks. We'll dive into that topic in this chapter when talking about peering in general.

- **Permissions**: It's important to properly design the access structure for your networks so that principals unrelated to a given service are not allowed to change or even read its network settings.

Let's now see how networks can be deployed in various scenarios.

Creating a virtual network with a subnet

We'll start with a simple scenario where we deploy a virtual network with a pre-configured subnet. To do that, we'll need a single command:

```
az network vnet create \
  --name <virtual-network-name> \
  --resource-group <resource-group-name> \
  --address-prefix 10.0.0.0/16 \
  --subnet-name default \
  --subnet-prefixes 10.0.0.0/24
```

Enter that command into your terminal and hit the *Enter* button. After a moment, you should see a standard JSON result containing most of the information related to the virtual network you created. As we provided parameters configuring a subnet, you should be able to immediately search for it using this command:

```
az network vnet subnet show \
  --name default \
  --vnet-name <vnet-name> \
  --resource-group <resource-group-name>
```

This command will confirm that a subnet is created within the network you created previously, by displaying its metadata. Remember that this command should be run within the context of a virtual network that contains the subnet you're looking for.

Adding a new address range to a virtual network

Once a virtual network is created, its address range is not locked. You can either change the existing range or add a new one. Let's see how we can deploy a new address range using the Azure CLI:

```
az network vnet update \
  --address-prefixes 10.0.0.0/16 10.1.0.0/24 \
  --name <vnet-name> \
  --resource-group <resource-group-name>
```

Note that when adding a new address range, you need to provide all the ranges that are already configured for a virtual network. If you provide only a new one, you may see the following error:

```
(NetcfgInvalidSubnet) Subnet <subnet-name> is not valid in virtual
network '<vnet-name>'.
Code: NetcfgInvalidSubnet
Message: Subnet '<subnet-name>' is not valid in virtual network
'<vnet-name>'.
```

Such an error is caused by the validation rules of the virtual network. Azure assumes that you'd like to erase other address ranges, but because there's already a subnet in that virtual network, this operation is disallowed.

> **Important note**
>
> Though in many scenarios Azure will block you from erasing existing address ranges, you may still accidentally remove them if they contain no resources. When using the command line for such an operation, make sure you're providing all ranges you want to have for that network!

If needed, the operation can be performed using other tools, including an IaC approach.

Configuring subnet delegation

Some Azure services require additional permissions to be set for them to be able to deploy service-specific resources. This includes services such as **Azure API Management**, **Azure App Service**, and even databases such as **Azure Database for MySQL** or **Azure Database for PostgreSQL**. To deploy those permissions, you will need to delegate a subnet to a specific Azure service. Once the subnet is delegated, you cannot allocate it for another service.

> **Important note**
>
> To be more specific, it's possible to have multiple delegations for a subnet. However, this is achievable only for compatible services; for example, you cannot delegate a subnet for both Azure App Service and **Azure SQL Database**.

To delegate a subnet, use the following command:

```
az network vnet subnet update \
    --resource-group <resource-group-name> \
    --name <subnet-name> \
    --vnet-name <vnet-name> \
    --delegations <delegation>
```

However, you may not be aware of valid values of the `<delegation>` parameter. As the list is dynamic, there's no point in listing it here. However, we can fetch it using a simple HTTP endpoint:

```
GET https://management.azure.com/subscriptions/<subscription-id>/
providers/Microsoft.Network/locations/<location>/
availableDelegations?api-version=2022-09-01
```

As this command is executed in a subscription context, we'll need a `Bearer` token sent as well in the `Authorization` header. You can easily obtain a token using the following Azure CLI commands:

```
az account get-access-token --query accessToken
```

To send a request, you'll need any **REST** client available (such as **cURL**, **Nightingale**, or **Postman**). The full request looks like this:

```
Method: GET, RequestUri: 'https://management.azure.com/
subscriptions/<subscription-id>/providers/Microsoft.Network/
locations/<location>/availableDelegations?api-version=2022-09-01',
Version: 2.0, Content: <null>, Headers:
{
   Authorization: Bearer <accessToken>
}
```

Remember to substitute `subscription-id`, `location`, and `accessToken` parameters. The result of such a request is an array of available delegations. A delegation's metadata will look like this:

```
{
      "name": "Microsoft.Web.serverFarms",
      "id": "/subscriptions/<subscription-id>/providers/Microsoft.
Network/availableDelegations/Microsoft.Web.serverFarms",
      "type": "Microsoft.Network/availableDelegations",
      "serviceName": "Microsoft.Web/serverFarms",
      "actions": [
        "Microsoft.Network/virtualNetworks/subnets/action"
      ]
}
```

As you can see, it consists of name, identifier, type, service name, and actions (which are an array of permissions) allowed to be performed by a service that gets delegation. Once you learn possible services for delegation, you can choose one and try to delegate a subnet for it. In my case, I chose the same service (*Azure App Service*) that I presented previously:

```
az network vnet subnet update \
    --resource-group <resource-group-name> \
    --name <subnet-name> \
    --vnet-name <vnet-name> \
    --delegations Microsoft.Web/serverFarms
```

Once the command completes, you'll receive a standard JSON response containing your subnet data, including the configured delegation. To check the current state of delegations for your subnet, use the following command:

```
az network vnet subnet show \
    --resource-group <resource-group-name> \
    --name <subnet-name> \
    --vnet-name <vnet-name> \
    --query delegations
```

As a result, you'll get an array of configured delegations (which, for many scenarios, will contain only a single item).

One thing worth remembering is if you want to configure multiple delegations (assuming they're compatible with each other), you can pass service types separated with a space:

```
az network vnet subnet update \
    --resource-group <resource-group-name> \
    --name <subnet-name> \
    --vnet-name <vnet-name> \
    --delegations <service-type1> <service-type2>
```

In fact, you can follow the same logic as we did for changing address ranges for virtual networks – if you'd like to change subnet delegation to another service, you can just use the `az network vnet subnet update` command but pass a different value for the `-delegations` parameter.

By now, you should have a basic understanding of working with virtual networks in Azure. We talked about design basics (non-overlapping address spaces, proper sizes), deployment of networks, and resize operations. Let's do one more step and learn something about NSGs.

Understanding NSGs

Virtual networks in Azure are used for segmentation and security boundaries for resources, but alone cannot be configured to define more granular access when it comes to defining which protocol and which port can be used for communication. To establish that level of control, you will need to use NSGs. This section is meant to give you a general overview of that resource type and possible use cases.

How do NSGs work?

Azure NSGs are a way to filter incoming and outgoing traffic for Azure networks. They allow you to decide how traffic should be handled depending on ports, protocols, or origin of traffic. NSGs can be assigned to either network interfaces or subnets, giving you flexible setup and granular configuration options.

It's important to remember that NSGs work differently depending on the resource to which they are attached. However, all instances of that service share some common features, which are set out as follows:

- `DenyAllInbound/AllowInternetOutbound` **rules**: Each NSG has a couple of default rules that are effective all the time (unless you explicitly override them). By default, NSGs deny all inbound traffic (so that no one/nothing can connect to your services) and allow outbound connectivity to the internet (so that your resources within a virtual network can connect to an internet service – for example, to download updates).

- **Priority**: Each rule defined for an NSG instance has a priority expressed as an integer. The lower the value, the higher priority that specific rule has. For example, let's say you defined one rule with a priority of `10` and a second rule with a priority of `1000`. In NSGs, a priority of `10` is higher than `1000`, so the second rule can be overridden by the first one.

- **Overriding**: Different rules can define a similar set of protocols and ports. If that is the case, rules with higher priority will override ones with lower priority, assuming they share part of the configuration. For instance, you define a rule that allows inbound connections within the `10000-11000` port range. If you define a rule with a higher priority that will block connections for `10023`, `10099`, and `10475` ports, it will override those individual ports, but leave the rest unaffected.

There's also a general suggestion to consider when working with NSGs – while you can attach them to both subnets and network interfaces, it's advised to avoid such a setup (in other words – select either a subnet or network interface, not both). This comes from the fact that configuring an NSG for both places may lead to unexpected traffic errors due to conflicting rulesets defined for multiple instances.

Let's now check how we can deploy, configure, and test NSGs.

Working with NSGs

In this section, we'll cover setting up an NSG along with custom rules and attaching it to both a network interface and subnet. This will give you a general overview of the service in connection to common scenarios.

Deploying an NSG for a network interface

A basic scenario when working with NSGs is attaching them to network interfaces that are then assigned to VMs in Azure. This allows you to control traffic on a host level and is mostly used when you have multiple machines serving different purposes.

We'll start with deploying an NSG that is not assigned to any resources:

```
az network nsg create -g <resource-group-name> -n <nsg-name>
```

Once completed, you'll get a standard JSON output containing the properties of a created resource. The next step is deploying a network interface and attaching the NSG we created to it:

```
az network nic create -g <resource-group-name> \
  --vnet-name <vnet-name> \
  --subnet <subnet-name>
  -n <nic-name>
  --network-security-group <nsg-name>
```

As you can see, to deploy a network interface, you'll need an existing virtual network and a subnet. Refer to the beginning of this chapter for detailed instructions on how to deploy one.

> **Important note**
>
> Make sure both the network interface and NSG are in the same region. Azure doesn't allow attaching an NSG to a network interface if they are in separate regions.

Once the commands are completed, you can verify the configuration by querying network interfaces that are linked to your NSG:

```
az network nsg show -n <nsg-name> -g <resource-group-name> --query
networkInterfaces[0].id
```

As the same NSG can be attached to multiple resources, we used a [0] index in our query. This means that we're looking for the first interface, which is listed here – this command obviously works in our scenario because we have only one place where the NSG is attached.

Deploying an NSG for a subnet

A second scenario where using NSGs is possible is deploying them for subnets. That approach is slightly different from the previous example where we used a network interface because it's meant for general control over connectivity to and from a subnet. This may become handy if you have a virtual network with various services that should be isolated from each other. By default, even if you put them in separate subnets, they will still be able to connect to each other (at least on the infrastructure level). By deploying an NSG for each subnet, you can achieve real isolation between them.

To deploy an NSG for a subnet, we'll need three components:

- Virtual network
- Subnet
- NSG

For the sake of our exercise, we'll enhance our scenario a little bit by deploying two separate subnets that will be used later when we'll be configuring rules for NSGs and testing the connection.

Let's start by creating all the resources we need:

```
az network nsg create -g <resource-group-name> -n <nsg-name>
az network vnet create -g <resource-group-name> -n <vnet-name>
```

Once both an NSG and a virtual network are created, we can proceed with creating a subnet:

```
az network vnet subnet create --name <subnet-name> \
   --resource-group <resource-group-name>
   --vnet-name <vnet-name>
   --network-security-group <nsg-name>
   --address-prefixes 10.0.0.0/24
```

As you can see, we're passing an additional parameter, --network-security-group, here, which will be linked to the subnet created. We omitted the rest of the optional parameters (such as --delegations), but they can be safely passed along if you need them. Otherwise, default values will be assumed.

> **Important note**
>
> When defining an NSG for a subnet or network interface using the –network-security-group parameter, you can pass either the name of the NSG or its identifier. Both options are valid when the NSG is in the same resource group as the resources you're linking it to, but if they're in separate resource groups, you need to pass the full identifier to make it work. The identifier looks like this: /subscriptions/<subscription-id>/resourceGroups/<resource-group-name>/providers/Microsoft.Network/networkSecurityGroups/<nsg-name>.

When your subnet is created, we can confirm the NSG is correctly assigned to it by using the following command:

```
az network nsg show -n <nsg-name> -g <resource-group-name> --query
subnets[0].id
```

Here, we're making the same assumption we made when assigning an NSG to a network interface – as we have only one subnet linked to our resource, we can just use a [0] index for our query. In other scenarios, you will need to learn which index should be used.

> **Important note**
>
> In many scenarios, we could write a more sophisticated query to find a resource we're looking for. Unfortunately, linking between subnets/network interfaces and NSGs doesn't provide much information besides their resource identifiers. This is why we cannot filter records using, for example, the resource name – this information isn't part of the data returned by Azure Resource Manager.

We've now learned how to attach an NSG for both a network interface and a subnet. Let's see how we can configure security rules for that resource.

Configuring security rules

Each NSG consists of multiple security rules that define how network traffic is handled. As mentioned previously, each rule has its priority value, which will tell us how important it is. Besides priority, rules describe the used protocol, origin and/or destination of traffic, and additional things such as integration with **application security groups** (**ASGs**), which we'll describe later in this chapter. To configure a rule, we can use the Azure portal, Azure CLI, Azure PowerShell, or even IaC. In this chapter, we'll focus on the use of the Azure CLI so that you learn the basics.

Creating a security rule for an NSG can be performed using the following command:

```
az network nsg rule create -g <resource-group-name> \
   --nsg-name <nsg-name> \
   -n <rule-name> \
   --priority <priority-value> \
   --source-address-prefixes <source-address-prefixes> \
   --source-port-ranges <source-port-ranges> \
   --destination-address-prefixes <destination-address-prefixes> \
   --destination-port-ranges <destination-port-range> \
   --access <access-type> \
   --protocol <protocol> \
   --direction <direction> \
   --description <description>
```

That's a lot, isn't it? The preceding example is almost a full example where you can define many different parameters of a security rule. Let's describe them briefly so that we're able to create a rule on our own:

- resource-group-name: A name of a resource group where the NSG was deployed.

- nsg-name: The name of the NSG where a rule should be created.

- rule-name: A friendly name for your rule.

- priority-value: An integer from 100 to 4096 indicating how important a rule is (the lower the number, the higher priority a rule has).

- source-address-prefixes: IP address prefixes, from where connections should be either allowed or denied.

- source-port-ranges: Individual ports or port ranges, from where connections should be either allowed or denied.

- destination-address-prefixes: IP address prefixes, to which connection should be allowed or denied.

- `destination-port-range`: Individual ports or port ranges, to which connection should be allowed or denied.

- `access-type`: A string indicating if a connection is allowed or denied for that configuration (accepts two values: `Allow` or `Deny`).

- `protocol`: A protocol for which that rule should be evaluated. Currently allowed values are `TCP`, `UDP`, `ICMP`, `ESP`, `AH`, or `Any`.

- `direction`: A value stating whether this rule should apply for inbound or outbound traffic (accepts two values: `Inbound` or `Outbound`).

- `description`: Optional text describing the rule.

> **Important note**
>
> If you use the Azure portal for creating a rule, ESP and AH ports won't be available. They can be used only if they interact with Azure using the CLI, **SDK**, or IaC.

We understand the theory – let's now see the process of creating a rule in practice. Use the following command to create it – make sure you replace some of the values with the names of your own resources:

```
az network nsg rule create -g <resource-group-name> \
  --nsg-name <nsg-name> \
  -n BlockAccessFromOtherSubnet \
  --priority 1000 \
  --source-address-prefixes 10.0.1.0/24 \
  --source-port-range * \
  --destination-address-prefixes * \
  --destination-port-ranges * \
  --access Deny \
  --protocol * \
  --description "Deny all connections from other subnet"
```

The rule we're creating will block all connections coming from the `10.0.1.0/24` IP address range, no matter which port was chosen to initiate a connection. What's more, it also doesn't matter what's the destination of that connection. Note that we're using an asterisk (`*`) here for some of the values. That character is evaluated as *any* value and can be used for address prefixes, ports, and protocol.

If you want to create a rule that blocks all connections but only for a specific subrange of address prefixes/port ranges, you can slightly modify the rule we used previously:

```
az network nsg rule create -g <resource-group-name> \
  --nsg-name <nsg-name> \
  -n BlockAccessFromOtherSubnetToSpecificService \
  --priority 1000 \
```

```
--source-address-prefixes 10.0.1.0/24 \
--source-port-range * \
--destination-address-prefixes 10.0.0.2 \
--destination-port-ranges 80 \
--access Deny \
--protocol * \
--description "Deny all connections from other subnet accessing web
server"
```

This rule would work in a very similar way to the previous one. The only difference is that we are making it more specific – it'll block connections only if they are targeting the 10.0.0.2:80 address (for example, a web server running on a VM on port 80). Let's see now how we can override defined security rules.

Overriding security rules

In some scenarios, you want a generic security rule that blocks access to a variety of services in your network. Such powerful rules may need to be overridden for a couple of services that are guaranteed to be secure. Let's deploy an example setup for that scenario to see how to configure it:

```
az network nsg rule create -g <resource-group-name> \
  --nsg-name <nsg-name> \
  -n BlockAccess \
  --priority 1000 \
  --source-address-prefixes 10.0.1.0/24 \
  --source-port-range * \
  --destination-address-prefixes 10.0.0.0/24 \
  --destination-port-ranges * \
  --access Deny \
  --protocol *

az network nsg rule create -g <resource-group-name> \
  --nsg-name <nsg-name> \
  -n AllowAccessForSecureServices \
  --priority 900 \
  --source-address-prefixes 10.0.1.12 10.0.1.23 \
  --source-port-range * \
  --destination-address-prefixes * \
  --destination-port-ranges * \
  --access Allow \
  --protocol *
```

We deployed two separate security rules in our NSG:

- The first one, named `BlockAccess`, will deny access for all traffic originating from the `10.0.1.0/24` network and targeting the `10.0.0.0/24` network

- The second one unblocks access if the source of traffic originates from `10.0.1.12` or `10.0.1.23` IP addresses

Note that we're overriding one rule with another by using different priority values. As in terms of importance, a value of 1000 is less important than 900, we can make sure that a small subset of services is allowed to make all the connections.

Validating connection

We deployed a couple of NSGs with security rules. Now comes the time to test the configuration. Depending on the IP addresses selected, protocols, and port configuration, validating our setup may be either a quick check or a sophisticated test suite. For the sake of providing an idea for doing such tests, we'll cover quite a simple scenario of trying to connect two VMs provisioned inside the same subnet. Let's start with deploying resources needed for our use case:

```
az vm create -n <first-vm-name> -g <resource-group-name> --image
Ubuntu2204 --vnet-name <vnet-name> --subnet <subnet> --admin-username
<username> --admin-password <password>
az vm create -n <second-vm-name> -g <resource-group-name> --image
Ubuntu2204 --vnet-name <vnet-name> --subnet <subnet> --admin-username
<username> --admin-password <password>
```

Those two commands will let us save some time as they will deploy two separate VMs with default configuration (which includes public and private IP addresses, NSGs, network interfaces, and disks). You only need to provide the same virtual network and subnet for them and the username and password you'd like to use to connect.

> **Important note**
>
> We're using a simplified version of the Azure CLI meant for deploying **Azure VMs** as we haven't covered that topic yet. We'll dive into the details of that process in *Chapter 5, Provisioning Azure Virtual Machines.*

After a moment, you should have two VMs deployed in the resource group you selected. They were created in the same network, so by default, there's nothing there to control the traffic between them. To test the connection between those two machines, we can use, for example, `ping`. However, before we do that, we need to make sure one of the NSGs allows connecting to a machine over **SSH** (port `22`).

> **Important note**
>
> In this section, we'll make the assumption that you deployed VMs to the same resource group and they are the only resources in it. We're doing that to simplify finding the values, as we'll be able to use indexes where querying resources.

Use the following command to check that:

```
az network nsg list -g <resource-group-name> --query [0].
securityRules[?destinationPortRange=='22'].access
```

Make sure that you get a result stating that such a connection is allowed:

```
[
  "Allow"
]
```

If that's not the case, we need to create a security rule that will allow connections from the internet using port 22. Such a rule needs to be created on one of the NSGs that were created along with the VM – it doesn't really matter which one you select if you'll use a proper VM for making connections.

> **Important note**
>
> If you wish, you may create the same rule for both NSGs. This will simplify your setup, though it's not something you should do in production environments.

To create a rule, use the following command:

```
az network nsg rule create -g <resource-group-name> \
  --nsg-name <nsg-name> \
  -n AllowSSHConnection \
  --priority 1000 \
  --source-address-prefixes * \
  --source-port-range * \
  --destination-address-prefixes * \
  --destination-port-ranges * \
  --access Allow \
  --protocol * \
  --direction Inbound
```

Once created, you'll be able to connect to the machine of your choice. Now, we can try to make a connection to one of the machines. First, let's obtain the public IP address:

```
az network public-ip list -g <resource-group-name> --query [0].
ipAddress
```

Then, I'll use my terminal for that and just try to connect to one of the hosts using the following syntax:

```
ssh <admin-username>@<public-ip-address>
```

If everything is correct, you'll be asked to confirm the connection (because, most likely, the host you're connecting to is not considered secure) and provide the user's password. Here's how it looked in my terminal:

```
The authenticity of host '20.16.64.188 (20.16.64.188)' can't be
established.
ECDSA key fingerprint is SHA256:d5rbnz...
Are you sure you want to continue connecting (yes/no/[fingerprint])?
yes
Warning: Permanently added '20.16.64.188' (ECDSA) to the list of known
hosts.
aach03@20.16.64.188's password:
Welcome to Ubuntu 22.04.2 LTS (GNU/Linux 5.15.0-1037-azure x86_64)
```

From now on, you can work in your terminal being connected to the VM, meaning all the commands you execute will be run remotely instead of your computer. We have one more thing to do – check whether we're able to connect to another machine we created. To do that, we'll leverage its private IP address, which can be found with a simple query:

```
az network nic list -g <resource-group-name> --query [1].
ipConfigurations[0].privateIpAddress
```

Then, while still connected via SSH to the first VM, we can run the `ping` command to see if we have connectivity:

```
ping -c 2 <private-ip-address>
```

If your setup is correct, you'll receive the following result:

```
PING 10.0.0.5 (10.0.0.5) 56(84) bytes of data.
64 bytes from 10.0.0.5: icmp_seq=1 ttl=64 time=1.88 ms
64 bytes from 10.0.0.5: icmp_seq=2 ttl=64 time=0.776 ms

--- 10.0.0.5 ping statistics ---
2 packets transmitted, 2 received, 0% packet loss, time 1002ms
rtt min/avg/max/mdev = 0.776/1.328/1.880/0.552 ms
```

Great – for now, everything works as expected. Our VMs can see each other, but actually, there's one gotcha here – we're allowed to communicate because the NSGs created for our machines have a default rule that allows connectivity between resources in the same network. This specific rule is named `AllowVnetInBound` and allows connections as long as both the origin and destination of a connection are set to `VirtualNetwork`. We can easily change that behavior by adding a new rule that will block communication – let's try to do it in a way that will block answering `ping` calls. First, obtain the name of the NSG attached to the second VM:

```
az network nsg list -g <resource-group-name> --query [1].name
```

Then, use that name to add a new security rule:

```
az network nsg rule create -g <resource-group-name> \
   --nsg-name <nsg-name> \
   -n BlockPing \
   --priority 900 \
   --source-address-prefixes * \
   --source-port-range * \
   --destination-address-prefixes * \
   --destination-port-ranges * \
   --access Deny \
   --protocol ICMP \
   --direction Inbound
```

Now, after a couple of seconds (needed to refresh the configuration of your network), try to run `ping` once again:

```
ping -c 2 10.0.0.5
PING 10.0.0.5 (10.0.0.5) 56(84) bytes of data.

--- 10.0.0.5 ping statistics ---
2 packets transmitted, 0 received, 100% packet loss, time 1031ms
```

As you can see, communication is now blocked – we denied communicating with that specific VM using the **ICMP protocol**, which is used by the `ping` command to send packets. Congratulations – you successfully configured your NSG and can now work on improving it with your own rules! In the next section, you'll learn about a topic that is similar to NSGs, called ASGs. As they may work with each other in the same moment, it's something worth learning, especially since it's a much simpler concept than NSGs.

ASGs

The last topic for this part of the chapter is a concept called **ASGs**. They work in a similar way to NSGs but are actually rather a complementary solution to them, meant to be an extension of your application's infrastructure. In other words, NSGs are very often used as a low-level mechanism of network security configured by dedicated network teams, while ASGs could be managed by application teams for better control over their services' connectivity. Let's visualize the concept:

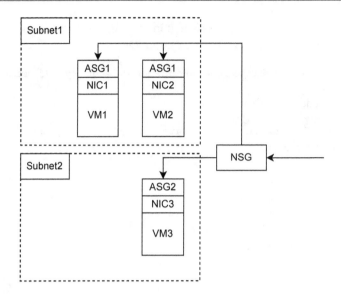

Figure 3.4 – High-level overview of ASGs

In the preceding diagram, you can see there are three separate VMs that are deployed in two separate subnets. We have a single NSG, two separate ASGs, and three different **network interface card** (**NICs**). As you can see, communication is controlled by an NSG and then validated by ASGs. In this setup, the NSG is meant to provide a baseline for network security, and ASGs are used as a target for security rules. Let's see how we can implement this using the Azure CLI.

We'll start by creating two separate ASGs – one named `AppWeb`, and a second named `AppDb`:

```
az network asg create --name AppWeb --resource-group <resource-group-
name>
az network asg create --name AppDb --resource-group <resource-group-
name>
```

Now, we'll create two network interfaces that will have those ASGs assigned:

```
az network nic create --name <nic-name>-01 --resource-group
<resource-group-name> --vnet-name <vnet-name> --subnet <subnet-name>
--application-security-group AppWeb
az network nic create --name <nic-name>-02 --resource-group
<resource-group-name> --vnet-name <vnet-name> --subnet <subnet-name>
--application-security-group AppDb
```

Once those commands are complete, we'll have two network interfaces with ASGs assigned to them. The only thing left is to create an NSG with security rules pointing to the ASGs we created:

```
az network nsg create -g <resource-group-name> -n <nsg-name>
az network nsg rule create -g <resource-group-name> \
```

```
--nsg-name <nsg-name> \
-n AllowInternetToWebConnection \
--priority 1000 \
--source-address-prefixes Internet \
--destination-port-ranges 80 8080 \
--access Allow \
--protocol Tcp \
--direction Inbound \
--destination-asgs AppWeb
```

We've now allowed connectivity to the network interface, which would be attached to a VM hosting a web server. Let's now unblock access from that VM to our database:

```
az network nsg rule create -g <resource-group-name> \
  --nsg-name <nsg-name> \
  -n AllowWebToDatabaseConnection \
  --priority 900 \
  --source-asgs AppWeb \
  --access Allow \
  --protocol Tcp \
  --direction Inbound \
  --destination-asgs AppDb
```

That's all! With this setup, instead of managing groups of rules and assigning them to new resources you created, you can just reuse the existing ASG and attach it to the network interfaces you provision. This simplifies your setup and helps when working in a dynamic environment.

You learned a lot about NSGs and different ways of working with that service. The next topic we're going to cover is network peerings, which will greatly improve your skills in setting up and managing network setups.

Working with virtual network peerings

In Azure, virtual networks work as a way of isolating your services. By default, there's no direct way of communicating between resources that span multiple networks. Of course, if you expose your services publicly (for example, via configuration in NSGs), you'll be able to make a connection between them. However, what if you want to keep them private and still be able to connect? To achieve such functionality, you need to use network peering. Let's discover that topic.

How does peering work?

When you set up a peering between networks, they will appear as a single network, even though they will be still separate Azure resources. This implies that your network cannot have overlapping address spaces – a problem we discussed at the very beginning of this chapter. Azure supports two types of peering – peering within the same region and global peering, which can be used if your networks are deployed to different regions. We'll discuss them separately.

The creation of a peering doesn't cause downtime in your applications and is supported by **Azure Resource Manager** (meaning you can use an IaC approach to configure it). The connection between peered networks is private – that is, no additional gateways are involved, and you don't need to encrypt communication or set up custom routing tables. Let's see how both types of peering can be configured.

Setting up peerings

To deploy a peering, we'll need virtual networks that we'd like to connect. Each network can have multiple peerings enabled, but a peering itself isn't transitive, meaning you always need to explicitly set it up for each pair of networks. Consider the following scenario – you have three different virtual networks named VNet1, VNet2, and VNet3. You set up peering between VNet1 and VNet2, then between VNet2 and VNet3. It'll look like this:

* VNet1 <--> VNet2
* VNet2 <--> VNet3

Now, to achieve a connection between VNet1 and VNet3, you need to configure peering between those networks. Even though VNet1 can communicate with VNet2, and VNet2 is able to communicate with VNet3, the communication channel is not established for VNet1 and VNet3.

To see how that feature works in practice, we'll start with defining a peering between networks in the same region.

Setting up peering for networks in the same region

We'll start that exercise by creating three separate networks, all in the same region and the same resource group. From the perspective of peering, whether a network is in the same or another subscription or resource group doesn't matter. All we need is to know its locations (defined as a combination of subscription and resource groups). Use the following commands to create your networks:

```
az network vnet create -g <resource-group-name> -n <vnet-name>-01
--address-prefixes 10.0.0.0/24 --subnet-name default --subnet-prefixes
10.0.0.0/26
az network vnet create -g <resource-group-name> -n <vnet-name>-02
--address-prefixes 10.0.1.0/24 --subnet-name default --subnet-prefixes
10.0.1.0/26
az network vnet create -g <resource-group-name> -n <vnet-name>-03
--address-prefixes 10.0.2.0/24 --subnet-name default --subnet-prefixes
10.0.2.0/26
```

Once those commands complete, we'll have three virtual networks created. Note that we explicitly provide the --address-prefixes parameter with our own ranges to be certain networks won't overlap.

Now, use the following commands to deploy three separate VMs, one per each created network. We'll use them to validate connection in a similar way to what we did in one of the previous exercises when talking about NSGs:

```
az vm create -n <vm-name>-01 -g <resource-group-name> --image
Ubuntu2204 --vnet-name <vnet-name>-01 --subnet default --admin-
username <username> --admin-password <password>
az vm create -n <vm-name>-02 -g <resource-group-name> --image
Ubuntu2204 --vnet-name <vnet-name>-02 --subnet default --admin-
username <username> --admin-password <password>
az vm create -n <vm-name>-03 -g <resource-group-name> --image
Ubuntu2204 --vnet-name <vnet-name>-03 --subnet default --admin-
username <username> --admin-password <password>
```

So far, so good – we have three separate hosts, each isolated from each other thanks to separate networks. However, each of those VMs has a public IP address assigned – we'll ignore that for the sake of simplicity for this exercise. In production environments, we'd most probably remove those IP addresses if a host didn't need to be available publicly.

Let's list all the private IP addresses assigned to our machines:

```
az network nic list -g <resource-group-name> --query
[].ipConfigurations[0].privateIpAddress
```

The result will be an array of IPs created for them:

```
[
  "10.0.0.4",
  "10.0.1.4",
  "10.0.2.4"
]
```

Now, we want to test the connection between any of those machines. Use the following command to find the public IP address of the first machine we created and use it to connect to it over SSH:

```
az network public-ip list -g <resource-group-name> --query [0].
ipAddress
<ip-address>
ssh <admin-username>@<ip-address>
```

After connecting to the VM use `ping` to send packets to the second or third private IP address you received using the previous command:

```
ping -c 2 10.0.1.4
PING 10.0.1.4 (10.0.1.4) 56(84) bytes of data.

--- 10.0.1.4 ping statistics ---
2 packets transmitted, 0 received, 100% packet loss, time 1013ms
```

As we expected, connection is not allowed – the IP address cannot be found, so there's no possibility to connect. Let's create a peering between the first two networks to see if that changes anything.

Creating a peering requires running the same command twice. The reason for that is quite simple – both networks need to *agree* on establishing a link before you can establish communication. See the following commands for an example:

```
az network vnet peering create -g <resource-group-name> -n <peering-
name> --vnet-name <vnet-name>-01 --remote-vnet <vnet-name>-02 --allow-
vnet-access
az network vnet peering create -g <resource-group-name> -n <peering-
name> --vnet-name <vnet-name>-02 --remote-vnet <vnet-name>-01 --allow-
vnet-access
```

Note that we reversed the --vnet-name and --remote-vnet values for the second run of that command. We're also using the --allow-vnet-access parameter so that traffic originating in each of the provided networks is allowed to access remote services. Use SSH to connect to the first VM once again, and try to connect to the second one using its private IP address:

```
ping -c 2 10.0.1.4
PING 10.0.1.4 (10.0.1.4) 56(84) bytes of data.
64 bytes from 10.0.1.4: icmp_seq=1 ttl=64 time=2.28 ms
64 bytes from 10.0.1.4: icmp_seq=2 ttl=64 time=0.816 ms

--- 10.0.1.4 ping statistics ---
2 packets transmitted, 2 received, 0% packet loss, time 1001ms
rtt min/avg/max/mdev = 0.816/1.548/2.281/0.732 ms
```

As you can see, the connection is now allowed, and our host can connect to the second machine, even though the used IP address is not available in the local network address range. However, if you try to call the third VM in the same way, it won't work:

```
ping -c 2 10.0.2.4
PING 10.0.2.4 (10.0.2.4) 56(84) bytes of data.

--- 10.0.2.4 ping statistics ---
2 packets transmitted, 0 received, 100% packet loss, time 1026ms
```

To fix that, you'd need to create a new peering, but this time between our first and third networks. Try to do that on your own before learning about global peerings in the next section!

Setting up peering for networks in different regions

Creating a peering between networks in different regions is slightly different from the previous scenario. The main difference comes from the parameters used to establish a connection. When connecting a virtual network from the same resource group, you can just use its name to configure a peering. For global peerings, you need to use the full resource identifier of the remote network.

> **Important note**
>
> The scenario and solution we're discussing here will work for setting up peerings between networks in separate resource groups or subscriptions as well.

Let's start by creating networks deployed to different regions:

```
az network vnet create -g <resource-group-name> -n <vnet-name>-01
--address-prefixes 10.0.0.0/24 --subnet-name default --subnet-prefixes
10.0.0.0/26
az network vnet create -g <resource-group-name> -n <vnet-name>-02
--address-prefixes 10.0.1.0/24 --subnet-name default --subnet-prefixes
10.0.1.0/26 --location <second-location>
```

For this exercise, make sure you're selecting a different location from the location of your resource group and pass it using the --location parameter.

> **Important note**
>
> You can use az account list-locations to list all locations that are available for your account.

Once both virtual networks are created, create two separate VMs in the same way as we did when creating a peering for networks in the same region. Make sure that the second machine is created in the same location as your network:

```
az vm create -n <vm-name>-01 -g <resource-group-name> --image
Ubuntu2204 --vnet-name <vnet-name>-01 --subnet default --admin-
username <username> --admin-password <password>
az vm create -n <vm-name>-02 -g <resource-group-name> --image
Ubuntu2204 --vnet-name <vnet-name>-02 --subnet default --admin-
username <username> --admin-password <password> --location <second-
location>
```

The last step is to set up a peering. As mentioned previously, we need to obtain the identifier of each network resource. To do that, use the following command:

```
az network vnet list -g <resource-group-name> --query [].id
```

Copy the provided value for both of your networks and then create the peering:

```
az network vnet peering create -g <resource-group-name> -n <peering-
name> --vnet-name <vnet-name>-01 --remote-vnet <remote-vnet-id>
--allow-vnet-access
az network vnet peering create -g <resource-group-name> -n <peering-
name> --vnet-name <vnet-name>-02 --remote-vnet <remote-vnet-id>
--allow-vnet-access
```

Remember that the `--remote-vnet` parameter must contain the identifier of a network you're peering with – the first command will point to the second network, and the second command will point to the first network. The last step is confirming that our configuration works. To do that, use SSH to connect to each VM and use the `ping` command to send packets to a private IP address assigned to one of the network interfaces (check the previous section to see how to do that). The result should look like mine:

```
ping -c 2 10.0.1.4
PING 10.0.1.4 (10.0.1.4) 56(84) bytes of data.
64 bytes from 10.0.1.4: icmp_seq=1 ttl=64 time=24.0 ms
64 bytes from 10.0.1.4: icmp_seq=2 ttl=64 time=20.7 ms

--- 10.0.1.4 ping statistics ---
2 packets transmitted, 2 received, 0% packet loss, time 1001ms
rtt min/avg/max/mdev = 20.708/22.372/24.036/1.664 ms
```

Congratulations! You successfully set up a connection between different networks, even though they're in separate Azure regions.

> **Important note**
>
> This example should help you understand why you need to configure peering for both ends. As the only thing needed to have it set up is to learn either the name of a virtual network or its identifier, both networks must accept the connection, so it's much harder to do it by mistake. Authorizing access to network configuration is an additional layer and should be done using RBAC.

In this section, we discussed the basics of working with peerings using a standard network-to-network connection. There are more advanced things to learn here (for example, using a network gateway instead), but they're out of the scope of this book. Let's jump to the last topic of this chapter – working with network routing and endpoints in Azure.

Network routing and endpoints

In Azure, basic networking setup is done automatically when you provision network components such as virtual networks and subnets. In many scenarios, the default setup can be enough, and you don't need to incorporate a custom configuration. For everything else, Azure gives you the possibility to introduce custom routes, use **Border Gateway Protocol** (**BGP**), and leverage service and private endpoints for improved security. We'll briefly characterize them in this section.

System routes

When a subnet is provisioned, Azure automatically assigns a set of default routes to that resource. Those default routes are called **system routes** and cannot be created manually or customized. You can, however, override them using custom routes. Before we dive deeper into that topic, let's quickly describe a route.

The easiest way to describe a **route** in Azure is by imagining a book's index. That part of a book contains specific words or topics and links them with a page number. An Azure route is a very similar thing – it contains an address prefix and a next hop, which defines where traffic should be routed.

Here are two examples of system routes in Azure:

- `0.0.0.0/0 ->` `Internet`
- `10.0.0.0/8 ->` `None`

You can read them as follows – each connection that doesn't target one of the IP addresses defined in the route table will be routed to `Internet`. Additionally, any connection targeting the `10.0.0.0/8` address range will be dropped. Any of those rules can be overridden if you want to use custom routes.

> **Important note**
>
> As system routes are added automatically for each subnet, each of them will contain additional rules pointing to defined address ranges within a network. This means that if you define, for example, a subnet with a `10.0.0.0/24` address range, a new route will be created containing the `10.0.0.0/24 ->` `Virtual network` rule.

There's also one additional behavior of defined routes in Azure. If the destination IP address is an address of one of Azure's services, traffic will be routed via Azure's backbone network. We'll discuss that in detail when talking about service and private endpoints.

Custom routes

In Azure, a **custom route** can be defined by either using a user-defined route or by leveraging BGP. Each of those features has its own set of use cases:

- User-defined routes are used mostly to override system routes. Use them if you feel you need more control over rules determining destinations of traffic in your network.
- BGP is used in hybrid environments where you're integrating an on-premises gateway with an Azure virtual network.

Depending on your setup, the use of one, both, or none mentioned capabilities may be necessary. Additionally, Azure has its own rules for determining the priority of routing in case you have multiple routes pointing to the same address prefix:

1. The most important route is a user-defined route.
2. If a user-defined route is not available, Azure looks for routes defined by BGP.
3. If none of the aforementioned methods is available, Azure will fall back to system routes.

To visualize that with an example, let's consider the following setup:

- `[Default] 0.0.0.0/0 -> Internet`
- `[User] 0.0.0.0/0 -> None`

This is an extreme configuration but will serve the purpose of showing us the implications of the discussed priorities. Here, we have two routes – one marked as `[Default]`, which is the system route. The second one is a user-defined route, hence the `[User]` prefix. The former routes traffic to `Internet`; the latter will drop it. As the latter is a user-defined route having precedence, all traffic will be dropped instead of being routed to `Internet` as the next hop.

> **Important note**
>
> There's one serious implication of overriding the `0.0.0.0/0` system route. If you leave it unchanged, Azure will make sure that even if you target the public IP address of the Azure service, traffic won't leave the internal Azure network. However, if you override it and point to a **virtual network gateway** or **virtual appliance**, all traffic will be routed there, meaning you may lose the benefit of staying within the backbone network. This doesn't have an effect when connecting with services with service endpoints enabled, as service endpoints have their own routing entries.

We'll be talking more about creating user-defined routes in the next chapters. For the last thing in this chapter, let's discuss service and private endpoints, as they're important networking features for improving the security of our infrastructure.

Service and private endpoints

In this chapter, we discuss service and private endpoints in the context of routes and routing in Azure in general. In the next chapters, we'll use them in practice, so there will be more space to see how they affect connectivity in terms of *living* infrastructure. In the previous parts of this section, we mentioned that endpoints may affect routing between our services. How can we understand that statement?

In Azure, we have two types of services when talking about their isolation level – a service can be either available publicly or privately. In other words, you may need only a public IP address to establish a connection (of course, ignoring authentication/authorization – we're considering network-level communication only here), or you need to be within a network to discover a service. When talking about **IaaS**, such a setup is easy to provision and configure. However, what if we want to use **PaaS** services such as Azure App Service, Azure SQL Database, or **Azure Container Registry**? Those are components that cannot be easily deployed to our virtual network due to technical limitations. If that's the case, how can we ensure that traffic between our systems and applications stays private when connecting to them?

This is where service and private endpoints come in handy. They allow us to determine the routing of requests our services make so that we can drop connections coming from outside of our virtual networks while keeping ones that are considered private.

> **Important note**
>
> Both service and private endpoints are concepts related to inbound connectivity. For outbound connectivity, Azure offers a separate set of features that won't be discussed in this book.

Let's see what the main differences between those two services in Azure are.

Service endpoints

A **service endpoint** is a special feature supported by a subset of Azure services, which allows you to easily configure private connectivity between your resources. They're used to make sure that inbound connectivity to Azure resources is allowed only from certain networks. The concept of a service endpoint is quite simple – once enabled, all traffic that originates from within a virtual network will start using the private IP address of a service for which a service endpoint was enabled. **DNS queries** will still be resolved to the public IP address of that service, but that won't matter as inbound connections are from outside of configured virtual networks.

The benefit of using service endpoints is that they don't incur additional charges and are easy to configure. Unfortunately, they cannot be used for security connections originating in on-premises networks, as they work with subnets configured in Azure virtual networks only.

Private endpoints

If you feel that service endpoints may lack the functionalities you seek, Azure offers a separate service called **Azure Private Link**. You can think about it as a *service endpoint on steroids* as it is much more advanced in terms of configurations and capabilities offered. Azure Private Link consists of **Azure Private Endpoints** and **Azure Private Link** services, which serve slightly different purposes.

The main difference between **private endpoints** and **service endpoints** is support for on-premises. While service endpoints cannot be used with on-premises networks and services, private endpoints don't have the same limitation. What's more, when a private endpoint is configured for a service, it remains truly private – that is, its public IP address is no longer available.

> **Important note**
>
> If you want, you can keep public access to your services, even though you enabled a private endpoint for them. In such a scenario, private endpoints can be used to secure inbound connectivity for either your own services (via integration with NSGs) or a subset of functionalities of a given service (for example, you can use a private endpoint to secure access to a `file` endpoint of Azure Storage while keeping other endpoints available for everyone).

To use private endpoints, you need to configure a private **DNS zone** that will be used to properly resolve the DNS name of a service. This is needed because normally, the IP address of a service is resolved using its name available in the public DNS server. Here's an example:

```
database.windows.net -> 168.12.13.15
```

When a private endpoint is enabled, all DNS queries will be resolved to private endpoints (for example, `privatelink.database.windows.net`) that need to be configured individually in another DNS zone (or host file if available).

When using private endpoints, you will be charged additionally for data routed via that service and DNS zones created in Azure. However, in exchange, you'll get a service that allows for much more granular configuration, provides on-premises support, and safely integrates different virtual networks, even if they're used by various customers.

Summary

That's all for *Chapter 3*! We discussed lots of different things, including fundamental topics when planning and structuring networks and resizing, deploying, and securing them using native services. Those topics will enhance your skills when working with networking in Azure and simplify learning more advanced concepts. After this chapter, you should be able to build your own networks, secure them using NSGs, and integrate them using peerings. You also learned some basics of routing and using endpoints in Azure for improved security when using managed Azure resources. You'll improve your knowledge in the next chapters when we leverage concepts from this chapter into real-world scenarios.

In *Chapter 4*, you'll learn about **Azure Load Balancer**, which is an important component of many Azure architectures, as it allows for distributing traffic between multiple VMs and services. This will also enable us to talk about scale sets and availability sets used for building clusters of machines.

Exploring Azure Load Balancer

In the previous chapter, we discussed topics related to networking in general but didn't focus on distributing incoming load across various Azure services. This part of this book is meant to give you a detailed overview of **Azure Load Balancer** – a managed solution that allows you to quickly configure how incoming network traffic should reach different parts of your infrastructure. Knowledge from this chapter will help you when you're managing more complex infrastructure setups that require low-level load-balancing solutions and focus on raw packets.

In this chapter, we're going to cover the following main topics:

- Overview of Azure Load Balancer
- Differences between public and internal load balancers
- Delving into backend pools
- Understanding load balancer rules
- Comprehending health probes

Technical requirements

To perform the exercises in this chapter, you'll need the following:

- Access to an Azure subscription
- The Azure CLI (`https://learn.microsoft.com/en-us/cli/azure/installazure-cli`)

The Code in Action video for this book can be viewed at: `https://packt.link/GTX9F`

Overview of Azure Load Balancer

When building software or computer systems in general, you may face a problem where a single instance of your server is just not enough. You may think about scaling that server up (that is, adding more compute power to it), but every machine has its physical limits. At some point, there's no more possibility to go up – you need to balance the load across multiple machines.

Once you deploy more machines to handle the load, a new problem arises – you have the infrastructure necessary to receive incoming traffic, but how do you point each connection to the appropriate machine? If you think about it, multiple challenges need to be overcome in such a scenario:

- Distributing the load evenly

- Making sure that the user is linked to a single server for the duration of their session (so-called *sticky sessions*)

- Redistributing the load in case one of your machines goes down

- Ensuring the machine responsible for distributing the load is highly available

That's a lot to take care of! Fortunately, in cloud environments, you can leverage a ready-to-use service – in our case, it'll be Azure Load Balancer. We'll discuss the major capabilities of this service that can be used to address these challenges, including alternatives to the service, individual components (such as IP configuration and pools), and the load balancing algorithm that's implemented in Azure Load Balancer.

Load balancing in Azure

Azure offers a couple of different load-balancing services, depending on your needs and the characteristics of the traffic you'd like to balance:

- Azure Load Balancer for distributing traffic at the **TCP/UDP** protocol level

- **Azure Application Gateway** for a generic load balancing solution that incorporates **Web Application Firewall** (**WAF**)

- **Azure Front Door** for global load balancing and improving the performance of your applications by moving some of your cloud infrastructure to the edge

- **Azure Traffic Manager** for **DNS-based load balancing** and improved reliability of your applications

As we're focusing on Azure Load Balancer in this chapter, we'll try to understand how it can fit a low-level infrastructure that includes resources such as VMs and virtual networks. To get started, we'll talk about individual components that can be used to configure your instance of Azure Load Balancer.

Components of Azure Load Balancer

To understand how Azure Load Balancer works, we need to talk a little about its components. Each component is a configurable feature with its own set of parameters and rules. Depending on your requirements and expectations, you'll need to use different values to achieve a setup that will work in your scenario. Let's discuss IP configuration, backend pools, health probes, and rules separately so that we have a better picture of their role in an Azure Load Balancer setup.

Frontend IP configuration

If we want to configure infrastructure where we have a load balancer responsible for distributing a load, we need to make it our entry point. To have it configured that way, we need to assign an IP address to it so that it can be discovered by other services and clients. Azure Load Balancer allows you to decide whether it's a publicly available service or an internal resource by assigning a public or private IP address. The decision will solely depend on the architecture of your solution – if you want to load balance requests only within a virtual network, you won't need an additional (public) IP address.

The part of Azure Load Balancer that is responsible for accepting requests is called the **frontend**. Each instance of that service can have multiple frontends, meaning you can have multiple IP addresses assigned to it. We'll discuss such setups later in this chapter (see *Delving into backend pools*) as it comes with some unique features and limitations.

Backend pool

Assigning an IP address to an instance of Azure Load Balancer makes it available to connect to. However, having only that won't make much difference for the services and clients connecting with it as there will be no destination to pass connections to. This is why we need a component called a **backend pool**. A backend pool is a set of resources that are load-balanced by an instance of Azure Load Balancer. They could be individual VMs or a VM scale set. Backend pools work in tandem with the frontend as we can have multiple frontends connecting to a single backend pool.

Health probes

Each load balancer needs to know if a backend pool is healthy. If that's not the case (that is, a pool is considered unhealthy), traffic won't be passed to that set of machines. In other words, **health probes** allow Azure Load Balancer to make correct decisions about possible destinations for distributing a load. Each health probe is an endpoint that you need to implement and ensure that it gives an instance of a correct Azure Load Balancer response.

Rules

Load balancing is all about rules. A **rule** is a simple item that connects the frontend with backend pools. It's up to you to define all the load-balancing rules and maintain them during the development and maintenance of your services.

There are also additional, more advanced components of Azure Load Balancer available – **high availability ports**, **inbound NAT rules**, and **outbound rules**. Those are features of a **Standard load balancer** in Azure (there are two tiers available – **Basic** and **Standard**); see *Understanding load balancer rules* for more information.

Algorithm of Azure Load Balancer

The algorithm that's used by Azure Load Balancer is called **tuple-based hashing** and is a fairly simple algorithm to understand. In general, tuple-based hashing means that there's N number of **tuples** (values). Then, a hash of those values is calculated, and the result of the hash calculation is used to determine where (and how) traffic should be distributed.

In the case of Azure Load Balancer, five tuples are used by default: **source IP address**, **source port**, **destination IP address**, **destination port**, and **IP protocol number** (for example, 6 for TCP, 17 for UDP). Let's see an example of such values:

- `172.32.0.0:80:10.0.1.57:80:6`

What we have in the preceding bullet is a combination of the aforementioned values containing the source IP address with a port (`172.32.0.0:80`), the destination IP address with a port (`10.0.1.57:80`), and the IP protocol number (6 for TCP). A load balancer may use any hashing algorithm to compute a hash (let's assume it's **SHA1**). The final hash may look like this:

- `f5f0190618cbd1ec901a95ca39b14ec90799983a`

Now, the load balancer will maintain a list of such hashes to know how requests within a session should be distributed. However, what will happen if a client initiates a new session? Well, most likely, a new session will be initialized using another source port that will invalidate the hash and probably route the connection to another machine. This is why a five-tuple hash distribution is considered to provide no session persistence.

To overcome this limitation (as you may need to achieve some level of session persistence), Azure Load Balancer supports two different modes for hash calculation:

- **Two-tuple** (using the source IP address and the destination IP address)
- **Three-tuple** (using the source IP address, destination IP address, and IP protocol number)

Depending on your use case, you may achieve session persistence for the combination of used IP addresses or IP addresses with the used protocol.

> **Important note**
> The correct hashing mode depends on the requirements of the services running on the load-balanced machines. You shouldn't change the default hashing mode of Azure Load Balancer unless you know that session persistence is necessary.

Different hashing modes of Azure Load Balancer are called **distribution modes**. It's possible to change them at any time without downtime of services behind a Load Balancer instance.

You should now have a general overview of what you can do with Azure Load Balancer, as well as its capabilities. Now, let's discuss the differences between public and internal load balancers.

The differences between public and internal load balancers

At the very beginning of this chapter, we mentioned that you can assign both private and public IP addresses to your instance of Azure Load Balancer. Depending on your configuration, we may talk about one of two types of load balancer:

- A **public load balancer**, which is used to provide outbound connections for VMs that don't have public IP addresses themselves.

- An **internal** (or **private**) **load balancer** (**ILB**), which is used to handle load balancing within a virtual network. This is helpful in hybrid infrastructure scenarios where on-premises infrastructure is involved as well.

> **Important note**
> An ILB can also be used in cloud-only scenarios, so there's no need to have an on-premises setup integrated with your cloud environment.

Both types of load balancers can coexist, as shown in the following diagram:

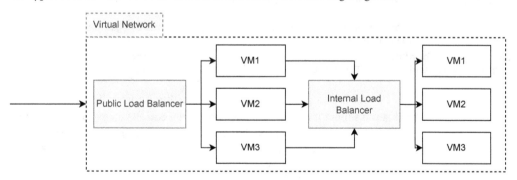

Figure 4.1 – Two types of load balancers in the same network

In general, there's very little difference between each type of load balancer – they mostly differ by their frontend's configuration, where the public load balancer has a public IP address assigned, and the ILB stays within a network by having a private IP address only. There's also no specific setting that would deploy Azure Load Balancer in public/internal mode – this makes the whole configuration much simpler as you can simply switch between the modes by modifying the frontend.

Let's start deploying and configuring Azure Load Balancers, starting with setting up backend pools.

Delving into backend pools

To get started with backend pools (or any other components in general), we need an instance of Azure Load Balancer we can configure. To deploy it, use the following command:

```
az network lb create -g <resource-group-name> \
   -n <load-balancer-name> \
   --sku Basic \
   --vnet-name <vnet-name> \
   --subnet default
```

This command will create a load balancer and a virtual network that will integrate with it. Of course, it's possible to create Azure Load Balancer with the existing network if you need to – in that scenario, make sure you're passing either its name or full resource identifier with the --vnet-name parameter.

> **Important note**
> The command we're using will only create a new virtual network if it cannot find another network with the name we provided in the same resource group.

Once created, your instance of Azure Load Balancer will already contain one front IP configuration and one backend pool. We can query them using the following commands:

```
az network lb show -n <load-balancer-name> -g <resource-group-name>
--query frontendIPConfigurations[0]
az network lb show -n <load-balancer-name> -g <resource-group-name>
--query backendAddressPools[0]
```

By default, the load balancer will have a private IP address assigned to it that will be based on the address space configured at the subnet level. The instance of Azure Load Balancer you just created will probably have the 10.0.0.4 address assigned, but you shouldn't assume that this value is by any means static (it relies not only on the address space but also the allocation method of that address, which can be either static or dynamic).

> **Important note**
> The default name of the frontend IP configuration and backend pool relies on default values provided by the Azure CLI. If you want, you can change those names when creating your Azure Load Balancer using the --frontend-ip-name and --backend-pool-name parameters.

Let's try to add one more frontend to make the configuration a little bit more complicated.

Adding a frontend IP configuration

We already have a private IP address assigned to one of the frontends of our load balancer. In this exercise, we'll try to add a new IP address to it so that there will be two frontends working on the same instance of our resource. We'll start by creating a new frontend IP configuration using a public IP address. Use the following command to create a public IP address resource in Azure:

```
az network public-ip create -g <resource-group-name> \
  -n <public-ip-address-name>
```

Once this has been created, we can try to add a new frontend:

```
az network lb frontend-ip create \
  -g <resource-group-name> \
  -n public-frontend \
  --lb-name <load-balancer-name> \
  --public-ip-address <public-ip-address-name>
```

Unfortunately, such an operation is not possible – the error we'll receive will tell us that we need to decide whether our load balancer is a public or an internal one:

```
(LoadBalancerReferencesBothPublicIPAndSubnet) LoadBalancer /
subscriptions/.../resourceGroups/.../providers/Microsoft.Network/
loadBalancers/... contains ipconfig /subscriptions/.../resourceGroups/.../
providers/Microsoft.Network/loadBalancers/.../frontendIPConfigurations/
LoadBalancerFrontEnd which references a subnet and ipconfig /
subscriptions/.../resourceGroups/.../providers/Microsoft.Network/
loadBalancers/.../frontendIPConfigurations/public-frontend which
references a public ip. All frontend ip should reference either a
subnet or publicIpAddress.
```

This is unfortunate, but at least we learned about some limitations of that service. Let's try to add a frontend with a private IP address instead:

```
az network lb frontend-ip create \
  -g <resource-group-name> \
  -n SecondFrontend \
  --lb-name <load-balancer-name> \
  --private-ip-address 10.0.0.5 \
  --vnet-name <vnet-name> \
  --subnet default
```

This operation should complete without an issue. Note that we explicitly pass an IP address here – it must be an address that is within the address range of the selected subnet and cannot be assigned to another resource within a network. With a new frontend created, let's check what is needed to create a new backend pool.

Adding a backend pool

Adding a backend pool is a simple operation, but before we can do this, we need to understand how it works under the hood. Backend pools are just configuration components of Azure Load Balancer and need to be connected to the resources you provision. This means that we need to create a backend pool upfront and then link resources that are meant to be part of the configured backend.

As we're using the Basic tier of Azure Load Balancer, we need to work with network interfaces instead of the IP addresses of our backend resources (it's a limitation of that tier, but you can safely switch to using IP addresses if you deployed your load balancer using the Standard tier). Before we deploy anything related to our host, let's configure a backend pool using this command:

```
az network lb address-pool create \
  -g <resource-group-name> \
  --lb-name <load-balancer-name> \
  -n SecondPool \
  --vnet <vnet-name> \
  --backend-addresses "[{name:vm1,ip-address:<private-ip-address}]"
```

If you're using the default address range for the virtual network you created previously, you can enter `10.0.0.6` as `private-ip-address` here; otherwise, find a correct IP address from the subnet where you'll deploy a VM.

The next step is creating a network interface:

```
az network nic create \
  -g <resource-group-name> \
  -n <nic-name> \
  --vnet-name <vnet-name> \
  --subnet default \
  --private-ip-address 10.0.0.6
```

Now, let's create a new machine in the same network as our load balancer that will leverage the network interface we created using the following command:

```
az vm create -g <resource-group-name> \
  -n <vm-name> \
  --nics <nic-name> \
  --image Ubuntu2204
```

The last step is adding our VM to the backend pool. To do that, we need to add an address pool to our network interface:

```
az network nic ip-config address-pool add \
  --address-pool SecondPool \
  --nic-name <nic-name> \
  -g <resource-group-name> \
```

```
--lb-name <load-balancer-name> \
--ip-config-name ipconfig1
```

After several seconds, the command should complete, and your load balancer should be configured with a new VM added to its backend pool. You can confirm your configuration with a simple Azure CLI query:

```
az network lb address-pool show \
  --id <resource-id-of-backend-pool> \
  --query backendIPConfigurations[0]
```

The result of this command shouldn't be empty. If it is, make sure you performed all the commands in the correct order.

> **Important note**
>
> When assigning our network interface to a backend pool, we used `ipconfig1` as the value of the `--ip-config-name` parameter. This is the default name of the IP configuration that is added to the network interface you create. If your network interface has an IP configuration object with a different name, make sure you provide the correct value here.

With that, we've successfully deployed and configured a backend pool for our instance of Azure Load Balancer. Now, let's learn how we can enhance that configuration with rules.

Understanding load balancer rules

So far, we have defined frontend and backend pools for our load balancer. Now, we need to connect those components by providing a set of rules that will tell Azure Load Balancer how to distribute the load. A rule is a simple map of values that links our frontend IP address with the set of machines defined for a given backend pool. In the upcoming sections, you'll create a rule and configure it. We'll also discuss more advanced topics, such as Floating IP and high-availability ports.

Creating a load balancer rule

Let's create our first rule using the following command:

```
az network lb rule create \
  -g <resource-group-name> \
  --lb-name <load-balancer-name> \
  -n WebServer \
  --protocol Tcp \
  --frontend-ip LoadBalancerFrontEnd \
  --frontend-port 80 \
  --backend-pool-name SecondPool \
  --backend-port 80
```

The rule we're creating will connect the default frontend we created previously with the backend pool we created by ourselves.

> **Important note**
> The examples in this section are based on the previous exercises. Adjust the names and values if you made any changes.

After a moment, a new rule will be created. To understand it better, let's describe it in detail:

- The rule maps the frontend port 80 to the backend port 80

- It will only apply to connections that are made using the TCP protocol

- No health probe will be assigned to that rule, as none are provided when creating it

- The rule will assume the default distribution mode (**five-tuple hashing**), meaning there will be no session persistence

Note that Azure Load Balancer rules are unable to read HTTP requests made on higher layers of the **OSI model** (Azure Load Balancer is itself a Layer 4 load balancer) and cannot be used for TLS offloading (instead, it gives you a highly scalable infrastructure component that can offload all the additional work to other components of your infrastructure). Let's check now how to create a rule that utilizes the high availability ports feature of Azure Load Balancer.

High availability ports

In Azure Load Balancer, you can configure a special rule that will be considered a **high availability ports rule**. Here's an example of how to do that:

```
az network lb rule create \
  -g <resource-group-name> \
  --lb-name <load-balancer-name> \
  -n WebServer \
  --protocol All \
  --frontend-ip LoadBalancerFrontEnd \
  --frontend-port 0 \
  --backend-pool-name SecondPool \
  --backend-port 0
```

As you can see, we made three changes to the process of creating a load-balancing rule:

- The frontend port was set to 0

- The backend port was set to 0

- The protocol was set to All

Once created, such a rule is considered a high availability ports rule.

> **Important note**
> Using the high availability ports feature is available only on Azure load balancers deployed in the Standard tier.

You might be wondering where or when you could leverage that feature of Azure Load Balancer. Well, there are a couple of scenarios where it becomes handy to be able to load balance incoming traffic on any port and any protocol:

- Simplifying the configuration of your load balancer where there's a large number of ports that need to be load-balanced

- Implementing high availability of your services (you can have multiple instances of an application running on multiple ports of the same machine)

- Dynamically allocating the ports of your services running on load-balanced machines

- Integrating with **network virtual appliances** (**NVAs**)

The downside of this feature is that it requires you to deploy a more expensive version of Azure Load Balancer (or redeploy an existing one if you have a load balancer in the Basic tier) and can work with internal load balancers only. So far, you've learned about high availability ports, which is a special type of rule in Azure Load Balancer. To continue this topic, we'll focus on Floating IP.

Floating IP

There's one more thing we must consider when it comes to configuring load balancer rules: **Floating IP**. Before we describe the feature itself, let's consider some scenarios where multiple instances of the same application need to reuse the same port on the same machine. This is true for the following services:

- Network virtual appliances

- **Clusters**, which need to be highly available

When Floating IP is enabled, Azure Load Balancer will no longer expose backends' IP addresses and instead change the IP address mapping to the load balancer itself. However, this will require introducing some changes to the OS running on the selected VMs.

The idea of Floating IP is based on reconfiguring the networking at the VM level. What you need to do is add a **loopback device**, which will have the load balancer's frontend IP address assigned to it. A loopback device is a virtual network interface that a machine can use to communicate with itself.

Once you have configured your machines in that way, Azure Load Balancer will be able to distribute traffic without worrying about **client–backend relation**, which will involve the destination IP address by default (as discussed when we mentioned distribution modes).

> **Important note**
> How you configure loopback devices will be different depending on the OS of the VMs being used.

Use of Floating IP in Azure Load Balancer may be necessary when you're configuring **Always On availability listeners** for **Azure SQL**. Unfortunately, this setup requires lots of preparation and is outside the scope of this book. If this topic interests you, you can read the following article from the Azure documentation: `https://learn.microsoft.com/en-us/azure/azure-sql/virtual-machines/windows/availability-group-listener-powershell-configure?view=azuresql`.

Remember that in many cases, you don't need those special rules for Azure Load Balancer to start working with it. They're limited to very specialized use cases, which are meant for very advanced infrastructure setups. However, to gain some more knowledge, we'll briefly discuss additional steps that are needed to configure Floating IP.

Example of configuring a loopback device

As a loopback device's configuration will be different for different OSs, we'll just check one of the easier examples to get an idea of how to approach this. If you want to perform this exercise, make sure you have a machine with **Ubuntu 22.04** that you can connect to.

Let's start by connecting to our machine and getting a list of available network interfaces:

```
ssh <username>@<public-ip-address>
ip addr
```

The result will contain multiple interfaces, but in our case, only loopback devices are important. Here's the result of running the command on my machine:

```
1: lo: <LOOPBACK,UP,LOWER_UP> mtu 65536 qdisc noqueue state UNKNOWN
group default qlen 1000
    link/loopback 00:00:00:00:00:00 brd 00:00:00:00:00:00
    inet 127.0.0.1/8 scope host lo
       valid_lft forever preferred_lft forever
    inet6 ::1/128 scope host
       valid_lft forever preferred_lft forever
2: eth0: <BROADCAST,MULTICAST,UP,LOWER_UP> mtu 1500 qdisc mq state UP
group default qlen 1000
    link/ether 60:45:bd:cd:af:fb brd ff:ff:ff:ff:ff:ff
    inet 10.0.0.8/24 metric 100 brd 10.0.0.255 scope global eth0
       valid_lft forever preferred_lft forever
    inet6 fe80::6245:bdff:fecd:affb/64 scope link
       valid_lft forever preferred_lft forever
```

As you can see, I have two interfaces, but only the first one will be important. Now, we need to assign a Floating IP to each loopback device found on the machine by running the following command:

```
sudo ip addr add 10.0.0.4/255.255.255.0 dev lo:0
```

Note that I used 10.0.0.4 as the IP and 255.255.255.0 as the network mask. These values should correspond to the frontend IP configuration of your instance of Azure Load Balancer. The last step is to open a port that has been selected for making connections (if the machine uses a firewall). This step will depend on the selected firewall solution.

In this section, we discussed lots of details related to load balancer rules. Now, let's switch focus to the last topic of this chapter, which is health probes.

Comprehending health probes

Azure Load Balancer needs to know which instances of our VMs are healthy so that it can safely distribute load there. The simplest idea is to just send a request to each machine and see whether it responds within the expected time frame. Health probes are exactly such a feature – it's an inbuilt component of Azure Load Balancer that, once configured, will automatically discover healthy instances.

Health probes have slightly different capabilities, depending on the selected **stock keeping unit** (**SKU**), which is the selected tier of our load balancer:

- Basic SKU supports TCP and HTTP only
- Standard SKU supports the TCP, HTTP, and HTTPS protocols

There are also different behaviors for established TCP flows once the probe is down. For the Basic SKU, once the probe fails, TCP flows to the given backend pool will be terminated. The Standard SKU load balancer is much more forgiving and will maintain a connection, assuming there's more than a single machine within a backend pool.

Let's learn how we can configure health probes by ourselves.

Creating a health probe

We'll start with a simple probe that will periodically check our machine using port 80 on the provided path:

```
az network lb probe create \
  -g <resource-group-name> \
  --lb-name <load-balancer-name> \
  -n HttpProbe \
  --protocol http \
  --port 80 \
  --path /
```

We can understand this probe as follows – check the health of the endpoint, which is exposed via port 80 and base URL (`/`). Of course, we're providing `--path` because we're configuring a probe with HTTP protocol. If TCP is used instead, `--path` won't be allowed as TCP is unaware of the paths of the requested endpoint.

Now that we have created our probe, we need to link it to one of the load-balancing rules.

Linking a health probe to a load-balancing rule

Health probes themselves don't provide any meaningful value until they're connected with instances defined within a backend pool. This is why we need to link them with backend pools – so that Azure Load Balancer can leverage them to determine which instances are healthy.

To create an assignment, we can use the following single command:

```
az network lb rule update \
  --probe HttpProbe \
  -n WebServer \
  --lb-name <load-balancer-name> \
  -g <resource-group-name>
```

Note that I used the name of a load-balancing rule from the previous exercises – you can use your own name here without implications.

Once the health probe has been assigned to a load balancing rule, your configuration of Azure Load Balancer will be complete. The service will be able to listen to incoming requests, load balance between multiple instances of VMs, and ensure that they are healthy. Now, let's learn about the differences between selected probe protocols, such as TCP and HTTP.

Differences between probe protocols

Each health probe can be configured using one of the available protocols (TCP, HTTP, or HTTPS). There are some differences when it comes to establishing connections, failed probing, and probe-up behavior.

TCP probes

When a TCP probe initiates a connection, it's done via a **three-way open TCP handshake**. The connection is established with a **configured port** and terminated using a **four-way handshake**. To clarify, a handshake is a general pattern for establishing communication between all the parties involved in the communication channel.

If a **TCP listener** on the probed instance doesn't respond within the specified timeout, the probe is marked *down*. Probe down behavior depends on the number of configured retries for a probe. Probing can also fail if a probe receives a TCP request from a probed instance.

A probe can be considered *up* if a connection with a machine was once again established successfully and it's eligible for new connections.

HTTP/HTTPS probes

These probes work differently than TCP probes as they utilize **GET requests** to establish a connection. They are especially useful in scenarios where you'd like to implement your own logic for removing particular instances from the backend pool (we're talking about traffic distribution here, not the configuration of a backend pool itself, which will still contain certain IP addresses).

For HTTP/HTTPS, a failed probe is a probe that receives a non-`200` status code. This means that HTTP status codes such as `404 Not Found`, `400 Bad Request`, `500 Internal Server Error`, or any other `3xx`, `4xx`, or `5xx` error will cause probing to fail. For those protocols, probing will also be considered a failure if a connection is closed via TCP reset.

Similarly to TCP probes, HTTP/HTTPS probes will be considered *up* if the probing mechanism receives an `HTTP 200` status code from an instance that was previously down. Finally, we'll talk about health probes and **network security groups** (**NSGs**).

Additional guidelines for health probes

Health probes, even though they're quite simple features, allow your instance of Azure Load Balancer to have sophisticated control over distributed traffic. They can be used to throttle incoming traffic or limit it as your services are undergoing maintenance. This applies to HTTP/TTPS health probes only, though it could theoretically be achieved with TCP probes as well by modifying firewall rules on machines.

When using NSGs, you need to make sure that security rules allow connections made by your instance of Azure Load Balancer. Otherwise, your setup will simply work as they will be rejected and won't be able to access VMs. You can configure an NSG using a concept called a service tag, as follows:

```
az network nsg rule create -g <resource-group-name> \
  --nsg-name <nsg-name> \
  -n AllowLoadBalancerProbes \
  --source-address-prefixes AzureLoadBalancer \
  --destination-address-prefixes '*' \
  --destination-port-ranges '*' \
  --direction Inbound \
  --access Allow \
  --protocol Tcp \
  --priority 900
```

This rule will whitelist all the incoming traffic from Azure Load Balancer to any destination within a subnet or network interface. Fortunately, by default, Azure adds a rule to each NSG that is deployed:

```
{
    "access": "Allow",
    "description": "Allow inbound traffic from azure load balancer",
    "destinationAddressPrefix": "*",
    "destinationAddressPrefixes": [],
    "destinationPortRange": "*",
    "destinationPortRanges": [],
    "direction": "Inbound",
    "name": "AllowAzureLoadBalancerInBound",
    "priority": 65001,
    "protocol": "*",
    "sourceAddressPrefix": "AzureLoadBalancer",
    "sourceAddressPrefixes": [],
    "sourcePortRange": "*",
    "sourcePortRanges": []
}
```

You're safe to override it if you want, but in most cases, it's not needed.

That's everything about Azure Load Balancer! You're now ready to explore this topic on your own (as there are still some topics that we didn't cover), but before that, let's summarize what we've learned.

Summary

This chapter was dedicated to Azure Load Balancer and gave you a detailed introduction to the topic of load balancing in Azure. Remember that this service is not the only Azure component that can be used for load balancing. However, as we're focusing on low-level infrastructure and administrative tasks in general, being familiar with the basics of Azure Load Balancer is crucial to be able to effectively manage resources in Azure. The topics that were presented in this chapter (setting up Azure Load Balancer, its configuration, health probes, and load balancing rules) will come in handy when you're setting up IaaS-based infrastructure in your projects.

This was also the last chapter of *Part 2* of this book. The next chapter will begin *Part 3 – Administration of Azure Virtual Machines*. Everything you've learned so far will be extremely important in the upcoming chapters, as lots of things related to Azure VMs are rooted in their networking components.

Part 3: Administration of Azure Virtual Machines

In *Part 3*, you'll learn about initial topics related to the administration of virtual machines in Azure. The main focus of this part is to give you a basic understanding of how virtual machines in Azure are deployed and configured. You'll also be able to read about performing various tasks related to day-to-day Azure administrator activities, such as configuring backups, managing disks, and enabling extensions for machines.

This part has the following chapters:

- *Chapter 5, Provisioning Azure Virtual Machines*
- *Chapter 6, Configuring Virtual Machine Extensions*
- *Chapter 7, Configuring Backups*
- *Chapter 8, Configuring and Managing Disks*

5

Provisioning Azure Virtual Machines

As mentioned before, **Azure Virtual Machines** are one of the most important services when working as an Azure administrator. Each VM requires much more attention than managed services (such as **Azure App Service**, **Azure SQL Database**, or **Azure Storage**) as they are the only resource that gives you access to the operating system. What's more, VMs are very often the backbone of advanced setups and services, thus requiring much more attention and knowledge.

The content of this chapter will help you understand how VMs in Azure are deployed and configured. We'll cover not only fundamentals regarding their setup parameters but also different options for making a connection and availability.

In this chapter, we're going to cover the following main topics:

- Exploring the sizes and families of Azure VMs
- Delving into Azure VM storage
- Deploying a VM
- Connecting to a VM
- The availability of Azure VMs

Technical requirements

For the exercises in this chapter, you'll need the following:

- The Azure CLI (https://learn.microsoft.com/en-us/cli/azure/install-azure-cli)
- A command-line tool of any kind (either available in your operating system or your favorite one)

The Code in Action video for this book can be viewed at: https://packt.link/GTX9F

Exploring the sizes and families of Azure VMs

Each cloud provider, when provisioning a VM, gives you a selection of available sizes and machine families to choose from. Some applications don't really care about the underlying hardware, while others may perform much worse if run on incompatible machines. Such workloads include **machine learning** (**ML**), video processing, and game development.

Azure offers 11 different series of VMs, ranging from entry-level VMs to advanced instances with dedicated **GPUs** and optimized networking setups. Let's review them for better understanding:

- **Entry-level VMs**: You don't always need a VM that comes with advanced hardware and functionalities. Sometimes, all you need is a small, generic machine that you can quickly set up and use for initial development or testing. Azure offers a small subset of all machines available as entry-level machines. As of the time of writing, you can select between **Basic** (**A0-A4**) and **Standard machines** (**A0-A7** and **Av2**).

  The benefit of using those VM families is low pricing – the cheapest machine (running Ubuntu) may cost as little as $13 monthly. However, note that there's one disadvantage of using such families – they may not be available for **VM reservations**.

- **Burstable VMs**: Azure also offers a selection of more specific VMs that provide the additional capability of delivering more performance if demanded. Those are called burstable VMs and are designed to handle low-to-moderate workloads but can also burst to handle increased load. This includes the **B-series** of VMs. The main disadvantage of those VM families is the lack of **hyperthreading**.

- **General-purpose VMs**: For generic workloads (which are not specified by a certain parameter, such as high CPU utilization, high memory demands, and increased network bandwidth), Azure offers a couple of generic VM series. This includes **D**, **Dv3**, **Dv4**, **Dv5**, **Dav4**, and **Dasv5** families (to name a few), which are run on various hardware. Generic series allows you to run a VM on **Intel**, **AMD**, and **ARM** processors, and some of them offer support for Premium and Ultra SSD disks, depending on region availability.

- **Memory-optimized VMs**: For more advanced scenarios, you may need to provision a VM with very specific capabilities. If you want to run workloads such as **SAP** databases (**Cassandra**, **MongoDB**, or **Redis**) or data warehouses, you'll need much more memory on your machine. This is where series such as **E**, **Ls**, **M**, or **Mv2** come in handy. They run both Intel and AMD processors and very often come with **Non-Volatile Memory Express** (**NVMe**) storage mapped locally. This gives you the possibility to run demanding services and applications without worries that they may be throttled by the underlying hardware.

- **Compute-optimized VMs**: For applications that require much better CPU (in terms of performance), Azure offers a variety of VM series – **F**, **H**, and **N**. They have a much better CPU-to-memory ratio than other families and may also be configured with a dedicated GPU for **deep learning** (**DL**), video editing, or graphics rendering. N-series can also be deployed with **InfiniBand** for a much better networking setup.

Now, with an understanding of the various families of Azure VMs, we will move on to exploring their prices.

Families and their pricing

Depending on your choice, pricing for a deployed VM will differ greatly. Let's compare two machines – one being an entry-level VM and the second being a compute-optimized machine (the same region and the same operating system):

- **Standard_A8_v2** (8 vCores + 16 GB RAM) – $279.59
- **Standard_NV6** (6 vCores + 56 GB RAM) – $996.45

As you can see, even though the second machine has fewer cores available (while having much more RAM), it is 3.5x more expensive. If we try to extrapolate available memory to 56 GB (for the first machine), we'll still have a huge difference.

For a better comparison, let's try to select similar machines:

- **Standard_NV6** (6 vCores + 56 GB RAM) – $996.45
- **Standard_E8_v5** (8 vCores + 64 GB RAM) – $443.84

Even though the VMs are similar, there's still a big pricing gap between them. You may wonder why there's such a difference. Well, it all depends on the underlying hardware. Listed VMs come from different series (**Av2**, **NV**, and **Ev5**) and may be configured and used with different capabilities. It's important to take that into consideration when planning used families and sizes so that you don't end up with an expensive setup, even though you don't utilize most of the allocated capacity of a machine. In the next part of this chapter, we'll discuss different options for operating systems available for Azure VMs. Each operating system offers a slightly different set of features that can be used depending on the context and requirements.

Operating systems

In Azure, you may deploy a VM with either Windows or Linux. Both operating systems can be deployed with various configurations and in different versions (or even distributions for Linux). You can run a VM with Windows, Windows Server, Ubuntu, **CentOS**, **SUSE**, or **Red Hat**. You can also prepare your own VM image and put it on **Azure Marketplace** for further distribution.

Selected operating systems affect not only what you can install on a machine but also the pricing. For some of the available operating systems, you may need to pay additional licensing costs. When comparing pricing between different VMs, make sure you include the license cost.

To avoid paying for a license, you may use Azure Hybrid Benefit, which is available for Windows and SQL Server machines.

Using Azure Hybrid Benefit

If you already own a license for your operating system (for example, Windows Server), you may transfer it to Azure. Not every license can be transferred that way, so make sure you understand the terms and conditions of the bought software before enabling Hybrid Benefit on a machine.

In general, you can think about using that feature when owning Windows Server, **SQL Server**, **RHEL**, or **SUSE Linux Enterprise Server** licenses. The benefit of using Hybrid Benefit looks like this:

- **Standard_D2_v5 with Windows** – $151.11 monthly
- **Standard_D2_v5 with Hybrid Benefit** – $83.95 monthly

As you can see, Hybrid Benefit can save you almost 50% of the initial cost, so it's worth checking out whether you can use it.

Unfortunately, Azure VM family and size are not the only parameters affecting the performance of a machine and its cost. Let's now discuss how VMs use attached storage as disks.

Delving into Azure VM storage

Each VM requires a disk that will be used by operating systems and applications run on it. In Azure, VMs have two types of disks:

- **OS disk**
- **Data disk**

Both types of disks have their own purpose, which we'll discuss shortly. What's more, each disk can be configured as either an HDD or an SSD disk, which will have a huge impact on the VM's performance.

Azure VMs have also additional disks called **temporary disks**. They're often labeled as `D:` disks and are not meant for storing data on them (that is, data stored there isn't replicated to Azure Storage). Their main purpose is to act as storage for swap files or similar operations. They get erased when rebooting a machine, performing a failover, or any other operation that restarts an operating system. What's more, some VMs in Azure don't have temporary disks created for them. You don't have control over that mechanism as it's something that's managed by Azure.

Important note

Some VM families (such as **D-series**) make it possible to leverage temporary disks for certain activities (such as storing `tempdb` or **Buffer Pool Extensions** (**BPEs**) when working with SQL Server). Those are, however, very limited scenarios and should be performed with care.

To better understand how to work with disks in Azure, we'll start by discussing the differences between operating system and data disks.

Types of disks

As mentioned previously, each Azure VM will have its own OS disks and optional data disk. OS disks store the operating system and are, in most cases, included in the image of a machine, which you can use to provision new resources. Data disks are used to extend the storage capabilities of your machines and can be dynamically attached and detached if you want.

Even though technically, your VM disks are stored in Azure Storage, you interact with them as if they were standard hard disks. This greatly simplifies the effort needed to manage your infrastructure, as most tasks are performed by **Azure Resource Manager**.

> **Important note**
>
> In the past, disks in Azure were an unmanaged resource, which made the whole setup much more difficult. As of the time of writing, using unmanaged disks is no longer recommended, and in this book, we'll focus on managed disks only.

Let's discuss the available disks and their capabilities for better understanding.

OS disks

Azure gives you two options when choosing an OS disk:

- **Persistent disk**
- **Ephemeral disk**

Both types have their pros and cons and, of course, different use cases. In general, both persistent and ephemeral OS disks are meant to store the operating system and its files. However, depending on the planned workload, they may be a better or worse fit. For example, if you're going to run a stateful service on a machine, an ephemeral OS disk wouldn't be a good choice as it offers no persistence for data stored on it.

So, how do both types of disks actually work? When you create a standard (persistent) OS disk, data saved on it gets replicated to Azure Storage for persistence. This means that even if the machine gets rebooted, erased, or broken, data will still be available and can be recovered. What's more, those disks offer an option to stop and deallocate VMs, which is especially important when looking for cost optimizations.

Why can stopping and deallocating a VM be used for cost optimization? It's related to the pricing model of Azure VMs and how their cost gets allocated. In general, VMs in Azure are priced per hour. If the machine is up for the whole month (approximately 730 hours), you get charged for each hour it's available. However, at any moment, you can stop and deallocate a machine, which has a very simple result – all the compute power reserved for your machine is detached from it and returned to the pool of the whole data center. As a result, you no longer pay for the machine itself – the only cost incurred will be related to additional services deployed in relation to that machine (for example, disks). A deallocated machine can be started at any time, just as with rebooting an operating system that has been shut down.

> **Important note**
> Be careful when deallocating Azure VM workloads running in production. Even though Azure data centers are considered to offer limitless capacity, there are still moments when there are fluctuations in the available compute power. This means that such power may not be available on demand. If you ever need to deallocate a production machine, make sure you're planning to power it on a couple of hours before the time it's needed.

Ephemeral OS disks, on the other hand, don't allow you to stop and deallocate a VM. They also cannot be resized. If you make a mistake when planning storage capacity for that disk upon creation of a VM, the only possibility to correct that mistake is to either recreate a machine or reassign the OS disk. This may lead to unplanned downtime of your services.

There are also additional behaviors of ephemeral OS disks worth mentioning:

- When resizing a VM, whole disks get reprovisioned, meaning data stored there will be lost
- When you want to redeploy a VM, an ephemeral OS disk will be recreated without data stored on it
- In case of any maintenance operations (related to unplanned downtime and **live migrations** performed by the Azure control plane), OS data stored on an ephemeral disk may not be preserved
- Not all sizes of VMs in Azure support ephemeral disks (the list includes the sizes supporting Premium disks, such as M, Fs, or Bs)

Persistent OS disks don't have those limitations and are a much easier component when starting your journey as an Azure administrator.

Data disks

Data disks, as opposed to OS disks, are optional disks that can be attached to your VM anytime. They're meant to provide an extension of available storage and offer much more flexibility when it comes to maintenance and operations performed on them.

A data disk has similar capabilities to any other disk that can be created and used in Azure (that is, it offers multiple performance options and can be migrated between machines). What's more, there are specific regions in which disks offer lower latency:

- Canada Central
- Central US
- East US

- East US 2

- South Central US

- West US 2

- Germany North

- Jio India West

- North Europe

- West Europe

> **Important note**
> The list of regions that offer lower-latency disks is subject to change. The preceding list presented was valid at the time the book was published.

If you plan to deploy a workload that requires higher performance and improved I/O, then those regions may be a good match for your infrastructure. To understand the topic better, let's talk about additional types of disks in Azure.

Additional types of disks in Azure

In Azure, there are five different types of disks (when talking about their performance, not use cases):

- Standard HDD

- Standard SSD

- Premium SSD

- Premium SSDv2

- Ultra disks

Each of those types will perform better in certain scenarios. Still, you need to remember that HDD disks will always be an option, which is worst from the perspective of performance, latency, and availability. This is caused by the physical layout of such disks – as they still have spinning elements inside, they're much more vulnerable to damage and cannot guarantee the same **service-level agreement** (**SLA**) as **SSD disks**.

To visualize those differences, let's look at the parameters of those disks:

- Max **input/output operations per second** (**IOPS**) – from 2,000 (HDD) to 160,000 (Ultra)

- Max throughput – from 500 MB/s (HDD) to 4,000 MB/s (Ultra)

As you can see, the difference is huge. The selection of a disk will make an impact on the performance of your VM; this is why the proper selection of VM size and disk type will make a difference.

> **Important note**
>
> Unfortunately, Ultra disks in Azure cannot be used as OS disks. They also have some additional limitations (they cannot be used with availability sets or disk encryption). What's more, when an Ultra disk is selected, you cannot change its type later.

When it comes to the availability of a given disk size and its type, you always need to consult the documentation; there are many limitations provided by Microsoft when it comes to the possible combination of VM size and disk type (plus its size), and keeping an eye on them is an impossible task. This is especially important when aiming for Ultra/Premium v2 disks, which are not available in all regions, can't be used in certain setups (availability sets, encryption, or recovery), and may not be available in any size.

On the other hand, remember that the selected disk type (mostly for OS disks) will impact the availability of your VM. In Azure, the desired SLA level for a single VM (99.9%) is achievable only if you deploy it with a Premium SSD disk at least. For Standard SSD, it's 99.5%, and for Standard HDD, you'll have a guarantee of 95% SLA.

So far, we've talked about different types of disks in Azure, including their performance tiers. Let's now switch our focus to data redundancy, which is an important topic in **high availability** (**HA**) scenarios.

Redundancy of disks

In Azure, each managed disk (as it's backed by Azure Storage) is replicated using **Locally Redundant Storage (LRS) replication mode**. LRS replication is a replication model where data gets replicated to three copies locally. This is fine for many generic workloads, but for some scenarios, you may look for improved resiliency.

If you can use Standard or Premium SSD disks, you can leverage a concept called **Zone-Redundant Storage (ZRS) disks**. Those disks are replicated across availability zones, making them much more resilient to outages affecting a single data center. On the other hand, the use of ZRS disks is limited not only to disk types but also to the following regions:

- Southeast Asia
- Australia East
- Brazil South
- West Europe
- North Europe
- France Central

- Qatar Central
- UK South
- East US
- East US 2
- South Central US
- West US 2

> **Important note**
> The list of regions that offer ZRS disks is subject to change. The preceding list was valid at the time the book was published.

What's more, ZRS disks are not available for Premium SSD v2/Ultra disks.

Let's now see how VMs and disks work together by learning about deployments of those resources.

Deploying a VM

In the previous chapters (*Chapter 3, Understanding Azure Virtual Networks*, and *Chapter 4, Exploring Azure Load Balancer*), we had a chance to deploy a couple of VMs using default parameters. We also made some connections and even ran some commands on them. In this chapter, we'll extend our knowledge and see what additional options there are when deploying VMs.

Deploying a single VM

When you want to deploy a single VM, you can use one of the commands available in the Azure CLI:

```
az vm create -n <vm-name> -g <resource-group-name> --image <os-image>
```

This will create a single machine with the selected operating system. If you want to learn what possible choices for the system are, you need to use another command:

```
az vm image list --all -o table
```

This command will display a big list of all images available, including additional information (such as publisher, offer, or SKU). The list itself may be a little too long to quickly find useful information. This is why you're allowed to use filtering using the --publisher, --offer, and --sku parameters.

When you don't provide additional parameters, a VM will be created with some default resources:

- Virtual network
- Subnet

- Public IP address
- OS disk
- **Network interface card** (**NIC**)

However, you may use more specific commands to create a resource that will integrate with already existing resources (this is especially important when deploying a VM in the context of an existing network). Remember that you can use the `az vm create -h` command to see possible options.

Let's see some of those options in action by deploying a VM with additional capabilities.

Deploying a single VM with a private IP address

When deploying a VM using the Azure CLI, by default it'll have a public IP address assigned to it. It's fine for cases where a machine needs to be available publicly, but of course, there are scenarios where you don't need it. For example, you may want to deploy a set of VMs enclosed in a virtual network that will be load-balanced internally and act as a backend for some frontend services.

To avoid the creation of a public IP address, you need to pass an empty value for the `--public-ip-address` parameter:

```
az vm create -n <vm-name> -g <resource-group-name> --public-ip-address
"" --image <os-image>
```

This will create a VM with all the necessary resources, but this time, a public IP address won't be assigned to it.

Deploying a single VM with a managed identity

In previous chapters (*Chapters 1* and *2*), we talked about the concept of managed identities. Let's quickly remind ourselves what it is – a **managed identity** is a feature of some Azure resources that enables them to act as a security principal when interacting with other resources and services. In other words – your resource becomes an entity in your **Entra ID** tenant, making it possible to assign it roles and permissions.

Azure VMs are one of many Azure resources that can have a managed identity configured. Depending on your scenario, you can select either a system-assigned or a user-assigned identity. The configuration of those types is slightly different.

For a system-assigned identity, all you need to do is to run the following command:

```
az vm create -n <vm-name> -g <resource-group-name> --image <os-image>
--assign-identity [system]
```

As you can see, we're passing `[system]` as an identity that will be assigned to the machine. This is a special value that will be identified as a system-assigned identity.

> **Important note**
>
> Remember that when a system-assigned identity is created, it'll automatically create a new principal in your Entra ID tenant. This principal will have an `objectId` value generated that you'll be able to refer to when assigning access, for example.

Using the Azure CLI, you can also configure a managed identity and assign a role in the same command. To do that, you need to provide the scope for a command to use:

```
az vm create -n <vm-name> -g <resource-group-name> --image <os-image>
--assign-identity [system] --scope <resource-id> --role <role-name>
```

For example, let's say we want our VM to have a `Reader` role on a storage account we created. To configure that, we could use the following commands:

```
az storage account create -g <resource-group-name> -n <storage-
account-name>
id=$(az storage account show -g <resource-group-name> -n
<storageaccount-name> --query id --output tsv)
az vm create -n <vm-name> -g <resource-group-name> --image <os-image>
--assign-identity [system] --scope $id --role Reader
```

This can be used when you want to quickly configure your infrastructure. Of course, the alternative would be to manually assign a role using a separate command (which would be a perfectly viable option), but sometimes you need to just get things done.

> **Important note**
>
> You need to have permission to assign roles for other principals to assign a role using the previous command.

If using a system-assigned identity is not your goal (because you want to reuse an identity across multiple VMs, for example), you can use a user-assigned identity. However, in this scenario, we need to create it before assigning it to a machine:

```
az identity create -n <identity-name> -g <resource-group-name>
id=$(az identity show -n <identity-name> -g <resource-group-name>
--query id --output tsv)
az vm create -n <vm-name> -g <resource-group-name> --image <os-image>
--assign-identity $id
```

As you can see, the only difference is providing an identifier of a resource (user-assigned identity) instead of [system] as a value. What's more, you can even configure both system- and user-assigned identities on the same VM:

```
az vm create -n <vm-name> -g <resource-group-name> --image <os-image>
--assign-identity [system] $id
```

This gives you lots of flexibility when building an automation script or just performing standard administrator tasks on a daily basis.

Selecting the VM size

At the beginning of this chapter (in the *Exploring the sizes and families of Azure VMs* section), we discussed multiple options when it comes to selecting a VM size and the implications of such a decision. Until now, we haven't really used a size selection parameter, so our machine ended up being created with a default size. To have more control over that process, let's use the `--size` parameter:

```
az vm create -n <vm-name> -g <resource-group-name> --image <os-image>
--size <vm-size>
```

For example, if you want to create a **Standard_A1_v2** machine, you'll run the following command:

```
az vm create -n <vm-name> -g <resource-group-name> --image <os-image>
--size Standard_A1_v2
```

If you're unsure about a certain size or you just want to learn more about the number of **vCores** and memory available, you can run the following command:

```
az vm list-sizes -l <location>
```

For obtaining names only, use query and output parameters:

```
az vm list-sizes -l <location> --query [].name -o table
```

This will give you an overall look at what's available in the selected region (as you need to remember that not all VM sizes are available in every region).

Configuring data disks

When a VM is created, by default it won't have any data disks assigned to it. If you want to create them, you have two options:

- Create them separately and assign them to a machine
- Create them when creating a VM

Let's start with creating them in the same command. To do that, use the `--data-disk-sizes-gb` parameter:

```
az vm create -n <vm-name> -g <resource-group-name> --image <os-image>
--data-disk-sizes-gb 10 20
```

The preceding command will create two data disks attached to a machine – one with 10 GB and the second with 20 GB. You can then list them with the following command:

```
az vm show -n <vm-name> -g <resource-group-name> --query
storageProfile.dataDisks
```

Depending on the VM size, you'll end up with disks of different types (if the size supports Premium SSD disks, such disks will be created).

The alternative would be to create a disk separately and then attach it to a VM:

```
az disk create -g <rsource-group-name> -n <disk-name> --size-gb <disk-
size> --sku <sku-name>
```

For the --sku parameter, you can use one of the following values:

- PremiumV2_LRS
- Premium_LRS
- Premium_ZRS
- StandardSSD_LRS
- StandardSSD_ZRS
- Standard_LRS
- UltraSSD_LRS

As you can see, creating a disk on your own will give you much more control over the configuration of a managed disk. For example, you may enable bursting on a disk, encryption type, or even reference an operating system image for the creation of an OS disk.

> **Important note**
> Remember that not every disk SKU is available in every region. For reference, check the documentation of Azure managed disks.

Now, the only thing that's left is to attach a newly created disk to our VM. Once again, we have two options here:

- Creating a VM with a disk linked to it
- Attaching a disk to an existing VM

If a disk was created before VM creation, we can use its identifier similarly to when assigning a role when configuring a managed identity:

```
az vm create -g <resource-group-name> -n <vm-name> --image <os-image>
--attach-data-disks <disk-resource-id>
```

Using the --attach-data-disks parameter, we can provide one or more data disks that will be automatically assigned to our VM. Note that passing more than one disk can be done by separating their identifier with a space:

```
az vm create -g <resource-group-name> -n <vm-name> --image <os-image>
--attach-data-disks <disk1-resource-id> <disk2-resource-id>
```

If you have an existing VM, attaching a data disk requires a slightly different command:

```
az vm disk attach --vm-name <vm-name> -n <disk-name> -g <resource-
group-name>
```

You can also use this command to create and attach a disk in a single command (so, you don't need to use the command we used previously as a separate step for creating a new resource):

```
az vm disk attach --vm-name <vm-name> -n <disk-name> -g <resource-
group-name> --new
```

Alternatively, if your disk is on a separate resource group or subscription, you need to use the following command:

```
az vm disk attach --vm-name <vm-name> -g <resource-group-name> --disks
<disk-resource-id>
```

This command allows you to also specify the size of a disk, SKU, or caching policy. If you need help, make sure you check its help using the az vm disk attach -h command.

Deploying a VM with an ephemeral OS disk

If you want to leverage the capabilities of an ephemeral OS disk, you can specify such an option when creating a VM. Configuring that option requires no special preparations – you just need to provide the correct parameter:

```
az vm create -g <resource-group-name> -n <vm-name> --image <os-image>
--ephemeral-os-disk true
```

If your size of VM supports ephemeral OS disks, a VM will be created with that type of disk for your operating system. However, always remember the implications of such a decision, which we discussed previously in this chapter (in the *Delving into Azure VM storage* section)!

Zonal placement of a VM

By default, your VM will be placed in one of the available availability zones configured in the selected region. This is, of course, true only for regions that support availability zones – otherwise, zonal placement is non-existent and won't affect your infrastructure.

Choosing a specific zone makes sense only if you plan to deploy more than one VM that will be integrated with other machines running the same workload. Having multiple machines in separate availability zones doesn't matter if each Azure VM runs a separate workload that has its own availability requirements.

> **Important note**
> Zonal placement for VMs is much easier to coordinate and manage when using **VM scale sets** (**VMSS**), discussed later in this chapter.

So, the question arises – when is zonal placement something you should worry about? Let's consider the following scenario – you deploy three separate VMs of different sizes. They may run different services, but the common thing for them is that they run one instance of the same service. If your machines are placed in the same zone, then an outage of that zone will cause all instances of the service to go down. If you place the machines in separate zones, then this specific service will have improved availability (thanks to placement on three separate machines running in different zones).

To specify an availability zone when creating a VM, use the following command:

```
az vm create -g <resource-group-name> -n <vm-name> --image <os-image>
--zone <1|2|3>
```

As you can see, the --zone parameter accepts a single value – 1, 2, or 3. Each of those numbers is a representation of a zone that will be used for the deployment of your machine. If you want to improve the availability of the machines running the same services, you should place them in separate zones.

We discussed lots of things related to the deployment of a single VM. Later in this chapter, we'll extend that knowledge by covering more advanced topics related to deploying multiple VMs at once. For now, let's change the subject to the methods of connecting with VMs.

Connecting to a VM

Each VM deployment can be used as a host to which you can connect. Depending on your infrastructure setup (availability of a public IP address and **network security group** (**NSG**) rules), such a connection is either a simple command in your terminal or a multi-step process including a variety of actions. In this section, we'll focus on different methods of connecting to a VM, covering differences between operating systems and security measures. Let's see how we can connect with a machine using SSH, RDP, and DNS name.

Connecting using SSH

A method of connection that works for both Windows and Linux is **SSH connection**. When connecting to a VM using this protocol, there is one prerequisite – port 22 accepting incoming connections. In the previous chapters (*Chapters 3* and *4*), we covered the topic of an NSG – a service that controls inbound and outbound access to the resource it's connected to. From a connection point of view, it doesn't matter whether the NSG is attached to a subnet of the network interface. In both scenarios, all you need is port 22 open.

To connect to a machine using SSH, you need an SSH client, which can be used for making a connection. In most operating systems, such a client is already installed and available in your terminal. If that's not the case, you can install anything that suits your needs. For the sake of this chapter, we'll assume that such a client is available to be called directly from a terminal using the following syntax:

```
ssh <username>@<ip-address>
```

By looking at this command, you may wonder two things:

- How do you obtain the username?
- Which IP address should you use?

The answers depend on your setup. Let's start with the IP address. If your VM (or, rather, its network interface) has a public IP address assigned, then you'll use it for making the connection. If a public IP address was not created, you can either create it and assign it to the machine or make a connection using a private address.

> **Important note**
> Even though we're using a VM with a public IP address attached to it, remember that such a setup is valid for development scenarios. You should never have a production workload running on a machine that is directly accessible from the internet.

Connecting with a private IP address is possible only if that address can be discovered within your network. When making a connection from a local computer that is not integrated with a virtual network in Azure, such a connection won't be possible. In this scenario, when using SSH to make a connection, you'll need an additional machine called a **jumpbox**. A jumpbox is a specialized machine that is deployed within your infrastructure and accepts connections from outside its network. When you connect to such a machine, you can make another connection from it using the private IP address of the destination machine. This is visualized in *Figure 5.1*:

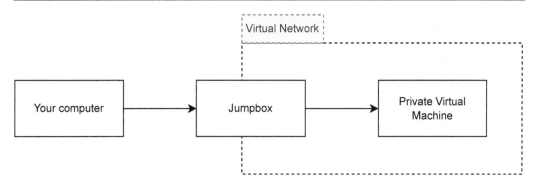

Figure 5.1 – Concept of a jumpbox connection

This setup may look a little bit naïve, but on a greater scale, it makes sense as it allows you to greatly reduce configuration effort when managing VMs and simplify the security setup. It has the following benefits:

- All machines can be kept in a private network, so there's no need to manage additional NSG rules
- You can set up a process of obtaining access to a jumpbox with proper monitoring and auditing
- Access can be quickly revoked by stopping a jumpbox machine

On the other hand, this setup has its disadvantages. The biggest concern is the ability to connect to any machine that is within a network from a jumpbox once you connect to it. This can be addressed by either placing private machines in separate subnets with additional NSGs or improving security controls over a jumpbox machine.

An alternative to a jumpbox would be setting up a VPN connection. This can be done in two models:

- **Point-to-site (P2S)**
- **Site-to-site (S2S)**

The former is dedicated to making connections from individual machines to a virtual network in Azure. The latter is a much more advanced setup whereby you connect your on-premises network with a network in Azure, making a hybrid infrastructure. From the perspective of a single user, those setups make connections much easier because you don't need to think about additional machines you need to use when making a connection. From the network perspective, a machine in Azure looks like a typical machine in your on-premises network. However, leveraging that setup requires much more effort as you need to properly set up all the networks (including a method of integrating them with, for example, a **VPN gateway**) and ensure that address ranges don't collide.

As an SSH connection is not always a desired choice, let's check an alternative – **Remote Desktop Protocol (RDP)**.

Connecting using RDP

Using RDP is another way of making a connection with your machine. This is one of the standard ways of connecting to machines running Windows, but it can also be configured for Linux machines (with additional setup). To connect to a machine with RDP, you need to open port 3389. Conceptually, you'll have the same challenges as if connecting using SSH. The difference comes from the user experience point of view. With RDP, you're gaining access to the user interface of your machine, which can be beneficial when struggling with the CLI or performing tasks that are cumbersome using the terminal only.

However, remember that not every operating system supports running the user interface, and even if it does, connecting to a machine using RDP requires much more CPU and memory to be available. Smaller VMs may struggle to handle such a connection, or making a connection may drain available resources, breaking running services.

To connect using RDP, we need to open our remote desktop client and pass the IP address of our machine plus the username and password. Here, the same challenges arise – if a machine has no public IP address configured, then you need to find a way to connect to it either using a jumpbox or connecting to the virtual network using a VPN connection (or any other integration method of your local and remote network).

To simplify obtaining the configuration, the **Azure portal** offers a quick way of obtaining an RDP file. After deploying your VM, find it in the Azure portal and click on the **Connect** menu:

Figure 5.2 – Connect menu in the Azure portal

It allows you to select an IP address used for making a connection (remember that a machine can have more than one) and the desired port number. The default port 3389 will suffice for most scenarios, but if you want to make a connection with a different port, make sure you change it there and in NSG rules defining access to your machine.

> **Important note**
>
> For making a connection to a Linux VM with RDP, you'll need to configure a desktop environment and remote desktop service on your VM. An example configuration (for Ubuntu) is described in the documentation: `https://learn.microsoft.com/en-us/azure/virtual-machines/linux/use-remote-desktop?tabs=azure-cli`. For different distributions, you'll need to find the appropriate tutorial.

Such a file contains basic connection information:

```
full address:s:<ip-address>:3389
prompt for credentials:i:1
administrative session:i:1
```

When you have an RDP client installed, such a file can be used as input, so you don't need to provide that information every time. In the next section, we'll check an alternative to connecting to a machine using the IP address – DNS name.

Connecting with the DNS name

So far, we talked about connecting to a VM using IP addresses. In Azure, it's also possible to leverage the **DNS name**, which can be configured for a public IP address of your machine. When creating such a resource, you can use an additional parameter called `--dns-name`, which will be used to add a prefix to the `.westeurope.cloudapp.azure.com` domain name available for each public IP address. The same parameter can be used for updating the address:

```
az network public-ip update -g <resource-group-name> -n <public-ip-name> --dns-name <dns-name>
az network public-ip create -g <resource-group-name> -n <public-ip-name> --dns-name <dns-name>
```

Once configured, you'll be able to point to that DNS name from your DNS server using a **CNAME record**. When involving DNS in making connections, we have two options:

- Make our public IP address static
- Have a dynamic IP address with the **fully qualified domain name** (**FQDN**) configured

Both options are viable but require a slightly different approach when configuring the rest of the components. For the static IP address, you may use a custom domain to make a connection with a VM, but to make it work, you'll need an A record added to your DNS server:

```
some-domain.com A <public-ip-address>
```

In this example, you could assign `some-domain.com` to the public IP address of your VM. This will allow people to connect to it using the domain instead of the assigned IP address.

> **Important note**
>
> We're discussing making a connection via SSH/RDP with a DNS name attached to your public IP address. This is only one of the available scenarios, as the same steps would be performed – for example, when setting up a public domain for a web server hosting your application on a VM.

As an alternative to having a static IP address, you may use a dynamic one, but for that to work, you'll need to configure the FQDN (which is basically what we got when setting up the DNS name on our public IP address) and use an A record with a slightly different configuration:

```
some-domain.com A <dns-name>.westeurope.cloudapp.azure.com
```

Here, instead of a public IP address, we're providing the FQDN as an alias of our main domain. This will once again resolve to the machine we're hosting in Azure, but people will be able to connect using our custom domain.

> **Important note**
>
> Using a public IP address or FQDN depends on your setup. If you have a static IP address, it doesn't really matter which option you choose. For a dynamic IP address, configuring the A record pointing to that dynamic address doesn't make much sense, as any change to the IP address would trigger a change in the DNS.

Once the DNS name is configured, you can connect to your machine using both SSH and RDP, but this time you won't use the IP address:

```
ssh <username>@some-domain.com
```

You could also modify the RDP file to reflect the changes:

```
full address:s:some-domain.com:3389
prompt for credentials:i:1
administrative session:i:1
```

This setup is less important from a connectivity point of view but will be helpful when allowing other people to connect to services hosted on that machine. To complete our lesson, let's discuss one more way of making a connection – a dedicated Azure service called Azure Bastion.

Connecting using Azure Bastion

The last option we'll discuss when talking about connecting to Azure VMs is **Azure Bastion**. This is a much more sophisticated way of making a connection as Bastion is a managed service that can be used to secure access to your machine. Conceptually, it's a similar setup to having a jumpbox machine and connecting to it using SSH or RDP. Technically, it has much more advanced capabilities.

The advantage of using Bastion is the ability to connect to a machine using its private IP address. Yes – even though it allows you to make a connection from outside of a network where a machine is deployed, the public IP address is not required. If you used it for making connections and decided to deploy a Bastion host, it'd be possible to safely remove it.

Azure Bastion has two main components:

- A **PaaS** service that is managed by Microsoft
- **A Bastion host** that you can install on your machine

It has the benefit of being a much simpler setup than maintaining your own service that would allow for making secure connections (for example, **Citrix**). On the other hand, Azure Bastion is not a free service – a basic instance will cost over $138 per month (West Europe). It's up to you and your technical requirements whether it should be enabled for each machine.

> **Important note**
>
> As Azure Bastion may incur additional charges, make sure you understand its pricing and capabilities before deploying it on a bigger scale. It's possible to deploy Azure Bastion using a couple of different methods – you can use the Azure portal, ARM templates, Azure PowerShell, or the Azure CLI. For the sake of this exercise, we'll use the Azure CLI.

Let's start by creating a resource group and virtual network where both Azure Bastion and our VM will be deployed:

```
az group create --name <resource-group-name> --location <location>
az network vnet create --resource-group <resource-group-name> \
   --name <vnet-name> \
   --address-prefix 10.1.0.0/16 \
   --subnet-name default \
   --subnet-prefix 10.1.0.0/24
```

Those commands will prepare the initial infrastructure for our setup. As you can see, we're creating a default subnet as well, as we need it to store our VM. The Azure subnet needs a subnet as well, but it needs to be a separate resource:

```
az network vnet subnet create --name AzureBastionSubnet \
   --resource-group <resource-group-name> \
   --vnet-name <vnet-name> \
   --address-prefix 10.1.1.0/26
```

> **Important note**
>
> The address ranges provided are just examples – you don't need to use the exact same ranges; they can be bigger or smaller. The general rule of thumb, however, is to avoid subnets smaller than /26 in size as it may be difficult to handle scaling your hosts if needed.

Once the subnet for Bastion is created, we need to create a public IP address for it:

```
az network public-ip create --resource-group <resource-group-name> \
  --name <public-ip-name> \
  --sku Standard
  --location <location>
```

As you can see, even though we don't need a public IP address assigned to our machine, we'll need it to make a connection to Azure Bastion. If that address is not provided, we won't be able to connect to it from outside of the virtual network. The last step is to deploy the actual Bastion host. We'll use the resources we created to complete the configuration:

```
az network bastion create --name <bastion-name> \
  --public-ip-address <public-ip-name> \
  --resource-group <resource-group-name> \
  --vnet-name <vnet-name> \
  --location <location> \
  --sku Basic
```

Azure Bastion has two SKUs – Basic and Standard – which differ in terms of their capabilities. The main differences are the following:

- You cannot use RDP to connect to a Linux VM with the Basic SKU

- You cannot use SSH to connect to a Windows VM with the Basic SKU

- You cannot upload and download files with the Basic SKU

- The standard SKU allows you to use a VM IP address to make a connection

In fact, the Basic SKU of Azure Bastion has some serious limitations that cannot be easily mitigated. If you're looking for a robust way of working when making a connection (for example, for remote working), the Basic SKU may not be sufficient. However, as SKUs can be upgraded, the Basic SKU is a good starting point for most scenarios.

Once Bastion is deployed (it may take up to 10 minutes), you can choose the right connection method, as there are a couple of those:

- SSH or RDP

- Native client from your local computer

For the Basic SKU, only SSH/RDP connections will be available. If you want to use a native client, you'll need to upgrade the SKU to Standard. Connecting using a native client is something that is also different for Windows and Linux (when making a connection locally). We'll cover that in the next section.

Native client – Windows

When using a local computer with Windows, you have two options (depending on the protocol):

```
az network bastion rdp --name <bastion-name> --resource-group
<resource-group-name> --target-resource-id <vm-resource-id>
az network bastion ssh --name <bastion-name> --resource-group
<resource-group-name> --target-resource-id <vm-resource-id> --auth-
type "ssh-key" --username <username> --ssh-key <path-to-ssh-key>
```

However, to make an SSH connection, you'll need an extension for your Azure CLI:

```
az extension add --name ssh
```

After completing the preceding commands, a native client will be opened on your computer, from which a session for a user will be started. For the second command, you may omit the last parameter – if the SSH key is not provided, you'll be prompted for a password.

Native client – Linux

On Linux, you can use an SSH connection only. The difference is that on Linux or other non-Windows hosts, you'll need to open a tunnel, which can then be used for making a connection:

```
az network bastion tunnel --name <bastion-name> --resource-
group <resource-group-name> --target-resource-id <vm-resource-id>
--resource-port <target-port> --port <local-port>
```

Once the tunnel is established, you'll be able to make a connection:

```
ssh <username>@127.0.0.1 -p <local-port>
```

As you can see, it's necessary to provide the same local port for both commands, so it's possible to use the created tunnel. This approach is also useful when you'd like to upload files over SSH.

Working with a VM via Azure Bastion

Once connected to your VM, you can interact with it as if it were a standard connection made over SSH or RDP. If the machine you're connecting to has a graphic interface enabled, then when connected, you'll see its desktop. Such a connection may be performed directly from the Azure portal – in that case, the browser will act as a proxy between your computer and the desired host.

> **Important note**
>
> Connecting to a machine from the Azure portal requires a browser supporting HTML5. Outdated or heavily customized browsers may not work in that scenario.

As mentioned previously, remember that Azure Bastion has some serious limitations for connecting with VMs depending on its SKU. If you face a scenario where the Basic SKU is insufficient, you can easily upgrade your Bastion host using the Azure CLI:

```
az network bastion update --name <bastion-name> --resource-group
<resource-group-name> --sku Standard
```

That's all about connecting with Azure VMs for this chapter. Let's move on to the last topic, which will help you understand what is possible to enhance the availability of VMs and deploy them as a single unit.

The availability of Azure VMs

When working with VMs, you'll face various scenarios:

- Deploying a single machine
- Deploying multiple machines as separate hosts
- Deploying multiple machines as connected hosts

Depending on your scenario, different approaches will be needed to achieve what you need. For example, up until now, we deployed multiple VMs, which were mostly unrelated hosts. This is the simplest scenario from a deployment point of view, but gives us no real resiliency. It's time to learn how to achieve HA in Microsoft Azure when deploying IaaS components. Learning about that topic will help in real-world scenarios, which very often require improved availability of your infrastructure due to business requirements.

Availability sets

Each deployed VM in Azure has specific hardware powering its capabilities. In other words, anytime you deploy something in Azure, the data center will select the proper placement for it in terms of physical location. You don't care about all that placement in most cases, but it's important to understand how it can affect the resilience of your services.

> **Important note**
>
> Some applications need to be placed as close to each other as possible. This is also true for infrastructure that is deployed for a service where latency must be as low as possible. For such scenarios, Azure has proximity placement groups, which guarantee that all the components are co-located and are as close to each other physically as possible. This has, however, a big trade-off of high risk of being affected by hardware outage.

When thinking about possible causes of an unstable environment, there are two major factors:

- Hardware outage
- Software errors

In Azure, these both happen from time to time, and if you're designing your system to be reliable, you need to take additional measures to ensure reliability. This is where the concept of availability sets comes in handy. However, before we dive deeper into it, you need to understand two additional concepts:

- **Update domain (UD)**
- Fault domain

Once you're familiar with them, you'll be ready to deploy your first availability set.

Update and fault domains

To protect against hardware and software issues, Azure services may leverage the concept of update and fault domains. Both domains have the same purpose but address slightly different issues:

- **FDs** are for hardware outages.
- **UDs** secure from software errors related to the operating system. They cannot secure you from application-related errors of a faulty configuration.

When deploying a single VM, it doesn't matter how you'd configure it – such a setup has little resiliency and shouldn't be considered from an HA point of view. However, if you have multiple machines, you may want to make them much more resilient. This is why such a cluster of machines should leverage placement in different domains, so if one domain fails, then the rest can handle the load.

Conceptually, it's simple – each VM should be placed in separate FDs and UDs. However, as there are only three FDs available, some machines will reuse the same domain. This is not ideal, but for many scenarios it will serve its purpose. The same is true for UDs – there are far more UDs than FDs, but still, they're not infinite. Let's now consider the following example – assume that you have five machines and would like to place them in separate domains:

- We have three FDs: FD1, FD2, FD3
- We'll use five UDs: UD1, UD2, UD3, UD4, UD5
- Here are our VMs: VM1, VM2, VM3, VM4, VM5

Once deployed, our placement should look like this:

- VM1 -> FD1, UD1
- VM2 -> FD2, UD2
- VM3 -> FD3, UD3

- VM4 -> FD1, UD4

- VM5 -> FD2, UD5

Such a setup will guarantee the following:

- If there are hardware failures, they will be mostly limited to one FD

- If machines should be updated (regarding software running on them, such as the operating system), the update process won't affect all the VMs at the same time

However, remember that those domains secure you only locally – if there's a much wider regional outage, FDs and UDs won't be able to ensure the availability of your machines. To increase availability in case of a wider local outage, we could use availability sets, covered in the next section.

Deploying an availability set

To deploy an availability set, you need a single command:

```
az vm availability-set create -n <availability-set-name> \
  -g <resource-group-name> \
  --platform-fault-domain-count <number-of-fault-domains> \
  --platform-update-domain-count <number-of-update-domains>
```

Once the availability set is deployed, you'll need to use it during the creation of new VMs. You cannot assign an existing VM to an availability set:

```
az vm create -n <vm-name> -g <resource-group-name> --image <os-image>
--availability-set <name-or-id-of-availability-set>
```

> **Important note**
>
> You can provide either a name or the resource ID of your availability set. The value depends on the placement of your resources – if both the VM and availability set are in the same resource group, you can use a name to link them.
>
> It's possible to attach an existing VM to an availability set, but this requires recreating it with a disk detached so that it can be reattached to a new machine.

The availability set will automatically assign UDs and FDs to the machines that are linked to it. As an alternative to availability sets, we can use VMSSs – let's dive into them.

VMSS

Availability sets will improve the resiliency of your machines, but they have a single flaw – each machine is still managed individually. This can be treated as an advantage – you can assign machines of different sizes – but many scenarios require deploying a set of the same machines with no real distinction between them. This is what VMSSs are for.

By default, VMSSs are not designed to provide improved resiliency of your services. They're deployed as a single unit that configures a common size for your machines with autoscaling capabilities. However, you can use availability zones to improve the availability of a cluster deployed using that method. To do that, you'll need to explicitly configure that when creating a VMSS:

```
az vmss create -n <vmss-name> -g <resource-group-name> --image
<os-image> --zones 1,2,3
```

Such a command will create a VMSS for which all the machines deployed will be spread across three availability zones. As the VMSS may contain more than three VMs, the resiliency concept is like availability sets – you may have more than one machine deployed to the same availability zone. However, this is fine from a configuration point of view as the VMSS is mostly used to deploy several machines sharing the same configuration (VM size, disk, and network). In many scenarios, it means that machines managed by a VMSS have the same services deployed. Using this service and the availability zones approach, you may achieve both easy scalability of your infrastructure and improved availability.

> **Important note**
>
> The use of availability zones is still a concept that guarantees availability in case of local failures. It's a much more resilient setup as it's less likely for Azure to have an outage of all availability zones at once when compared to availability sets, which don't provide **zonal deployment mode**.

Such a setup has its disadvantages as well – in Azure, egress (which is outgoing traffic from your services) incurs additional charges. This charge is applicable to traffic across availability zones, so such infrastructure will most likely cost more than a similar setup using availability sets.

Remember that it's possible to manually configure VMs to be deployed across zones. In general, you may not need a VMSS unless you want to manage those machines as a single unit.

That's all about the availability of VMs in this chapter. Let's summarize our findings and see what's waiting for us in the next chapters.

Summary

This chapter concentrates on general knowledge about VMs, including sizing, disks, deployment modes, and their availability. We discussed different ways of connecting to machines, including the differences between SSH, RDP, and Bastion. The knowledge gained from this chapter should help you in further investigating other capabilities of Azure VMs and possibilities when using them in your infrastructure.

The next chapter will focus on installing and configuring extensions for VMs. We'll see what's possible to do when you want to configure a deployed machine or automate its management operations.

6

Configuring Virtual Machine Extensions

After learning about **Azure Virtual Machines**, it's time to see how one can extend their capabilities by installing additional extensions and plugins. In Azure, you can quite easily add a service or a component to any deployed instances of Azure Virtual Machines – the only requirement is to do so according to the platform's requirements.

Basic knowledge of setting up and configuring extensions for Azure Virtual Machines will come in handy when deploying additional components used, for example, for monitoring or auditing your infrastructure.

In this chapter, we're going to cover the following main topics:

- How to use virtual machine extensions
- How to implement a Custom Script Extension
- What is the **Desired State Configuration** (DSC)?

Technical requirements

For the exercises from this chapter, you'll need the following:

- The Azure CLI (`https://learn.microsoft.com/en-us/cli/azure/install-azure-cli`)
- A command line of any kind (either the one available in your operating system by default or your favorite one)

The Code in Action video for this book can be viewed at: `https://packt.link/GTX9F`

Using virtual machine extensions

Once your virtual machine is deployed, it's ready to be used and configured. In many scenarios, you don't need to do anything besides installing some basic software needed by your services. However, there are use cases where you need a certain functionality for your virtual machine – this can be implemented in various ways, but very often, the easiest path is by using an extension.

Azure offers a couple of predefined extensions available for most virtual machines. However, availability depends on a couple of factors:

- Region
- Operating system
- Additional capabilities of the virtual machine

The easiest way to learn what is available for your setup is to run the following command in the Azure CLI:

```
az vm extension image list --location <location> --output table
```

This command will return a list of available extensions per given location. It'll also include additional information, such as the name, publisher, and version of the given extension.

Now, depending on your operating system, you'll need to work through different steps to install and use these extensions. We'll start with machines based on Windows and then proceed to the Linux operating system.

Employing an extension in a Windows Azure Virtual Machine

Each Azure Virtual Machine running Windows will require an additional component to run extensions. This component is called the **Azure Virtual Machine Agent for Windows** and needs to be installed separately from the standard infrastructure configuration.

> **Important note**
> The Azure Virtual Machine Agent for Windows doesn't support all versions of Windows. You need an x64 architecture for the selected CPU, and the machine needs to support .NET Framework 4.0 at a minimum.

To install the agent, you have two possible paths:

- Installing via the **Infrastructure-as-Code approach** (e.g., **ARM templates** or **Azure Bicep**)
- Manual installation

Let's see how to perform those operations.

Installing via the Infrastructure-as-Code approach

At the beginning of this book, we discussed the benefits of the **Infrastructure-as-Code** (**IaC**) approach and possible use cases. While you may not need to be an expert on every aspect of the administration of Azure resources, there are some scenarios where this knowledge is very beneficial. One of those scenarios is installing the Azure Virtual Machine Agent for Windows.

To install the Azure Virtual Machine Agent for Windows, you need to set the `provisionVmAgent` property to `true`:

```
{
    "resources": [{
        "name": "<vm-name>"
        "type": "Microsoft.Compute/virtualMachines",
        "apiVersion": "2016-04-30-preview",
        "location": "<location>"
        "properties": {
            "osProfile": {
                "windowsConfiguration": {
                    "provisionVmAgent": "true"
                }
            }
        }
    }]
}
```

The preceding code snippet is, of course, just a subset of a final Azure Virtual Machine configuration. To be able to deploy a machine, you'll need to additionally pass the rest of the required parameters, which are described in the documentation.

However, for any Windows virtual machine deployed via **Azure Marketplace**, the agent is enabled by default, meaning you don't need to activate this property by yourself. On the other hand, it is possible to disable it. However, note that if the agent is disabled (i.e., not installed), you won't be able to run certain services such as **Azure Backup**.

Manual installation

If you're provisioning a virtual machine in Azure from a custom image, you might need to install the Azure Virtual Machine Agent for Windows manually. Each available version of the Azure Virtual Machine Agent for Windows can be downloaded directly from its GitHub project page at `https://github.com/Azure/WindowsVMAgent`. From there, go to the **Releases** page and download either the **MSI installer** (`.msi`) or **ZIP archive** (`.zip`) options.

▼ Assets   6

⊕Win7_Win8_IaaS_amd64_2.7.41491.1095_2307171095_GuestAgentPackage.zip	13.5 MB	3 weeks ago
⊕Win7_Win8_IaaS_arm64_2.7.41491.1095_2307171095_GuestAgentPackage.zip	10.1 MB	3 weeks ago
⊕WindowsAzureVmAgent.amd64_2.7.41491.1095_2307171095.fre.msi	14.5 MB	3 weeks ago
⊕WindowsAzureVmAgent.arm64_2.7.41491.1095_2307171095.fre.msi	11.2 MB	3 weeks ago
🗋Source code (zip)		Sep 16, 2021
🗋Source code (tar.gz)		Sep 16, 2021

Figure 6.1 – Available assets for virtual machine agents

> **Important note**
> Machines with the `provisionVmAgent` property disabled must be updated with an additional setting – `AllowExtensionOperations`. This is required in order to enable an extension to perform operations on a machine where the extension is installed.

After installing the Azure Virtual Machine Agent for Windows manually, you can update your virtual machine resource with the following operations:

```
az vm update -n <vm-name> -g <resource-group-name> --set osProfile.
allowExtensionOperations=true
```

This is required to tell the virtual machine that it should allow the running of operations initiated by installed extensions. The same property could also be updated via ARM templates, Azure Bicep, or **Azure PowerShell**. Let's now discuss the network requirements that need to be in place to get extensions up and working.

Network requirements

Agents running on your virtual machines need a special IP address – 168.63.129.16. This IP address is used in Azure for multiple purposes (including DNS services and health probing in load balancer scenarios) and should be allowed when configuring network rules for a machine.

In virtual machine agent scenarios, the 168.63.129.16 address is used to communicate with Azure as a platform and notify it that the agent is in its *ready* state. This communication flows over **TCP** using ports 80 and 32526. As this is an infrastructural concept of Azure, you should not interfere with this communication or try to manage it using **network security groups**, for example.

As a point of contrast, let's now examine how extensions are used in the context of Linux.

Using extension in Linux Azure Virtual Machines

Similarly to Windows, Linux machines in Azure also need an agent installed to run extensions. The installation method for the Linux agent is slightly different – the preferred method is to install it via the **RPM** or **DEB** package managers, as in the following example:

```
sudo apt-get install walinuxagent
```

To install the agent manually (or provide a more advanced configuration), you can use installation directly from the source. It'll require some additional configuration and installation of dependencies (including Python), so the best way to be successful is to follow the instructions in the project's repository at `https://github.com/Azure/WALinuxAgent`.

Note that in Azure, there's a limited list of Linux distributions with official support. The same limitation applies to the Linux agent (Azure states that the agent may run on other distros as well – it's just not tested against them). Currently supported distributions include **Red Hat**, **SUSE**, and **Canonical** (**Ubuntu**).

Let's now see a number of methods for installing the extensions themselves.

Installing extensions

Extensions can be installed and managed using the Azure CLI, Azure PowerShell, or the **IaC approach**. You can choose any extension available in your region, such as the following:

- Disk encryption
- **Desired State Configuration (DSC)**
- Custom script extensions

Depending on your chosen method, there are small differences between tools when it comes to running an extension on your machine. For example, to enable an extension using the Azure CLI, run the following command:

```
az vm extension set \
  --resource-group <resource-group-name> \
  --vm-name <vm-name> --name <extension-name> \
  --publisher <extension-publisher> \
  --protected-settings <path-to-settings-file>
```

The same can be done using an ARM template as follows:

```
{
  "name": "<resource-name>",
  "type": "extensions",
  "location": "[resourceGroup().location]",
  "apiVersion": "2019-03-01",
```

```
"properties": {
  "publisher": "<publisher>",
  "type": "<type>",
  "typeHandlerVersion": "2.1",
  "autoUpgradeMinorVersion": true,
  "settings": {},
  "protectedSettings": {
    "commandToExecute": "<command>",
    "fileUris": ["<file-url>"]
  }
}
}
```

We'll dive deeper into that topic in the next section, where we'll focus on running an extension called the Custom Script Extension.

Implementing the Custom Script Extension

One of the most useful extensions is the Custom Script Extension. This extension allows you to run scripts on your virtual machines to provide custom logic or install additional software. Often, this extension is used to complete the configuration of your machine when it isn't possible to use the standard deployment options.

> **Important note**
>
> Use of the Custom Script Extension shouldn't replace tools such as **Ansible**, **Chef**, or **Puppet** when configuring a machine. If you need to configure a large number of machines or require advanced control tools, the Custom Script Extension will become cumbersome and difficult to maintain.

Let's see how to use this extension for basic scenarios.

Installing software with the Custom Script Extension

To get started, we'll need to create an Azure Virtual Machine that we will then configure later using the extension. Use the following commands to deploy an empty Linux machine:

```
az group create -n <resource-group-name> -l <location>
az vm create -g <resource-group-name> -n <vm-name> --admin-username
<username> --admin-password "<password>" --image "Ubuntu2204" --size
"Standard_ B1s"
```

Once the virtual machine is deployed, make sure you can connect to it using **SSH**:

```
ssh <username>@<vm-public-ip-address>
```

Once connected to the virtual machine, terminate the SSH session to proceed.

> **Important note**
>
> If you can't connect to the machine, make sure you have port 22 opened for SSH connections.

Once you're able to connect to the machine, it's time to configure the extension to install **nginx** on our machine and get it running:

```
az vm extension set \
  --resource-group <resource-group-name> \
  --vm-name <vm-name> --name customScript \
  --publisher Microsoft.Azure.Extensions \
  --settings "{'commandToExecute': 'apt-get -y update && apt-get
install -y nginx'}"
```

After running the command, wait a moment until it completes. Once the CLI returns the result of running your command, open port 80 on your machine by adding a new security rule to your network security group:

```
az network nsg rule create -g <resource-group-name> \
  --nsg-name <nsg-name> \
  -n Http \
  --priority 4096 \
  --destination-address-prefixes '*' \
  --destination-port-ranges 80 \
  --access Allow \
  --protocol Tcp
```

After a moment, point your browser to the public IP address of your machine. You should see the default welcome page of nginx:

Welcome to nginx!

If you see this page, the nginx web server is successfully installed and working. Further configuration is required.

For online documentation and support please refer to nginx.org.
Commercial support is available at nginx.com.

Thank you for using nginx.

Figure 6.2 – Welcome page of nginx

As you can see, we were able to install a web server using an extension configured on our virtual machine. Let's next see how we can operate on files or perform other operations with the Custom Script Extension.

Executing a script

In the previous exercise, we passed a couple of commands inline to be executed by the extension. This will work in scenarios where there's no complex logic involved, but for more advanced use cases, you may need to provide a script to be executed at runtime. To do that, you'll need two things:

- A custom script
- The location from which the script can be downloaded

As sometimes it may not be ideal to pass a script via a file location, the Custom Script Extension also allows you to pass a script inside a parameter. We'll try that in the next section.

Executing a script from a location

When configuring the Custom Script Extension, you have the option to pass the `--protectedSettings` parameter. This parameter allows you to pass the same set of parameters as `--settings` used previously, but this time they will be treated as sensitive values that cannot be presented as plain text. See the following code snippet to see the structure of the passed object:

```
"protectedSettings": {
        "commandToExecute": "<command-to-execute>",
        "script": "<base64-script-to-execute>",
        "storageAccountName": "<storage-account-name>",
        "storageAccountKey": "<storage-account-key>",
        "fileUris": ["https://.."],
        "managedIdentity" : "<managed-identity-identifier>"
}
```

Note that you have the option to pass both **storage account** and **managed identity** values – but you cannot use them both simultaneously. In other words, you need to select whether to authorize access using a storage account key or a role assigned to a managed identity.

Now, if you want to run a script from a location, you'll need to decide where it'll be stored. If it's a generic location (e.g., a public file share or a repository), no additional actions are required on your side. However, if you decide that you'd like to store files in Azure Storage, you'll need to configure an authorization method (key/managed identity).

> **Important note**
>
> While this extension natively supports integration with Azure Storage only, you can use any storage you want. To do that, you'd need to create a starting script and make it publicly available, then include the logic for downloading the *real* script from a custom location. For authorization purposes, you could leverage something like the environment variables defined on the virtual machine, for instance.

Let's try to configure a virtual machine to download a script created by us from Azure Storage using a managed identity. To get started, we need a storage account set up:

```
az group create -l <location> -n <resource-grouo-name>
az storage account create -g <resource-group-name> -n <storage-account-name>
az storage container create -n <container-name> --account-name <storage-account-name> --public-access off
```

This command will create three resources:

- Resource group
- Storage account
- Container with public access disabled

Now, we need a script, so let's use the following one:

```
!#/bin/bash

echo "Creating directories ..."
mkdir /data
mkdir /appdata

echo "Creating files ..."
touch /data/data.dat

echo "Setting permissions ..."
chmod 777 /data/data.dat
```

Next, we'll upload that script to the container. Save the script in your working directory as `script.sh` and use the following command to upload it:

```
az storage blob upload -f ./script.sh -c <container-name> -n script.sh --account-name <storage-account-name>
```

We now have our basic setup complete. The next step is to deploy a virtual machine with the Custom Script Extension, which will run our script. However, as we decided that we want to leverage a managed identity, we'll need to do this in three steps:

- Deploy a virtual machine with an identity assigned

- Assign a role for the identity

- Run the extension

The first step is quite easy – we deploy a machine as usual, remembering that we need to enable the identity:

```
az vm create -n <vm-name> \
  -g <resource-group-name> \
  --image Ubuntu2204 \
  --assign-identity [system] \
  --role "Storage Blob Data Reader" \
  --scope "<storage-account-resource-id>"
```

However, you may get an error stating that the Azure CLI is unable to perform the preceding operation due to an API version mismatch:

```
{"status":"Failed","error":{"code":"DeploymentFailed","target":"/
subscriptions/…/resourceGroups/…/providers/Microsoft.Resources/
deployments/…","message":"At least one resource deployment
operation failed. Please list deployment operations for details.
Please see https://aka.ms/arm-deployment-operations for usage
details.","details":[{"code":"UnsupportedApiVersionForRoleDefinition
HasDataActions","message":"Assignments to roles with DataActions and
NotDataActions are not supported on API version '2015-07-01'. The
minimum required API version for this operations is '2018-01-01-
preview'."}]}}
```

If that's the case, use the following two commands:

```
az vm create -n <vm-name> \
  -g <resource-group-name> \
  --image Ubuntu2204 \
  --assign-identity [system]

az role assignment create \
  --assignee-object-id "<managed-identity-object-id>" \
  --role "Storage Blob Data Reader" \
  --scope "<storage-account-resource-id>"
```

The last stage of your setup is to enable the extension on your virtual machine:

```
az vm extension set -n customScript \
  --publisher Microsoft.Azure.Extensions \
  --vm-name <vm-name> \
  --resource-group <resource-group-name> \
  --protected-settings "{'managedIdentity':{},'fileUris':['<path-to-
file>'],'commandToExecute':'sh script.sh'}"
```

After a moment, the script should run on the machine. You can verify this by connecting to the machine via SSH and checking the main directory:

```
drwxr-xr-x    2 root root  4096 Jun 13 12:37 appdata
lrwxrwxrwx    1 root root     7 Jun  1 02:09 bin -> usr/bin
drwxr-xr-x    4 root root  4096 Jun  1 02:14 boot
drwxr-xr-x    2 root root  4096 Jun 13 12:37 data
drwxr-xr-x   18 root root  4000 Jun 13 12:09 dev
drwxr-xr-x   97 root root  4096 Jun 13 12:34 etc
drwxr-xr-x    4 root root  4096 Jun 13 12:34 home
drwxr-xr-x   13 root root  4096 Jun  1 02:11 var
aach06@aach0601:/$ cd data
aach06@aach0601:/data$ ls -la
total 8
drwxr-xr-x  2 root root 4096 Jun 13 12:37 .
drwxr-xr-x 21 root root 4096 Jun 13 12:37 ..
-rwxrwxrwx  1 root root    0 Jun 13 12:37 data.dat
```

As you can see, both the `appdata` and `data` directories were created. The `data.dat` file is also available. Before we continue, let's discuss some remarks:

- When passing the value of the managed identity, we passed an empty object as `'managedIdentity':{}`. This tells the extension that we want to use a system-assigned identity. To use a user-assigned identity, pass the `clientId` or `objectId` parameters in the object.

- Make sure you're running the correct script by passing it via the `commandToExecute` parameter.

Let's now see how we could execute our script without uploading it to any storage beforehand.

Executing a script inline

Instead of deploying a script to storage, we could run it directly using a value of a parameter. To do that, we need to hash the script using `base64` encoding:

```
cat script.sh | base64 -w 0
```

If your script is huge, you can additionally compress it with `gzip`:

```
cat script.sh | gzip -9 | base64 -w 0
```

The Custom Script Extension always tries to decode and decompress scripts when passed in, so you don't need to worry about additional parameters. Once the script is ready (note that its size cannot exceed 256 KBs), you can run it with the following command:

```
az vm extension set -n customScript \
  --publisher Microsoft.Azure.Extensions \
  --vm-name <vm-name> \
  --resource-group <resource-group-name> \
  --protected-settings "{'script':'<base64-encoded-value>'}"
```

The result of running the script will be the same as previously – it'll create new directories and files. This way of running a script is useful for simpler scenarios, where your script is intended for a single machine only (or doesn't need to be shared across different infrastructure components). If you'd like to build a registry of scripts, the better option would be to upload them to a common location and download them from there.

That's all on the Custom Script Extension! Let's now switch our focus to the last topic of this chapter – *What is the Desired State Configuration?*.

What is the Desired State Configuration?

There are two possible definitions for **Desired State Configuration** (**DSC**) in the context of Azure:

- An extension for PowerShell used for bootstrapping and managing Azure Virtual Machines
- A general concept where you work toward developing an automated solution for configuration management of your infrastructure

In this section, we'll focus on both definitions for a better understanding of the whole concept.

Azure Automation State Configuration

In Azure, you can automatically manage the desired state of your virtual machines by leveraging **Azure Automation State Configuration**. This feature is basically a configuration file that you create and pass to your infrastructure. Your infrastructure will handle the passed configuration via an installed DSC agent and apply all the changes defined in it.

Such a configuration looks something like the following:

```
configuration IISInstall
{
    node "localhost"
```

```
    {
        WindowsFeature IIS
        {
            Ensure = "Present"
            Name = "Web-Server"
        }
    }
}
```

However, before you start planning on using this functionality, you need to consider a couple of factors. First is the question of support for the DSC extension by the operating systems running in Azure. For Linux distributions, support for this extension will cease by the end of 2023. This means that if you intend to use it, you need to switch to **Azure Automanage** as soon as possible. This will also affect current users of DSC, so, in fact, there's very little time to try out this feature on Linux.

> **Important note**
>
> The general recommendation is to use the newer version of DSC for both Linux and Windows. This new version is called Azure Automanage **Machine Configuration**.

The second thing to consider is a comparison of DSC available in Azure with similar tools, such as Chef or Ansible, discussed in the next section.

Sample configuration of DSC as an extension

To configure and enable the DSC extension on your machine, you can use, for instance, the following configuration passed via an ARM template:

```
{
    "type": "Microsoft.Compute/virtualMachines/extensions",
    "name": "Microsoft.Powershell.DSC",
    "apiVersion": "2018-10-01",
    "location": "<location>",
    "properties": {
        "publisher": "Microsoft.Powershell",
        "type": "DSC",
        "typeHandlerVersion": "2.77",
        "autoUpgradeMinorVersion": true,
        "settings": {
        },
        "protectedSettings": {
        }
    }
}
```

The preceding configuration has the same syntax as the extensions discussed previously but will require additional, more detailed configuration passed in via the `settings` / `protectedSettings` object. You can find examples and the full syntax for it at `https://learn.microsoft.com/en-us/azure/virtual-machines/extensions/dsc-template`.

To understand the topic better, let's quickly explore the general concept of DSC.

Understanding DSC – general concepts

When managing infrastructure, the *desired state* is a general concept that applies to a range of different cloud vendors and on-premises setups. In fact, many companies leverage this idea to automate activities related to the infrastructure of their systems. Examples of this automation include the following:

- Providing a common schema for defining configuration

- Monitoring execution of scripts

- Reusing parts of configuration files as modules

- Detaching users from the execution of automation processes

To implement DSC as a concept in Azure, you don't need the DSC extension – you can use any of the typical, publicly available configuration tools such as Chef, Puppet, or Ansible. Indeed, all of these tools can fulfill most of the necessary requirements on most platforms. What's needed, however, is familiarity with the concepts and solutions provided by different tools (e.g., some tools are installed as agents, some require connectivity over SSH, etc.), so there's no single tool that can solve all problems.

That closes our exploration of extensions for Azure Virtual Machines. Let's summarize the chapter and set the stage for the next one.

Summary

As we've seen in this chapter, extensions for Azure Virtual Machines can be used to automate a selection of management activities and operations (e.g., backups or monitoring) and to help initialize a machine with additional services and applications. One of the most useful extensions is the Custom Script Extension, which allows you to run any logic contained within a script you provide. It's a powerful feature, though do note that it's not meant for setting up configuration at a large scale.

Remember that extensions in Azure Virtual Machines can be used for a wide variety of use cases, starting with installing monitoring agents or **Configuration-as-Code** agents (such as **Puppet**). What's more, they're generally pretty straightforward features to set up, meaning that you don't need to provision additional infrastructure to get them working.

In the next chapter, we'll focus on configuring and using backups for virtual machines in Azure.

7
Configuring Backups

By now, you should be familiar with lots of basic concepts related to building and managing infrastructure with Azure. This time, we're going to cover a more advanced topic that is very important in all production-ready systems – backup. Just to be clear – in this chapter, we won't dive into backing up databases or applications' data and instead focus on **virtual machines** (**VMs**), their disks, and additional components that can be used to provide **disaster recovery** (**DR**) and secure their data.

Throughout this chapter, we'll be discussing how Azure can help you back up and restore the state of VMs. We'll cover not only generic topics such as general infrastructure and authorization setup but also specific solutions leveraging native components such as Azure Backup Server and Azure Site Recovery.

In this chapter, we're going to cover the following main topics:

- Protecting VM data
- Understanding backup and restore for Azure VMs
- Using Azure Backup Server
- Exploring Azure Site Recovery

Technical requirements

For the exercises from this chapter, you'll need:

- The Azure CLI (https://learn.microsoft.com/en-us/cli/azure/install-azure-cli)
- A command-line tool of any kind (either available in your operating system or your favorite one)

The Code in Action video for this book can be viewed at: https://packt.link/GTX9F

Protecting VM data

VMs provisioned to run workloads needed for your applications (or applications themselves) need to be protected against accidental deletion, misconfiguration, or loss of data. Azure, as a platform, offers multiple ways to do that, depending on your configuration, technical requirements, and available technologies. Some scenarios can be covered by third-party solutions as well – we won't cover them in this chapter as it'd be difficult to select tools generic enough to serve everyone. Let's get started with securing VMs by making sure that the infrastructure itself is secure.

Coping with accidental deletion

At any moment in time, a user, script, or application can accidentally delete some components of your infrastructure. This is, of course, true, assuming some basic prerequisites:

- Resources can be removed (are not locked)
- An actor (user/script/application) has enough permissions to perform a deletion

When talking specifically about **Azure VMs**, there's one more thing to consider – the most important part of your infrastructure is disks, which store the configuration of the operating system and data of your applications. It's worth considering treating them separately, so restoring a VM is a much simpler process, thanks to additional steps you may have considered to secure yourself. We'll cover all those topics as separate actions to have a clearer picture.

Implementing locks

As mentioned previously, if you don't secure yourself against accidental deletion, some resources may be deleted by an accident or an error in one of the scripts running against your infrastructure. This also includes the removal of resources on purpose as a form of attack on your infrastructure. To lower the chance that a resource (such as a VM, data disk, or even database) could be removed, we can leverage the concept of locks.

> **Important note**
> Accidental deletion of resources may also be caused by **Infrastructure as Code** (**IaC**) tools such as **Terraform** if somebody fails to properly review the deployment plan. That's something that is even more likely to happen than an attack based on the removal of resources on purpose.

A **lock** in Azure is an additional resource that is deployed as an extension of an existing resource and prevents certain actions from happening. There are two types of locks available:

- A ReadOnly lock blocks modifications
- A CannotDelete lock will block deletion

Locks can be mixed; that is, you can define both types on the same resource and define them on different scopes (such as subscription, resource group, or resource). Locks defined on a higher scope will be inherited, meaning a `ReadOnly` lock on a resource group will block any update on any resource contained within that resource group.

So, now you know how locks work, let's deploy two data disks in a new resource group:

```
az group create -l <location> -n <resource-group-name>
az disk create -g <resource-group-name> -n <disk-name-1> --size-gb 10
az disk create -g <resource-group-name> -n <disk-name-2> --size-gb 10
```

Once disks are created, let's obtain an identifier of the first disk – we'll use to it assign a lock to it:

```
az disk show -n <disk-name-1> -g <resource-group-name> --query id
```

Now, we'll create a lock using that identifier:

```
az resource lock create --lock-type CannotDelete -n CannotDelete
--resource <resource-id>
```

Great – we have a lock created. As you can see, the type of that lock is defined as `CannotDelete` – it's supposed to block delete operations performed on the configured disk. Let's see if it really works – to do that, we'll perform the same delete operation on both disks:

```
az disk delete -n <disk-name-1> -g <resource-group-name>
az disk delete -n <disk-name-2> -g <resource-group-name>
```

While the second disk can be deleted without a problem, for the first disk, you'll see the following error:

```
(ScopeLocked) The scope '/subscriptions/…/resourceGroups/…/providers/
Microsoft.Compute/disks/… cannot perform delete operation because
following scope(s) are locked: '/subscriptions/…/resourcegroups/…/
providers/Microsoft.Compute/disks/…. Please remove the lock and try
again.
Code: ScopeLocked
```

The only way to remove that disk is to remove the lock first. Unfortunately, it seems that's not a difficult task – when using a standard role such as **Contributor**, you can delete a lock in a second. This is why we'll discuss the second challenge – a proper permissions model.

Establishing a permissions model

In many standard Azure setups, many companies leverage a basic **permissions model**; that is, they leverage in-built roles (with a focus on **Owner/Contributor/Reader** roles). This works for an initial couple of months, but as new projects are onboarded, and more people start working on Azure infrastructure, it becomes clear that such an operational model won't give us lots of security control.

To overcome that problem, we need to establish a permissions model that will be controlled and implemented by a dedicated team. The most important rule is following the **least-privilege principle (LPP)**. In short, this principle states that any actor in a system should have access to the least possible number of resources and data. Let's see an example – here's a definition of an in-built Contributor role in Azure (for the sake of clarity, I removed fields that are not important for the topic):

```
[
    {
    "permissions": [
        {
        "actions": [
          "*"
        ],
        "dataActions": [],
        "notActions": [
          "Microsoft.Authorization/*/Delete",
          "Microsoft.Authorization/*/Write",
          "Microsoft.Authorization/elevateAccess/Action",
          "Microsoft.Blueprint/blueprintAssignments/write",
          "Microsoft.Blueprint/blueprintAssignments/delete",
          "Microsoft.Compute/galleries/share/action"
        ],
        "notDataActions": []
        }
      ]
    }
]
```

By looking at the `actions` and `notActions` fields, you can see that the assignee can do anything unless it's forbidden by the `notActions` configuration. This role works flawlessly in initial scenarios because it gives anyone almost admin-like access to the underlying resources and, at the same time, prevents them from making new role assignments. However, in more advanced scenarios, it's not enough – we need more control over the removal of resource locks. To do that, we could introduce a custom role with the following permission added to the `notActions` field:

`Microsoft.Authorization/locks/delete`

On the other hand, when you look at the resource provider defined in that permission – `Microsoft.Authorization` – it seems that the Contributor role is already configured not to be able to remove locks. That's good, but we could improve our setup. To make sure that disks cannot be deleted, even if a resource lock is not present, we could disallow the following action:

`Microsoft.Compute/disks/delete`

Of course, to do that, we'd need to introduce a custom Contributor role and assign it to our users. On the other hand, it'd be worth doing if you really don't want to let people delete disks (or any other resource) within a given scope (such as a production environment).

Utilizing images and snapshots for securing data

When talking about securing data for Azure VMs, we need to describe the difference between VM images and VM snapshots. However, before we dive into the details, let's introduce a generic problem we need to handle. Securing data may be related to two different areas:

- Securing configuration
- Securing data stored and processed on a VM

While the areas are not directly comparable, we need to take them both into consideration when improving the reliability of data in relation to our VMs. Let's discuss them individually.

Securing configuration

Each deployed VM will have its configuration, which is a living thing. When faced with the task of protecting configuration from being deleted or improperly modified, it is important to identify specific moments when these mechanisms should be put in place:

- VMs can be redeployed with common configuration using prebuilt images, as we have learned in previous chapters
- VMs can be configured and adjusted without using a prebuilt image (that is, using **Configuration-as-Code** (**CaC**) solutions or generic deployment scripts)
- Configuration of VMs can be altered manually or automatically through their lifetime

The important thing now is understanding possible solutions and their impact on our workload and capacity. In general, the easiest thing to do (with scalability and value over time in mind) is to have all the configuration managed via a CaC solution (**Chef**, **Puppet**, **Ansible**, or even **Desired State Configuration** (**DSC**), discussed in the previous chapter). Why is that? Well, if you establish a process where any change applied on deployed machines can be done via script or desired state description, you can restore the state of any machine anytime. However, this has some sidenotes to consider.

Using CaC will secure the desired state of your machines but won't secure data saved on attached disks. This approach is also a little bit cumbersome if you can't control whether somebody is making manual changes. In fact, any manual change applied on a machine level will be overwritten once you redeploy the configuration. This can be a good thing (because it always returns the configuration to the desired state) but may not work in all scenarios.

Using images

Instead of using CaC, you may go for prebuilt images (created with tools such as **Packer**), which will help you provide boilerplate configuration for any deployed machine. Such images are often called **golden images** and very often have improved security (in other words, they're hardened images). The downside of this approach is losing control after the machine is deployed. On the other hand, you may use both CaC and images. Such a solution becomes helpful if the initial configuration is very complex or takes lots of time. If you want to shorten deployment times (which will be prolonged by a need to configure everything upfront), you can just set up a VM image containing all the base dependencies and manage the rest using CaC.

To somehow control things changing on a disk level, instead of using images or CaC, you'd need to use snapshots, which we'll describe in a second.

To secure data saved on a disk attached to your VM (including both the application's data and OS data), you'd need to **snapshot** the state of a disk at some point in time. Choosing the frequency of snapshots (and scope, because you don't always want to save everything) is something that should be reflecting the importance of that data. If a machine runs a critical workload (such as a database), you'll make snapshots much more often than for a non-production machine running a small web server.

> **Important note**
> Images and snapshots mustn't be used as an alternative to services and patterns ensuring **high availability (HA)** of VMs (such as **Availability Sets**, **Availability Zones**, **Load Balancer**). The former is applicable when implementing DR/**business continuity (BC)** scenarios, while the latter is related to the availability of infrastructure.

When working with DR/BC scenarios, make sure that you don't treat snapshots as backups, as those concepts are not interchangeable.

In the next parts of this chapter, we'll discuss how snapshots (backups) can be used to improve the reliability of your data and how to secure it from being deleted permanently.

Understanding backup and restore for Azure VMs

In one of the previous chapters (*Chapter 5, Provisioning Azure Virtual Machines*), we had a chance to deploy Azure VMs in different scenarios, but we never mentioned how one can back up and restore a machine if something goes wrong or a machine is lost. Let's see what the options in Azure are when it comes to backups.

Setting up backup for Azure VMs

To get started, we'll need a machine – use the following script to create an empty resource with a known configuration:

```
az group create -l <location> -n <resource-group-name>
az vm create -g <resource-group-name> --image Ubuntu2204 --name
<vm-name>
```

However, to enable backup for our machine, we'll need one more resource – a **Recovery Services vault**. You can think about it as a place that holds the configuration of backups for a given VM and is responsible for performing them according to a configured backup policy. To create a vault, use the following command:

```
az backup vault create --name <vault-name> -g <resource-group-name> -l
<location>
```

After a moment, a vault should be created in the resource group you selected. From now on, it can be used for any service that supports integration with Recovery Services for providing backups or other DR scenarios (meaning you can reuse it across multiple VMs). Once our vault is deployed, we can configure a VM to use it:

```
az backup protection enable-for-vm \
   --resource-group <resource-group-name> \
   --vault-name <vault-name> \
   --policy-name DefaultPolicy \
   --vm <vm-name>
```

While the preceding command is quite straightforward, there's one parameter that we'll describe in a second – `policy-name`. As mentioned previously, backups can be performed with a certain schedule that should reflect the importance of a resource. Azure has a default policy available in each vault (named `DefaultPolicy`), which can be checked with the following command:

```
az backup policy show --name DefaultPolicy --resource-group <resource-
group-name> --vault-name <vault-name>
```

In response, you'll receive a JSON result containing lots of useful information, with the most important part covering retention and schedule of a backup:

```
"retentionPolicy": {
    "dailySchedule": {
        "retentionDuration": {
            "count": 30,
            "durationType": "Days"
        },
        "retentionTimes": [
```

```
            "2023-06-24T04:00:00+00:00"
        ]
    },
    "monthlySchedule": null,
    "retentionPolicyType": "LongTermRetentionPolicy",
    "weeklySchedule": null,
    "yearlySchedule": null
},
"schedulePolicy": {
    "hourlySchedule": null,
    "schedulePolicyType": "SimpleSchedulePolicy",
    "scheduleRunDays": null,
    "scheduleRunFrequency": "Daily",
    "scheduleRunTimes": [
        "2023-06-24T04:00:00+00:00"
    ],
    "scheduleWeeklyFrequency": 0
}
```

As you can see, the default policy has the following properties:

- Each daily backup is stored for 30 days
- Each backup is run daily
- Each run is scheduled at 4 A.M.

Such a policy will work in many common scenarios, but of course, it's not meant to reflect every possible case. We'll discuss policies in the next section.

Backup policies

When created, the Azure Recovery Services vault has three inbuilt policies:

- `HourlyLogBackup` (for backing up a database log)
- `DefaultPolicy` (backs up a VM once per day)
- `EnhancedPolicy` (for fine-grained backup schedules and retention rules)

Policies added to a vault can be listed using the following command:

```
az backup policy list -g <resource-group-name> -v <vault-name> -o
table
```

When executed, it should give you a result similar to mine:

```
Name               Resource Group     Type
---------------    ----------------   -------------
HourlyLogBackup    aach07             AzureWorkload
DefaultPolicy      aach07             AzureIaasVM
EnhancedPolicy     aach07             AzureIaasVM
```

As you can see, each policy has one additional parameter that represents it – a type. As vaults can be used to secure more than Azure VMs (they work with other workloads such as **Azure SQL**, **file shares**, and **SAP HANA**), backup policies can be different types to be much more aligned with the type of workload they refer to.

When creating a backup policy, you need to write it as a **JSON** document, which will then be used by the CLI command (or entered in the **Azure Portal** or **IaC** solution). Such a document has too big a schema to describe it in one go, so we'll need to do it in parts. Each policy is an object with defined properties:

```
{
   "properties": {
   }
}
```

Then, you need to define both management type and time zone:

```
{
   "properties": {
     "backupManagementType": "AzureIaasVM",
     "timeZone": "Pacific Standard Time"
   }
}
```

For `backupManagementType`, you can use a couple of available values – `AzureIaaSVM`, `AzureSQL`, or `AzureWorkload`. This parameter is used to decide which properties of a policy should be available for the rest of the policy body.

> **Important note**
> For working with a **REST API**, you could include an additional parameter in the body of a policy – `workLoadType`. It represents the same value as `Type` returned by the Azure CLI.

Then, we can define a schedule policy:

```
"schedulePolicy": {
      "schedulePolicyType": "SimpleSchedulePolicy",
      "scheduleRunFrequency": "Weekly",
      "scheduleRunTimes": [
        "2023-06-26T10:00:00Z"
      ],
      "scheduleRunDays": [
        "Monday",
        "Wednesday",
        "Friday"
      ]
},
```

This part of a backup policy defines the frequency of backups. As you can see in the example, the defined schedule would run three times a week – on Monday, Wednesday, and Friday. The scheduleRunTimes parameter is used to determine at what time a backup should run (note that it accepts an array of values, so you can set up a backup to be performed more than once).

The last part is defining a retention policy. That policy is used to configure how long backups should be kept:

```
{
  "properties": {
    "backupManagementType": "AzureIaasVM",
    "timeZone": "Pacific Standard Time",
    "schedulePolicy": {
      ...
    },
    "retentionPolicy": {
      "retentionPolicyType": "LongTermRetentionPolicy",
      "weeklySchedule": {
        "daysOfTheWeek": [
          "Monday",
          "Wednesday",
          "Friday"
        ],
        "retentionTimes": [
          "2023-06-26T10:00:00Z"
        ],
        "retentionDuration": {
          "count": 1,
          "durationType": "Weeks"
```

```
          }
        }
      }
    }
}
```

The `retentionPolicyType` parameter accepts two possible values:

- `LongTermRetentionPolicy`

- `SimpleRetentionPolicy`

Both types are used for the same purpose, but the former accepts much more advanced configurations (as you can define weekly, monthly, and yearly schedules). The latter is configured with only two parameters – `count` and `durationType`:

```
"retentionPolicy": {
  "retentionPolicyType": "SimpleRetentionPolicy",
  "retentionDuration": {
     "count": 7,
     "durationType": "Days"
  }
}
```

It's up to you to decide which form is the best for your infrastructure. In many scenarios, the simpler configuration may be enough to achieve the expected level of security. For more sophisticated workloads, you may need to use more advanced configuration.

> **Important note**
> For an overview of the backup policy schema, look at the following web page: `https://learn.microsoft.com/en-us/rest/api/backup/protection-policies/create-or-update?tabs=HTTP`

Once your policy is ready and saved locally on your computer, you can add it to a vault using the following command:

```
az backup policy create --policy <path-to-policy-file>.json -g
<resource-group-name> -v <vault-name> --name <name-of-your-policy>
--backup-management-type AzureIaaSVM
```

Once created, you should be able to see that policy and use it when configuring backup for the selected workload type.

Using a created policy

We created a custom policy and added it to our vault. Let's now see how we can use it for the selected VM. In the previous section, we did that operation using an inbuilt policy. Using a custom one won't change much in the process – the only change is the name of a policy we'd like to use:

```
az backup protection enable-for-vm \
   --resource-group <resource-group-name> \
   --vault-name <vault-name> \
   --policy-name <policy-name> \
   --vm <vm-name>
```

As policies are created in the context of a vault, we need to make sure that the selected policy name exists in the provided vault. This is the only requirement for setting up a custom policy for our machine (besides having a policy that is compatible with the selected workload, that is, the Azure VM). Let's talk now about the process of recovering a VM, which is a crucial part of restoring your infrastructure from an invalid state or outage.

Recovery of Azure VM

Once a backup is configured for your VM, Azure will automatically create a resource group, which will store a collection of restore points representing backups of our resources. This resource group is created in the same subscription and will have a standard name such as `AzureBackupRG_westeurope_1` selected for it.

> **Important note**
>
> If you don't like the default naming convention for the resource group created for your backups, you can customize it by using the Azure portal. Just go to your policy for which you'd like to provide a custom name and fill in the **Azure Backup Resource Group** field.

It's possible to adjust it by entering custom values in the textbox presented in *Figure 7.1*:

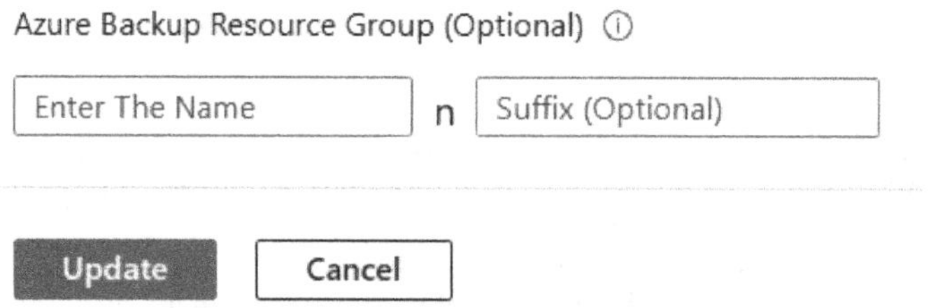

Azure Backup Resource Group (Optional) ⓘ

| Enter The Name | n | Suffix (Optional) |

[Update] [Cancel]

Figure 7.1 – Entering a custom resource group name and suffix

Let's see how we can work with our recovery data to restore a VM to a certain point in time.

Listing restore points

To see restore points, we need to learn what's the name of a container that is used to store recovery data for our workload. To do that, use the following command:

```
az backup container list -g <resource-group-name> -v <vault-name>
--backup-management-type AzureIaasVM
```

In return, you'll receive an object that should represent the VM we used for the exercises from this chapter:

```
[
    {
        "eTag": null,
        "id": "/subscriptions/.../resourceGroups/.../providers/Microsoft.
RecoveryServices/vaults/.../backupFabrics/Azure/protectionContainers/
IaasVMContainer;iaasvmcontainerv2;...;...",
        "location": null,
        "name": "IaasVMContainer;iaasvmcontainerv2;aach07;aach0701",
        "properties": {
            "backupManagementType": "AzureIaasVM",
            "containerType": "Microsoft.Compute/virtualMachines",
            "friendlyName": "...",
            "healthStatus": "Healthy",
            "protectableObjectType": "Microsoft.Compute/virtualMachines",
            "registrationStatus": "Registered",
            "resourceGroup": "aach07",
            "virtualMachineId": "/subscriptions/...d/resourceGroups/.../
providers/Microsoft.Compute/virtualMachines/...",
            "virtualMachineVersion": "Compute"
        },
        "resourceGroup": "...",
        "tags": null,
        "type": "Microsoft.RecoveryServices/vaults/backupFabrics/
protectionContainers"
    }
]
```

The preceding code block contains the metadata of a backup container, which contains basic information. However, the most important part is the `"properties"` object:

```
"properties": {
        "backupManagementType": "AzureIaasVM",
        "containerType": "Microsoft.Compute/virtualMachines",
        "friendlyName": "...",
        "healthStatus": "Healthy",
        "protectableObjectType": "Microsoft.Compute/virtualMachines",
```

```
      "registrationStatus": "Registered",
      "resourceGroup": "aach07",
      "virtualMachineId": "/subscriptions/…d/resourceGroups/…/
providers/Microsoft.Compute/virtualMachines/…",
      "virtualMachineVersion": "Compute"
    }
```

This block consists of information related to the configured features of a backup container (such as what kind of object is secured with it, what is used to manage it, and what is its health).

Now, to list restore points, we'll need a name or a friendly name of a container. Both values are acceptable, and it only depends on your way of working on selecting one of them (in many cases, it may be much easier to use a friendly name as it may represent the name of your VM). To list those points, use the following command:

```
az backup recoverypoint list \
    --container-name <name-or-friendly-name> \
    --backup-management-type AzureIaasVM \
    --item-name <vm-name> \
    -g <resource-group-name> \
    -v <vault-name> \
    -o table
```

In response, you'll get a list of all available restore points that are available for the given machine:

```
Name                Time                                        Consistency
----------------    -----------------------------------------   -------------------
446082638977647     2023-06-26T04:07:22.985885+00:00            FileSystemConsistent
448707461894781     2023-06-25T04:14:55.326448+00:00            FileSystemConsistent
443807712822437     2023-06-24T04:02:56.822010+00:00            FileSystemConsistent
```

The number of available restore points may differ depending on the selected backup policy assigned for the machine.

> **Important note**
>
> If you don't see any available restore points, make sure you wait until the first backup is performed. For the backup policies used in this chapter, you may need to wait 24 hours until the first backup comes up.

Now we know which backups are available; we can proceed with restoring a machine to a certain point in time.

Restoring a VM

Restoring a VM using a backup is a process called recovery, or DR. In most cases, you'll be performing that operation to recover from outages, software and hardware failures, or misconfigurations of your machines. To restore a machine, we'll need the following command:

```
az backup restore restore-disks
```

However, before we use it, we need to create one additional resource – an **Azure Storage account**. You may wonder why Azure Storage is needed to restore a VM – it's used by Azure Backup to store backups of a VM so that they are available for the service when needed. If that's a requirement, let's create an empty storage account for our restore operations:

```
az storage account create -g <resource-group-name> -n <storage-
account-name>
```

Next, let's schedule a `restore` operation on our vault:

```
az backup restore restore-disks \
  --container-name <name-or-friendly-name> \
  --item-name <vm-name> \
  -g <resource-group-name> \
  --rp-name <restore-point-name> \
  --storage-account <storage-account-name> \
  -v <vault-name>
```

After this command completes, you'll see that it doesn't immediately restore a machine. Instead, it creates a backup job on our vault, which will run in the background. We can fetch its status with the following operation:

```
az backup job show --ids <backup-job-id> --query properties.status
```

The value of the `backup-job-id` parameter can be found in the result of the previous command – it's the value of the `id` parameter.

> **Important note**
> Backup jobs take several minutes to complete, depending on the size of a restore point.

Once the command completes, you'll be able to find the container name storing your restored VM disk with a simple command:

```
az backup job show --ids <backup-job-id> --query
properties.extendedInfo.propertyBag
```

The result should look like this:

```
{
   "Config Blob Container Name": "<vm-name>-2b7b0f62a61c43d4b3569006ae
ebe347",
   "Config Blob Name": "config-<vm-name>-682df2ad-5079-4180-98ca-
f94769dee138.json",
   "Config Blob Uri": "https://<storage-account-name>.blob.core.
windows.net/<vm-name>-2b7b0f62a61c43d4b3569006aeebe347/config-<vm-
name>-682df2ad-5079-4180-98ca-f94769dee138.json",
   "Job Type": "Recover disks",
   "Recovery point time ": "6/24/2023 4:02:56 AM",
   "Target Storage Account Name": "<storage-account-name>",
   "Target VM Name": "vmName",
   "Template Blob Uri": "https://<storage-account-name>.blob.
core.windows.net/aach0701-2b7b0f62a61c43d4b3569006aeebe347/
azuredeploy682df2ad-5079-4180-98ca-f94769dee138.json"
}
```

Based on that information, you can find a container in your storage account that stores a restored managed disk. That disk can be used to restore the whole VM (by either deploying a new one with that disk or reattaching the OS disk on an existing machine).

Let's now see how we can configure and manage backups using Azure Backup Server.

Using Azure Backup Server

Until now, we discussed backup capabilities in Azure using managed resources. This path allows us to secure workloads that work natively in Azure (that is, Azure VMs; Azure SQL runs as SQL Server on Azure VM; Azure Files storage), but in scenarios where we have non-native resources, we need to seek another solution. This is where **Microsoft Azure Backup Server** (**MABS**) comes into play.

Using Azure Backup Server is a more advanced operation as it involves installing additional software and managing it by ourselves (as opposed to using Azure Recovery Services vaults integrated with managed workloads). In general, this approach can be used for the following services:

- VMs managed by Hyper-V
- VMs managed by VMware
- Azure Stack HCI
- Microsoft SQL Server
- SharePoint Server
- Microsoft Exchange

As you can see, those workloads are mostly connected to services running on-premises in many common setups available in lots of projects. For some of those, you could consider performing a migration to Azure so that they can be integrated with managed backups, but that's not always the case. If you cannot migrate (or just don't want to) but still want to leverage Azure capabilities, you need to understand how Azure Backup Server may satisfy your requirements.

Installation platforms

Azure Backup Server can be used to secure two generic workloads:

- Machines running on-premises
- Azure VMs

You may wonder why you'd use it for securing Azure VMs when there are Recovery Services vaults available for that. It all depends on the characteristics of your infrastructure and the type of workloads that are the majority of available machines. If most of your workloads are services not supported by standard vaults, you may want to go for Azure Backup Server for a consistent user and configuration experience. What's more, Azure Backup Server works with the Classic deployment mode of resources in Azure (which is a **legacy mode**), which makes it suitable for older workloads.

No matter which installation platform is chosen, you need to remember that a machine running Azure Backup Server and machines you'd like to back up need to be in the same domain. There's also a requirement that this machine should have at least 2 cores and 8 GB of RAM available. Let's see how to approach the process of installing Azure Backup Server and configuring it on a machine.

Installation of Azure Backup Server

To install and configure Azure Backup Server, we'll need a dedicated vault for the selected workloads. To create it, we'll use the Azure portal, as a download link for the server won't be available when creating the vault using the Azure CLI or Azure PowerShell:

1. Let's start by going to the Azure portal, finding your **Recovery Services vault** instance, and clicking on the + **Backup** button:

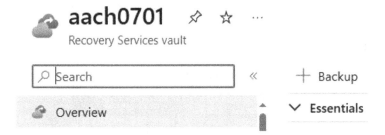

Figure 7.2 – Creating a backup vault

2. From the next screen, select **On-Premises** as our environment and desired workloads to back up:

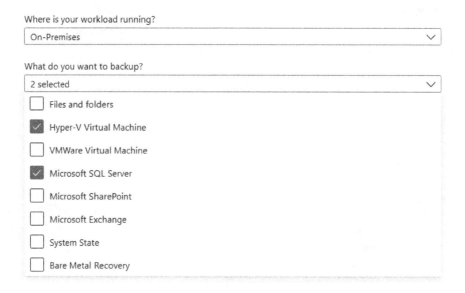

Figure 7.3 – Selecting workloads for backup

3. On the next screen, click on the **Download** link, which will redirect you to the **Download Center**, from where you can download all the files needed:

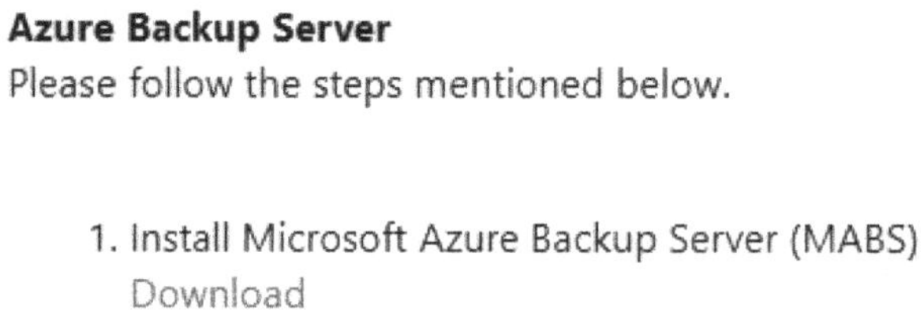

Azure Backup Server
Please follow the steps mentioned below.

1. Install Microsoft Azure Backup Server (MABS)
   Download

Figure 7.4 – Instruction for MABS containing the Download link

4. The last step is to click on the **Download** button and wait for the files to be downloaded:

Figure 7.5 – Downloading files from the download website

> **Important note**
>
> To perform those steps much quicker, download the files from the machine supposed to run Azure Backup Server.

5. While files are being downloaded, obtain vault credentials from the Azure portal by checking the checkbox shown in *Figure 7.6* and clicking on the **Download** button:

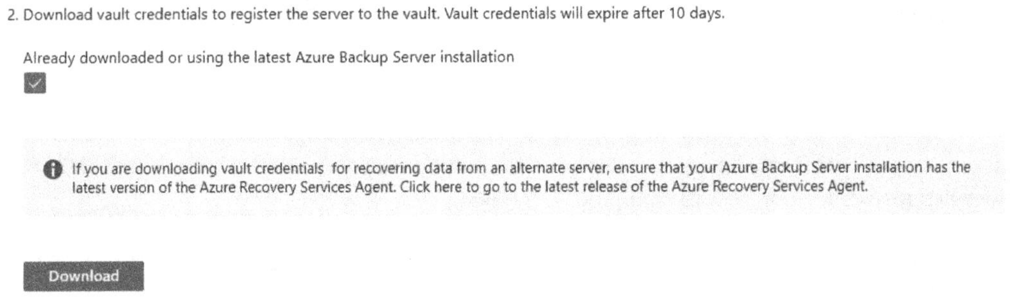

2. Download vault credentials to register the server to the vault. Vault credentials will expire after 10 days.

Already downloaded or using the latest Azure Backup Server installation

☑

ⓘ If you are downloading vault credentials for recovering data from an alternate server, ensure that your Azure Backup Server installation has the latest version of the Azure Recovery Services Agent. Click here to go to the latest release of the Azure Recovery Services Agent.

Download

Figure 7.6 – Downloading credentials

6. After you download all the files and copy them onto the machine that is supposed to be the backup server, run the executable file to open the installation wizard. Follow the instructions of the installer. Once it completes, you'll need to start one more installation, which will add Azure Backup Server to the machine. To do that, go to the directory where the installation files were extracted (by default, it's `C:\Microsoft Azure Backup Server V4`) and double-click the `Setup.exe` file. You should see the following installation screen:

Figure 7.7 – Installation screen of Azure Backup Server

Click on the **Microsoft Azure Backup Server** option and once again follow the instructions of the installation wizard.

> **Important note**
>
> Installation steps may be different depending on the selected workloads for backup. This implies that for some of them, additional dependencies may be required. Follow the information reported by the installation wizard to set up Backup Server correctly. If you find it difficult to follow the process, see this documentation for reference: `https://learn.microsoft.com/en-us/azure/backup/backup-azure-microsoft-azure-backup`.

Once Azure Backup Server is installed, you can start using it for performing backups for your workloads. As there are many different configuration options and solutions, it's best to check the documentation for detailed instructions on how to configure the workload you selected:

- `https://learn.microsoft.com/en-us/azure/backup/back-up-hyper-v-virtual-machines-mabs`

- `https://learn.microsoft.com/en-us/azure/backup/backup-azure-backup-server-vmware`

- `https://learn.microsoft.com/en-us/azure/backup/backup-azure-sql-mabs`

Let's now switch our focus to the next component of backup and recovery in Azure – Azure Site Recovery.

Exploring Azure Site Recovery

The last topic of this chapter is a service called Azure Site Recovery. It's part of Azure Recovery Services, which we already discussed when talking about Azure Backup for our workloads. While backups allow us to provide improved security for VMs and databases, Azure Site Recovery is meant to grant us the possibility to provide BC in case of unexpected failures. We'll discuss various options when it comes to recovering from outages and prerequisites to achieve continuity.

Replication

When talking about BC, we need to consider how our workloads are replicated. **Replication** is a process that will be performed automatically for most scenarios (especially in **active-active architectures**) and should ensure that we have a working environment we can migrate to. There are three different possibilities when thinking about replication:

- Azure to Azure

- Azure to on-premises

- Azure to Hyper-V/VMware environments

Each of those options will provide replication capabilities, but we need to make sure that they're reliable before we choose them as our replication method.

Let's talk now about recovery targets for IT systems and infrastructure, which will help us understand how critical our configuration is and what means of security should be taken to avoid disruptions to business.

RTO and RPO targets

Recovery Time Objective (RTO) and **Recovery Point Objective (RPO)** are two major factors affecting our recovery and continuity process. In short, they define how long our system may be unavailable (RTO) and how much data can be lost (RPO). Depending on their values, we'll approach the problem of BC in different ways.

For example, if we set RTO to 0 seconds, it means that our system must be available no matter what. To achieve this, we'd need to host a copy of our system up and running all the time and load balance all the traffic between multiple instances. We cannot perform a failover in such a scenario, as failover always takes some time.

> **Important note**
> In a scenario where RTO is set to 0 seconds, Our Load Balancer will also become a critical component for BC.

On the other hand, if we decide that we cannot lose data (which would be represented by RPO set to 0), everything must be replicated synchronously at any point in time. This is achievable in some scenarios (for instance, **Azure Cosmos DB** can be configured for **Strict consistency mode**, resulting in data replicated in multiple regions), but it's quite difficult to implement on your own.

Network integration

If we're talking about replication, we need to also make sure that replicated workloads are accessible over the network for the solution that performs replication. In Azure-to-Azure scenarios, this mostly involves setting up proper rules in **network security groups (NSGs)**, **virtual network peerings**, or **VNet gateways**. In Azure-to-on-premises scenarios, you need to configure hybrid networking whitelisting traffic between cloud and local workloads.

Configuring Azure Site Recovery

To configure Azure Site Recovery, you'll need an **Azure Recovery Services** vault – the same resource we created at the beginning of this chapter to work with backups. Once you have it deployed, deploy two resource groups – make sure they are in separate regions and the source resource group region is not the same as your Recovery Services vault region!

> **Important note**
>
> Azure Site Recovery can replicate resources across the same region, but this should be an explicit decision. As opposed to replication across regions, **intra-region replication** is performed across Availability Zones, which won't give you as much reliability as inter-region replication.

We use the following steps:

1. We'll start by creating two separate resource groups in two different locations:

   ```
   az group create -n <resource-group-name-1> -l <location-1>

   az group create -n <resource-group-name-2> -l <location-2>
   ```

   Now, deploy a single VM to the first of the deployed resource groups:

   ```
   az vm create -n <vm-name> -g <resource-group-name-1> --image
   Ubuntu2204
   ```

2. Once the VM is deployed, go to the Azure portal, find your Recovery Services vault, and look for **Site Recovery** in the menu:

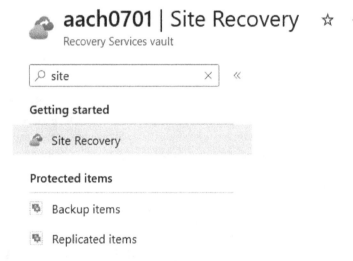

Figure 7.8 – Site Recovery menu in Recovery Services

3. We'll need to select our workload. For the sake of this exercise, choose replication for Azure VMs by clicking on the **1: Enable replication** link, as presented in *Figure 7.9*:

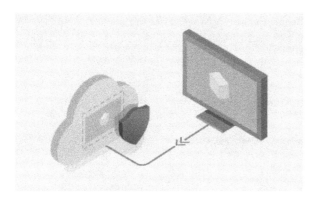

Azure virtual machines

Protect your Azure virtual machines for disaster recovery by replicating to another Azure region.

1: Enable replication

2: Manage recovery plans

Figure 7.9 – Enabling replication for Azure VMs

4.   The first step of our configuration is choosing the source of replication. Provide the **Resource group**, **Region**, and **Subscription** values for where you deployed your VM:

Enable replication   ⋯

① Source	② Virtual machines	③ Replication settings	④ Manage	⑤ Review

Region * ⓘ	East US ⌄
Subscription * ⓘ	MCT ⌄
Resource group * ⓘ	aach0703 ⌄
Virtual machine deployment model * ⓘ	○ Classic ● Resource Manager
Disaster recovery between availability zones? * ⓘ	○ Yes ● No

Figure 7.10 – Choosing replication source

5. On the second screen, select the VM you'd like to replicate:

Figure 7.11 – Choosing a VM for replication

6. On the third screen, we'll configure the **Replication settings** section. Select the location and subscription of the second resource group we created and choose it as the target in the **Target location/Target subscription** fields. Azure Site Recovery will automatically create a failover network and subnet as well (you can provide your own parameters if you want):

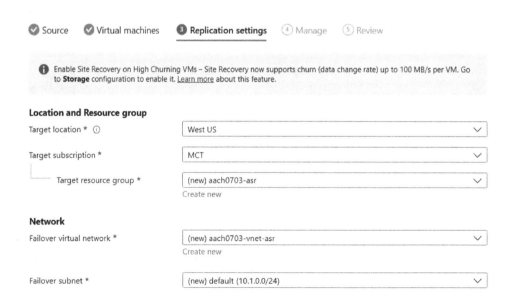

Figure 7.12 – Configuring replication settings

7. The last step is management configuration, including **Replication policy** options (how often a resource should be replicated) and optional automated management of extensions (we can disable it for now by choosing the **Manage manually** option):

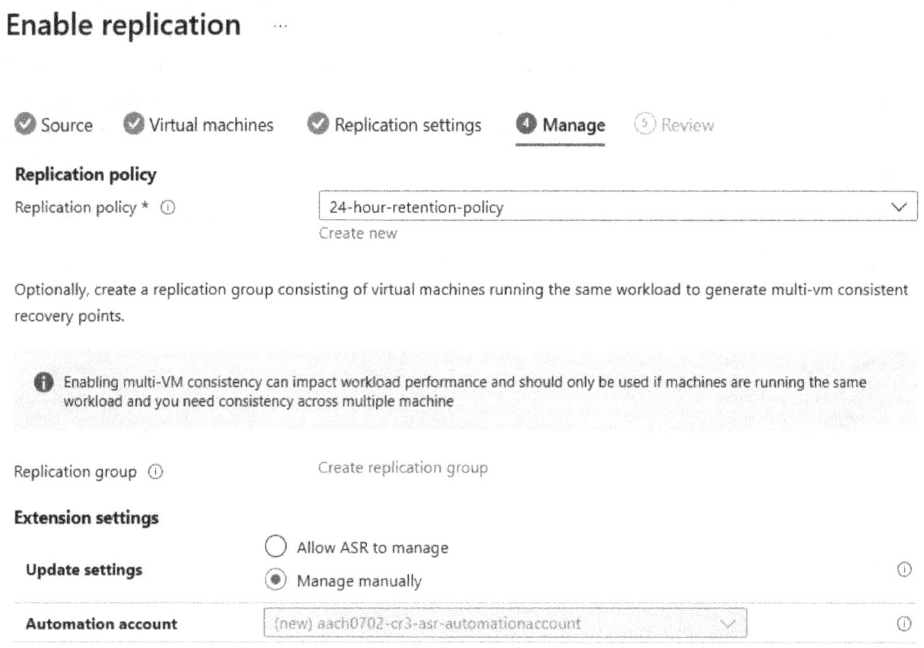

Enable replication ···

Source   Virtual machines   Replication settings   **4 Manage**   (5) Review

Replication policy

Replication policy * (i)
```
24-hour-retention-policy                                    ∨
```
Create new

Optionally, create a replication group consisting of virtual machines running the same workload to generate multi-vm consistent recovery points.

> (i) Enabling multi-VM consistency can impact workload performance and should only be used if machines are running the same workload and you need consistency across multiple machine

Replication group (i)   Create replication group

Extension settings

Update settings   ◯ Allow ASR to manage
                            ● Manage manually   (i)

Automation account   (new) aach0702-cr3-asr-automationaccount   ∨   (i)

Figure 7.13 – Management configuration

Once everything is ready, review your configuration and enable it. This may take a while, so be patient!

After some time, Azure will finish configuring replication settings for the selected resources and will take care of replicating them across selected resource groups. Remember that once replication is enabled, you will start paying for extra resources that are created (mostly replicated Azure VMs). This should be taken into consideration when planning for BC/DR scenarios (that is, the cost of such solutions cannot exceed possible money and time loss in a scenario where they're non-existent).

That's all about Azure Site Recovery planned for this chapter. Let's summarize our findings and lessons learned.

Summary

In this chapter, we focused on improving the reliability of our services running on Azure VMs by discussing options for securing data via snapshots and backups. When implementing those features, make sure you plan for additional storage capacity needed (as backups will need additional disk space to be stored) and increased cost of your Azure infrastructure. Anytime BC and DR are considered, pay extra attention to cost calculation. It's very easy to lose control over Azure spending when implementing those services, and you never want to spend more on them when compared to potential financial loss during outages.

In the next chapter, we'll revisit managed disks in Azure by diving into more advanced topics such as attaching/detaching disks, resizing, and swapping OS disks on the fly.

8

Configuring and Managing Disks

We had a chance to talk about **Azure managed disks** in *Chapter 5*, where we discussed **Azure Virtual Machines**. In this chapter, we'll extend our knowledge by diving into more advanced and more detailed topics. Knowledge from this chapter will be helpful when you're managing **VM-based infrastructure** in Azure, as lots of the operations we'll perform are often the bread and butter of day-to-day Azure administrator tasks.

The topics that will be covered in this part of this book are aimed at operations related to Azure disks, which we can swap, optimize, and reuse across multiple machines. These operations are also important for backup and restore processes as, sometimes, you may need to move a disk from one machine to another to recover from an error or outage.

In this chapter, we're going to cover the following main topics:

- Expanding on OS and data disks

- Exploring ephemeral OS disks

- Adding, detaching, and expanding disks

- Swapping OS disks

Technical requirements

For the exercises in this chapter, you'll need the following:

- The Azure CLI (`https://learn.microsoft.com/en-us/cli/azure/install-azure-cli`)

- A command line of any kind (either available in your OS or your favorite one)

The Code in Action video for this book can be viewed at: `https://packt.link/GTX9F`

Expanding on OS and data disks

You should be already familiar with two types of disks that can be provisioned in Azure (we discussed them in *Chapter 5*):

- **OS disk**

- **Data disk**

In Azure, each virtual machine can have a single OS disk attached to it, plus several data disks, which are used as additional storage units for a machine. The number of possible data disks attached to the machine relies on its family and size:

- Memory-optimized **Dv2** and **Dsv2-series** – **8–64** data disks

- **Ev4** and **Esv4-series** – **4–32** data disks

- **Mv2-series** – **64** data disks

- **B-series burstable series** – **2–32** data disks

You can find the full list in the Azure documentation: `https://learn.microsoft.com/en-us/azure/virtual-machines/sizes`. When planning your infrastructure (and considering its capabilities and capacity), this should be the first place where you consult your assumptions. Azure Virtual Machines, with their families and sizes, are living organisms, so the exact information will change over time.

Remember that, in Azure, most virtual machines also have a third disk type called **temporary disk**. The amount of space available for such disks will also depend on the virtual machine's size and family (it can be from 10 GB to over 2,000 GB).

> **Important note**
> Remember that temporary disks are non-persistent. This means that you cannot use them for storing data that needs to be available all the time (such as database files). A rule of thumb is to avoid storing any data there unless necessary.

Let's talk about some additional features of managed disks used for virtual machines in Azure. They are useful when you need to improve the performance of your machines or increase their security. When building basic infrastructure based on virtual machines, you probably don't need them. However, as you progress with your experience and the complexity of the solutions you're managing, they will become more and more helpful.

Shared disks

Azure offers a way to share managed disks between multiple virtual machines. This capability is implemented using the **Small Computer Systems Interface (SCSI) Persistent Reservations** feature, which is a standard that's used not only in the cloud but also on-premises setups. In Azure, this capability is not enabled by default – you need to enable and configure it yourself. What's more, this feature has some limitations that you must consider:

- Not all disks can be shared (it works for **Ultra**, **Premium**, and **Standard** SSD disks)

- Shared disks need to be individually attached to virtual machines

- You cannot access shared disks directly – they need to be managed via external software designed for **cluster management**

Because of these limitations, shared disks are not something you should use out of the box. They are very specific features that are used mostly in cluster-related scenarios. They limit our options for the type of disk and require an additional toolset that you need to understand and configure. They also imply a different way of charging you for infrastructure, which may lead to unexpected charges if you're not aware of their functionalities. While there are scenarios where shared disks are helpful in terms of improved system performance or simplified sharing capabilities, always proceed with caution when choosing this way for configuring your infrastructure.

> **Important note**
> Shared disks may impact the billing of your infrastructure. An additional charge doesn't exist for Ultra disks, but for Premium and Standard disks, there's an additional charge based on the disk's size (see `https://azure.microsoft.com/en-us/pricing/details/managed-disks/` for more details). On the other hand, while shared Ultra disks don't incur additional costs, their billing is based on a monthly charge that's based on the disk's capacity and throughput. When sharing is enabled, additional metrics will be published by a disk, which will eventually impact the cost of a resource.

A shared disk can be enabled from the Azure CLI using the `--max-shares` parameter:

```
az disk create -g <resource-group-name> -n <disk-name> --size-gb
<disk-size> --sku UltraSSD_LRS --disk-iops-read-only 200 --disk-mbps-
read-only 30
```

The preceding command will create an Ultra SSD disk that can be shared by a maximum of four virtual machines. If you set this parameter to `1`, it will disable disk sharing. Note that you can update this parameter at any time, meaning you can enable sharing even for already existing disks.

Now, let's talk about disk encryption, which is another advanced topic. It becomes handy when you need to deploy your infrastructure in secure environments (such as financial or medical institutions), as they often imply customized ways of hardening their infrastructure.

Encryption

In Azure, you can encrypt your disks using a variety of tools:

- Encryption at rest

- Encryption at host

- Azure Disk Encryption

- Confidential disk encryption

Each of these tools can be used for most disk types and sizes, though they have their limitations. The most limited option is encryption at rest, which is the most basic option for disk encryption. It allows you to encrypt both data and OS disks but cannot be used for temporary disks. It also doesn't encrypt data flow between the compute part of your virtual machine and storage, meaning data can travel unencrypted at some point in time.

The improved version of this encryption option is encryption at host. It encrypts both temporary disks and data flows but cannot be used for Ultra disks and Premium SSD v2 disks. It also introduces some operational challenges as, while you can enable it for existing machines, you'll need to deallocate and allocate them once again to enable encryption.

Azure Disk Encryption is a service that works for both Windows and Linux virtual machines by using **BitLocker** and **DM-Crypt**, respectively. It has similar capabilities to the previous two solutions, but it also has some potential challenges. You need to consider CPU utilization when using it (as it'll use the CPU of your machine). It also doesn't work for custom Linux machines, making it difficult to use in customized scenarios.

Confidential disk encryption is a specialized feature available for machines with confidential computing enabled (for example, the **Dcasv5** and **Ecasv5** families). It can only be used with OS disks, and similarly to Azure Disk Encryption, it will use your machine's CPU.

All these solutions can be integrated with **Azure Key Vault** (**Premium/Managed Hardware Security Module (HSM)**) for storing encryption keys. This approach is called **Bring Your Own Key (BYOK)** and is a concept that can be used for other services as well (for instance, Azure Storage or Azure Machine Learning).

Next, we'll cover a topic you should already be familiar with, as we briefly addressed it in *Chapter 5 – ephemeral OS disks*.

Exploring ephemeral OS disks

In a standard scenario (no additional performance requirements, OS disk data persistence), you can use a typical OS disk that will be provisioned as a managed disk stored on a remote Azure Storage account. This simplifies setup and management but will also impact the latency of the **input/output**

operations per second (**IOPS**) of a disk. If you're looking for improved performance, Azure offers ephemeral OS disks, which are configured and managed differently.

An ephemeral OS disk is provisioned directly on a machine. This means that they're collocated with your virtual machine, giving some boost to the latency of disk operations. They also have some additional traits:

- No additional cost – ephemeral disks are free because they don't use Azure Storage.
- Not all virtual machine families support them.
- The maximum size depends on the maximum size of the temporary disk of the virtual machine cache. In general, they cannot exceed 2,048 GB.
- OS disk data is not persistent, meaning resizing a machine or redeployment will delete data and reprovision the OS.
- Virtual machines with ephemeral disks cannot be stopped.

As you can see, ephemeral disks are quite special and cannot be used as a generic solution for OS data storage in Azure. Now, let's learn how to deploy a machine using this type of disk.

Deploying a virtual machine with an ephemeral OS disk

To deploy a virtual machine using an ephemeral OS disk, use the following command:

```
az vm create \
    --resource-group <resource-group-name> \
    --name <vm-name> \
    --image Ubuntu2204 \
    --ephemeral-os-disk true \
    --ephemeral-os-disk-placement ResourceDisk \
    --os-disk-caching ReadOnly \
    --admin-username <admin-username> \
    --admin-password <admin-password>
```

However, before we proceed, let's discuss some of these parameters. We can enable an ephemeral OS disk using the --ephemeral-os-disk parameter. Then, we need to configure disk placement using the --ephemeral-os-disk-placement parameter. We have two options available:

- CacheDisk
- ResourceDisk

Placement allows us to determine which disk will be used as storage for our ephemeral disk (which uses locally provisioned storage). By default, the ephemeral disk will be placed on a cache disk (if available). Otherwise, it will be stored on a standard temporary disk. Cache disks are only available for a subset of Azure Virtual Machines and can be used to improve the performance of a disk even more.

> **Important note**
>
> Ephemeral OS disks can be used for **Virtual Machine Scale Sets** as well. If you deploy a cluster of virtual machines, use the same parameters that we're using for a single machine to configure that type of disk.

When using ephemeral disks, consider the following limitation – as those disks use locally provisioned storage, you need to make sure that the selected virtual machine family and size support a **temp/ cache disk** so that it can store the selected **OS image**. For example, if the selected virtual machine has only 30 GB of local storage available and the selected OS image needs more than that, you won't be able to provision an ephemeral disk for it. In that case, you need to either select a smaller image or a bigger machine.

Now, let's talk about the operations we can perform on disks in Azure.

Adding, detaching, and expanding disks

When working with infrastructure in Azure, you rarely make a one-time setup. Some resources, including Azure Virtual Machines with disks, require constant maintenance and monitoring of utilized compute and storage. It's important to know how to perform basic maintenance operations daily so that you can then automate them if possible.

To get started with some exercises, let's deploy a single virtual machine using the following command:

```
az group create -l <location> -n <resource-group-name>
az vm create -g <resource-group-name> -n <vm-name> --image Ubuntu2204
--admin-username <username> --admin-password <password>
```

Once the virtual machine has been created, it'll have no data disk and a single OS disk with default parameters. Let's try to add new data disks to it.

Adding a disk to a virtual machine

To attach a new disk to a virtual machine, we can use two paths:

- We can create a disk separately and then attach it with the `az vm disk attach` command
- We can use the `az vm disk attach` command with a `--new` parameter to create and attach a disk with a single command

In this chapter, we'll go for the second option. Use the following command to create and attach a disk:

```
az vm disk attach -g <resource-group-name> --vm-name <vm-name> --name
<disk-name1> --size-gb 30 --sku Standard_LRS --new
```

It'll create an HDD disk containing 30 GB of free space, which will be automatically attached to your machine. Confirm that the disk is attached by using the following command:

```
az vm show -g <resource-group-name> -n <vm-name> --query
storageProfile.dataDisks -o table
```

It should return a result similar to the following:

```
Lun Name       Caching CreateOption DiskSizeGb ToBeDetached DeleteOption
--- ----       ------  -----------  ---------  -----------  ------------
0   aach0801   None    Empty        30         False        Detach
```

Note that by using default parameters for the command that created our virtual machine, we created a **Standard_DS1_v2** machine, which supports a maximum of four data disks. Let's confirm that by deploying an additional four disks:

```
az vm disk attach -g <resource-group-name> --vm-name <vm-name> --name
<disk-name2> --size-gb 30 --sku Standard_LRS --new
az vm disk attach -g <resource-group-name> --vm-name <vm-name> --name
<disk-name3> --size-gb 30 --sku Standard_LRS --new
az vm disk attach -g <resource-group-name> --vm-name <vm-name> --name
<disk-name4> --size-gb 30 --sku Standard_LRS --new
az vm disk attach -g <resource-group-name> --vm-name <vm-name> --name
<disk-name5> --size-gb 30 --sku Standard_LRS --new
```

When running the fourth command (resulting in adding a fifth disk to the machine), you should see the following error:

```
(OperationNotAllowed) The maximum number of data disks allowed to be
attached to a VM of this size is 4.
Code: OperationNotAllowed
Message: The maximum number of data disks allowed to be attached to a
VM of this size is 4.
Target: dataDisks
```

In such cases, if you'd like to proceed, you'd need to resize the virtual machine to a bigger size or another family so that you can attach more than four data disks.

Now, let's learn how to mount a disk that we've attached to a virtual machine.

Mounting a disk

After attaching a disk to a virtual machine, it will not be immediately available for use. To make it usable, we need to mount and format it using the selected filesystem. Let's perform that operation to complete our setup. To get started, you'll need to use SSH or **Remote Desktop Protocol** (**RDP**) to connect to the virtual machine. In the previous section, we created a Linux virtual machine, so we'll use an SSH connection with the configured admin username and password:

```
ssh <admin-username>@<public-ip-address>
```

Now, let's list the available disks to see whether they can be seen by the OS:

```
lsblk -o NAME,SIZE,MOUNTPOINT | grep -i "sd"
sda         30G
├─sda1    29.9G /
├─sda14      4M
└─sda15    106M /boot/efi
sdb          7G
└─sdb1       7G /mnt
sdc         30G
sdd         30G
sde         30G
```

As you can see, I have three unmounted disks (sdc, sdd, and sde) and two mounted disks, which represent the OS disk (sda) and the temporary disk (sdb). Note that with the command we used, it may be difficult to determine which disk is which (as we attached more than a single disk to the machine). To differentiate disks, you can use the following command:

```
lsblk -o NAME,HCTL,SIZE,MOUNTPOINT | grep -i "sd"
```

By including HCTL (**HCTL** stands for **Host:Channel:Target:Lun**), you'll be given a value, which includes a **logical unit number** (**LUN**). The output of that command would look like this:

```
sda        0:0:0:0       30G
├─sda1                 29.9G /
├─sda14                   4M
└─sda15                 106M /boot/efi
sdb        0:0:0:1        7G
└─sdb1                    7G /mnt
sdc        1:0:0:0       30G
sdd        1:0:0:1       30G
sde        1:0:0:2       30G
```

Now, you can use the following command to find the LUN of the Azure disk:

```
az vm show -n <vm-name> -g <resource-group-name> --query
"[storageProfile.dataDisks[].{lun:lun,name:name}]"
```

This advanced query will return an array of objects containing the LUN and the name of a disk attached to your machine. Now that you've learned what LUN is assigned to the data disk, we can format and mount it. To format a disk, you can use any tool that is available and known to you. In our case, we'll use `parted`:

```
sudo parted /dev/<device-name> --script mklabel gpt mkpart xfspart xfs
0% 100%
```

Make sure you're providing the proper device name (which is linked to the LUN you checked previously). Once the command completes, you'll see that the disk has a single partition:

```
sda        0:0:0:0        30G
├─sda1                    29.9G /
├─sda14                     4M
└─sda15                   106M /boot/efi
sdb        0:0:0:1         7G
└─sdb1                      7G /mnt
sdc        1:0:0:0        30G
└─sdc1                     30G
sdd        1:0:0:1        30G
sde        1:0:0:2        30G
```

In my case, it's represented by `sdc1` and based on a disk with LUN 0. Now, let's make the kernel aware of the partition:

```
sudo partprobe /dev/<partition-name>
sudo mkfs.xfs /dev/<partition-name>
```

Once those commands complete, the last step is mounting the disk. To do that, use the following command:

```
sudo mkdir <local-directory>
sudo mount /dev/<partition-name> /<local-directory>
```

At this point, the disk has been fully configured and is ready to be used. You can start storing data on it, configuring backups, and replicating if you want to.

> **Important note**
>
> The mounted disk won't be remounted after rebooting a machine until you add it to the `/etc/fstab` file. This is important from the perspective of improving the reliability of a machine, as removing a disk without editing that file (assuming the disk was added to it) may lead to the failure of a virtual machine, which means it will be unable to boot. This is only true for Linux VMs.

Now, let's learn how to detach a disk.

Detaching disks

So far, we've created and attached disks to a virtual machine. Let's see how we can perform the opposite – detach a disk from a machine. To do that, we'll use a similar command to what we used previously. The only difference is that we'll be using the `detach` operation instead of `attach`:

To detach a disk, use the following command:

```
az vm disk detach -g <resource-group-name> --vm-name <vm-name> --name
<disk-name>
```

Once the command completes, you can verify what data disks are attached to your machine:

```
az vm show -g <resource-group-name> -n <vm-name> --query
storageProfile.dataDisks -o table
```

If you performed those commands on the virtual machine we created in this chapter, you should see that it now has three data disks attached instead of four. We could also check whether we're able to create and attach a disk that failed previously:

```
az vm disk attach -g <resource-group-name> --vm-name <vm-name> --name
<disk-name5> --size-gb 30 --sku Standard_LRS --new
```

It turns out that no error is returned, which means one of the previously attached disks was detached successfully. A detached disk will persist all the data saved on it, meaning you can safely leave it as-is until it's needed.

> **Important note**
>
> Remember that a detached disk can be accidentally removed as it's no longer a direct dependency of a running virtual machine. Refer to *Chapter 7*, where we talked about securing virtual machine storage by using **management locks** and an **appropriate permissions model**.

The commands we performed will work just fine if a disk wasn't added to the `/etc/fstab` file. If it was, we need to edit that file and then detach it using Azure CLI commands. To check whether it's required to go that route, connect with your machine using SSH:

```
ssh <admin-username>@<public-ip-address>
```

Now, use the following command to find the **universally unique identifier** (**UUID**) of the disk you'd like to detach:

```
sudo -i blkid
```

It will return a result similar to mine:

```
/dev/sdb1: UUID="6ba22e85-8198-426e-b0bc-f0d203483474" BLOCK_
SIZE="4096" TYPE="ext4" PARTUUID="1d563c0a-01"
/dev/sda15: LABEL_FATBOOT="UEFI" LABEL="UEFI" UUID="B6C3-B75F" BLOCK_
SIZE="512" TYPE="vfat" PARTUUID="a295d76d-648c-4a4b-a3e0-b6307dd6e209"
/dev/sda1: LABEL="cloudimg-rootfs" UUID="1c12acfb-8f0c-440f-b6b7-
6c22c1f36e1e" BLOCK_SIZE="4096" TYPE="ext4" PARTUUID="ee1583fb-fd94-
4b13-98b6-5f25e7fa4580"
/dev/loop1: TYPE="squashfs"
/dev/loop2: TYPE="squashfs"
/dev/loop0: TYPE="squashfs"
/dev/sdc1: UUID="9c402d97-6ef7-45b3-8106-3b6a76f9dc0d" BLOCK_
SIZE="4096" TYPE="xfs" PARTLABEL="xfspart" PARTUUID="4d9e65a4-cde6-
448c-8ed2-62b1f0733974"
/dev/sda14: PARTUUID="b857fc35-18dc-48df-b3f0-ae83aa33b319"
/dev/loop3: TYPE="squashfs"
```

Assuming I'd like to detach /dev/sdc1, I need to write down its UUID and then remove the corresponding line from the /etc/fstab file using a text editor of my choice. Then, I need to unmount the disk:

```
sudo umount /dev/<partition-name> /<mounted-directory>
```

After completing all those operations, you'll be safe to detach the disk from your Azure Virtual Machine using Azure CLI commands. Now, let's proceed to the last operation I want to discuss with you.

Expanding a disk

So far, you've learned about attaching and detaching disks using Azure CLI commands. There's one more operation that you can perform on a disk that's quite common – expanding a disk. This operation will be helpful when you run out of disk space and don't want to migrate data from one disk to another. To save some time (and make the process much simpler), we can just extend a disk, giving it some additional free space.

> **Important note**
> Even though expanding a disk is not a complicated operation, always make sure your disk (and data) is healthy. Before making any changes, back up your data and check what disk partition type you have – you must verify whether it will support the new disk size.

Resizing (expanding) a disk can be performed with and without downtime.

Zero downtime resizing

If your disk satisfies the following conditions, you'll be able to resize it without downtime:

- It's a data disk

- It's not a shared disk

- It's not an Ultra/Premium SSD v2 disk

- If you'd like to resize your disk to 4 TiB or beyond, it's recommended to deallocate your virtual machine first

If your machine meets those requirements, you can resize it with a single Azure CLI command:

```
az disk update \
    --resource-group <resource-group-name> \
    --name <disk-name> \
    --size-gb <new-disk-size>
```

After this command completes, your Azure disk will have a new size available.

Resizing with downtime

If you need to resize a disk with downtime, you'll need to use two additional commands before updating the size of a disk. First, you need to deallocate your machine:

```
az vm deallocate --resource-group <resource-group-name> --name
<vm-name>
```

Deallocating a machine stops it completely and detaches compute from it. Once the machine is down, you can update the disk in the same way as described in the previous section. After resizing a disk, start a machine with the following command:

```
az vm start --resource-group <resource-group-name> --name <vm-name>
```

Now, your machine can use the new disk size.

> **Important note**
>
> Resizing with downtime requires deallocating your virtual machine. Remember that once a virtual machine is deallocated, you don't have a guarantee that you'll be able to start it at any time. Possible causes of failures when allocating compute once again for your machine include capacity limits for the selected Azure region, local or regional outages, and high demand hours. This operation should be performed during the off-hours of your business units if possible.

Before we proceed to the last topic of this chapter, we need to perform one more operation – make our OS aware of the new disk size.

Expand partitions and filesystems

In general, the OS of our virtual machines is unaware of changes we perform outside of the scope of our machine. This includes resizing the attached disk, so we need to make sure that those changes are reflected in the registries of our system. It's very easy to notice this by listing the disk space after performing a resize operation in Azure:

```
aach08@aach0801:~$ df -Th
Filesystem      Type    Size  Used Avail Use% Mounted on
/dev/root       ext4     29G  1.7G   28G   6% /
tmpfs           tmpfs   1.7G     0  1.7G   0% /dev/shm
tmpfs           tmpfs   682M  972K  681M   1% /run
tmpfs           tmpfs   5.0M     0  5.0M   0% /run/lock
/dev/sda15      vfat    105M  6.1M   99M   6% /boot/efi
/dev/sdb1       ext4    6.8G   28K  6.5G   1% /mnt
/dev/sdc1       xfs      30G  247M   30G   1% /data1
tmpfs           tmpfs   341M  4.0K  341M   1% /run/user/1000
```

In my case, I resized the /dev/sdc disk from 30 GB to 60 GB, but that change is still not visible within my virtual machine. I can confirm this with one more command:

```
aach08@aach0801:~$ sudo fdisk -l /dev/sdc
Disk /dev/sdc: 30 GiB, 32210157568 bytes, 62910464 sectors
Disk model: Virtual Disk
Units: sectors of 1 * 512 = 512 bytes
Sector size (logical/physical): 512 bytes / 4096 bytes
I/O size (minimum/optimal): 4096 bytes / 4096 bytes
Disklabel type: gpt
Disk identifier: 841D9FA8-76F0-4344-8148-B60B5F9E2F3A
```

This is still 30 GB. Let's enforce the rescanning of the disk:

```
echo 1 | sudo tee /sys/class/block/sdc/device/rescan
```

After a moment, you can check the disk once again:

```
Disk /dev/sdc: 60 GiB, 64424509440 bytes, 125829120 sectors
Disk model: Virtual Disk
Units: sectors of 1 * 512 = 512 bytes
Sector size (logical/physical): 512 bytes / 4096 bytes
I/O size (minimum/optimal): 4096 bytes / 4096 bytes
Disklabel type: gpt
```

```
Disk identifier: 841D9FA8-76F0-4344-8148-B60B5F9E2F3A

Device      Start      End  Sectors Size Type
/dev/sdc1    2048 62912511 62910464   30G Linux filesystem
```

The only thing left would be either adding a new partition to the disk for the remaining free disk space or reconfiguring the existing partition to cover the whole disk.

That's all about attaching, detaching, and expanding (or shrinking) a disk in Azure! Now, let's go to the last section of this chapter, where we'll talk about swapping OS disks.

Swapping OS disks

Swapping OS disks is a simple operation that can be performed without stopping or deallocating a virtual machine. The decision of whether to stop a machine or perform a swap without downtime relies on the type of workload you have running on a machine. It's not guaranteed that swapping operations won't interfere with your services, so to be on the safe side, it's recommended to plan downtime upfront. No matter whether you go for downtime or not, the operation will be performed in the same way.

The only command you need to swap OS disks is the command for updating a virtual machine's properties:

```
az vm update \
   -g <resource-group-name> \
   -n <vm-name> \
   --os-disk <os-disk-resource-id>
```

The only difficulty in performing that operation is making sure that the virtual machine and disk are compatible. Remember that not all virtual machines support Premium disks. If your machine doesn't, and you want to swap disks using Premium storage, you'll need to resize your virtual machine before performing the swap.

> **Important note**
> Remember that the chosen OS disk cannot be in use. If you choose the disk that's currently in use, the swap operation won't succeed.

That's all about disks and their operations for *Chapter 8*! Let's summarize what you've learned.

Summary

In this chapter, we talked about performing various operations with Azure disks. You had a chance to attach and detach disks by not only performing those operations in Azure but this time, you needed to go deeper. As you learned, when administering infrastructure in Azure, you cannot just rely on cloud knowledge – experience from managing on-premises or other cloud vendors will be helpful since managing infrastructure at the OS level is cloud-agnostic.

We also talked a little bit about advanced topics surrounding disks in Azure (sharing and encryption) and realized that swapping the OS disk for a virtual machine in Azure is a piece of cake. In the next chapter, we'll switch focus to another Azure service called **Azure Storage**, where we'll talk about things such as **blob storage** and **file shares**.

Part 4:
Azure Storage for
Administrators

Part 4 of the book covers storage-related topics in Azure, such as the Azure Storage service, file shares, and data security. In this part, you'll learn about storing files using Blob Storage and Azure Files, configuring the life cycle of files, and replicating them using custom life cycle rules.

This part has the following chapters:

- *Chapter 9, Configuring Blob Storage*
- *Chapter 10, Azure Files and Azure File Sync*
- *Chapter 11, Azure Storage Security and Additional Tooling*

9

Configuring Blob Storage

We have talked a lot about infrastructure in Azure, covering topics such as **Azure Virtual Machines**, (**VMs**), **virtual networks** (**VNets**), load balancing, and disks. That knowledge will help you build and manage solutions based on **Infrastructure-as-a-Service** (**IaaS**) services in Azure. This time, we'll focus on a slightly different type of service – a managed storage solution for data called **Azure Blob Storage**.

Information presented in this chapter will enable you to explore architecture that requires less typical administrative work (such as managing the OS, updates, and software) and focuses more on providing business value thanks to a much easier infrastructure setup and smaller cognitive load.

In this chapter, we're going to cover the following main topics:

- Exploring storage accounts, containers, and **Binary Large Objects** (**blobs**)
- Configuring access tiers in Blob Storage
- Configuring lifecycle and replication in Blob Storage
- Uploading blobs to Blob Storage

Technical requirements

For the exercises from this chapter, you'll need the following:

- The Azure CLI (`https://learn.microsoft.com/en-us/cli/azure/install-azure-cli`)
- A command-line tool of any kind (either available in your operating system or your favorite one)
- AzCopy (`https://learn.microsoft.com/en-us/azure/storage/common/storage-use-azcopy-v10`)

The Code in Action video for this book can be viewed at: `https://packt.link/GTX9F`

Exploring storage accounts, containers, and blobs

In Azure, there's a variety of different services that allow you to work with data. Depending on your needs, there are various databases (Azure SQL Database or Azure Cosmos DB), **orchestrators** (**Azure Data Factory**, or **ADF**), or **data ingestion streams** (Azure Event Hubs or Azure Stream Analytics). What's more, even Azure VMs, which we covered in *Chapters 3-8*, need a storage solution where they can keep their data. All those services have one thing in common – they leverage or integrate with one of the most important Azure services called **Azure Storage**.

Lots of other available services use Azure Storage as one of the key components they are based on. You can think about that service as a part of Azure's service backbone (Azure VMs can also be included in that category). Why is Azure Storage that important? Let's characterize its capabilities:

- It's a general-purpose storage, meaning it can cover lots of different business and technical cases
- It offers decent performance, which can be further improved by the use of Premium tiers and careful crafting of data schema
- It's available in all Azure regions and is a well-tested and easy-to-understand solution
- It supports multiple **replication models** (local/zonal/geographic), so it can be used in **high-availability** (**HA**) scenarios
- Its pricing is based on usage (average amount of data stored monthly, number of operations performed against the service), so it can easily scale with your solution

What's more, Azure Storage consists of four different services:

- **Table Storage**
- **Blob Storage**
- **File Service**
- **Queue Storage**

In this book (as we're focusing on an administrator's tasks), we'll cover two of those: Blob Storage and File Service. Table Storage and Queue Storage are services that relate to application development for most use cases. Of course, it doesn't mean you cannot use them or find a use case for them if you're an Azure administrator. They're just not as useful as the other two if you're not an application developer, as using queues or key-value storage are services that are mostly related to building business applications.

To get started with Azure Storage, we'll discuss the first layer of that service, which is the storage account.

Storage accounts

Each Azure Storage instance is called a **storage account**. Once created, it'll automatically give you access to the four aforementioned services. You cannot opt out of creating them when provisioning an instance, but don't worry – you won't be charged for them until you start using their functionalities.

> **Important note**
>
> In the previous versions of Azure Storage, you were allowed to create a storage account that had Blob Storage only. Nowadays, it's still possible to create an instance that will provide Blob Storage capabilities only, but for most use cases, you'll be using generic-purpose accounts, which offer a full spectrum of functionalities.

A storage account is a logical container for all the data stored within an instance. It also hosts the configuration of the service, including things such as **identity and access management (IAM)**, **networking**, **replication settings**, and **auditing options**. To better understand its purpose, let's create an instance using the Azure CLI.

Creating an Azure Storage instance using the Azure CLI

To create an instance of Azure Storage, we'll use the following command:

```
az group create -l <location> -n <resource-group-name>
az storage account create --name <storage-name> --resource-group
<resource-group-name> --location <location> --sku Standard_LRS
```

First, we're creating a resource group that will store the Azure Storage instance. Then, we create a storage account by providing its name, resource group, location, and **stock keeping unit (SKU)** parameter. Before we proceed, let's discuss both the name and the SKU parameter, as they may be a little bit tricky the first time they're used.

Azure Storage has some unique ways of validating whether its name is valid. You can only use alphanumeric characters, and the full name must be at least 3 characters long while not exceeding 24 characters. This may be a challenge in some environments, especially if they enforce naming conventions. Unfortunately, that problem has existed since the beginning of that service, and it's highly unlikely Microsoft will do anything about it.

The SKU parameter accepts one of the available replication modes:

- `Premium_LRS`
- `Premium_ZRS`
- `Standard_GRS`
- `Standard_GZRS`
- `Standard_LRS`
- `Standard_RAGRS`
- `Standard_RAGZRS`
- `Standard_ZRS`

Initially, they may be difficult to distinguish. They are, however, quite important from your perspective as an administrator, as well as the application using that Azure service. We'll characterize them now to have a better understanding of the possible implications.

Replication modes

Azure Storage offers three different replication options:

- Local
- Zonal
- Geographic

Those options are included in the name of the selected SKU. This is why we have **locally redundant storage (LRS)**, **zone-redundant storage (ZRS)**, and **geo-redundant storage (GRS)**. Besides those three generic modes, we have two more variants:

- **Geo-zone-redundant storage (GZRS)**
- **Read-access geo-redundant storage (RA-GRS)/read-access geo-zone-redundant storage (RA-GZRS)**

Does it look a little bit confusing? Well, initially, they may look intimidating to you. Fortunately, they're much easier to understand than you may anticipate. In Azure, your infrastructure may be deployed as either a local instance (which is deployed to one of the data centers available in a selected region), replicated across Availability Zones, or replicated across regions. The same applies to Azure Storage – if you select LRS, your storage account (and stored data) will be replicated only locally. If you select ZRS, the infrastructure and data will be replicated across Availability Zones, introducing much more reliability. As zonal replication is still a local replication (as it doesn't go beyond the boundaries of a single Azure region), you may use GRS replication to have data replicated across two paired Azure regions.

> **Important note**
>
> To learn about paired regions, read an additional article in the Azure documentation: `https://learn.microsoft.com/en-us/azure/reliability/cross-region-replication-azure`. As regions are paired statically, it's always a good idea to know where data may be replicated if you choose the GRS option for Azure Storage.

Read-access replication adds one more feature to the storage account. Normally, you don't have access to replicated data. This means that if there's an Azure outage in your primary region, you either wait for Azure engineers to fix it or perform a manual failover for your storage account. If you don't want to do that, you can opt in for read-access replication, which will give you read-only access to replicated data in the secondary region. We'll talk more about that feature in the *Configuring lifecycle and replication in Blob Storage* section. Let's now have a brief introduction to Azure Storage endpoints, which are basically **REST** entry points used to connect to the service.

Storage account endpoints

When you create a storage account using the `az storage account create` command, it'll return a JSON response containing various data related to the service. Look at one of the returned fields called `primaryEndpoints`:

```
"primaryEndpoints": {
    "blob": "https://<storage-account-name>.blob.core.windows.
net/",
    "dfs": "https:// <storage-account-name>.dfs.core.windows.net/",
    "file": "https:// <storage-account-name>.file.core.windows.net/",
    "internetEndpoints": null,
    "microsoftEndpoints": null,
    "queue": "https:// <storage-account-name>.queue.core.windows.
net/",
    "table": "https:// <storage-account-name>.table.core.windows.
net/",
    "web": "https:// <storage-account-name>.z6.web.core.windows.net/"
}
```

As you can see, Azure Storage exposes a bunch of different endpoints – one for each service that is enabled for the storage account. Here, we can also see `dfs` and `web` endpoints, which are meant for the **Data Lake service** (`dfs`) and a **static website** (`web`). Those are, however, individual features of Azure Storage rather than whole services; hence I didn't list them at the beginning of this chapter. What's important here is that any interaction between a client and an Azure Storage instance is performed via those endpoints. Now, you may also notice why the naming of Azure Storage is so tricky – it must be a valid DNS name, so special characters are disallowed.

> **Important note**
>
> Though *RFC 1034* and *RFC 1035* define exact rules for domain names and allow some special characters, Microsoft implies some internal rules for the naming of Azure Storage instances so that their resources don't interfere with those created by Azure users. This causes much more strict naming rules for Azure Storage, which you can see when creating a new instance.

Those endpoints will be visible when connecting with Azure Storage using connection strings. Let's see the possibilities for making a connection to see how an endpoint can be used.

Connecting with Azure Storage

Azure Storage allows you to connect using one of three available methods:

- **Access key**
- **Shared access signature (SAS) token**
- **Azure Active Directory (Azure AD)**

Each of those methods has a different purpose and limitations. When building a solution based on Azure Storage, you'll need to consider the following questions before making a choice:

- Are all services using Azure Storage deployed in Azure? If not, how they will authenticate?
- Do you want to manage access via access policies, tokens, or **role-based access control** (**RBAC**)?
- How do you revoke access to the storage account?

Let's see now how you can leverage each of those methods to make a connection with the service, starting with access keys as the simplest option.

Connecting using access keys

In general, the easiest way to connect with Azure Storage is based on access keys. Each storage account has two access keys that can be used interchangeably – the point of having two of those, however, is to be able to revoke access and use another key as an authorization method.

You can list the access key with the following Azure CLI command:

```
az storage account keys list -g <resource-group-name> -n <storage-
account-name>
```

You'll then receive the following result:

```
[
  {
    "creationTime": "2023-07-29T20:44:48.299346+00:00",
    "keyName": "key1",
    "permissions": "FULL",
    "value": "K4gPP5UuDwl2/…+AStZ6ODSw=="
  },
  {
    "creationTime": "2023-07-29T20:44:48.299346+00:00",
    "keyName": "key2",
    "permissions": "FULL",
    "value": "E3HEFMiy57injDHYYsNz0bE0PYXR2LgS/…+ASthHHukA=="
  }
]
```

Of course, `creationTime` and `value` fields for your keys will be different than mine as they are generated specifically for a storage account. As you can see, a key is just a string – to use it, we'd need to combine it with the proper Azure Storage endpoint to make a connection string. The easiest way of doing so is with one more Azure CLI command:

```
az storage account show-connection-string -g <resource-group-name> -n
<storage-account-name>
```

Running it will return a couple of parameters combined into a single connection string:

```
{
  "connectionString":
"DefaultEndpointsProtocol=https;EndpointSuffix=core.windows.
net;AccountName=<storage-account-name>;AccountKey=K4gPP5UuDwl2/…+AStZ6
ODSw==;BlobEndpoint=https:// <storage-account-name>.blob.core.windows.
net/;FileEndpoint=https://<storage-account-name>.file.core.windows.ne
t/;QueueEndpoint=https://<storage-account-name>..queue.core.windows.
net/;TableEndpoint=https://<storage-account-name>..table.core.windows.
net/"
}
```

Such a connection string can be then used to connect with a storage account from scripts and applications. It doesn't require additional configuration or setting up access for a client – instead, it provides full access to the Azure Storage instance (which may not be the best option in some cases). If you want to specify more granular access, you could use SAS tokens.

Connecting using a SAS token

A SAS token is another method of making a connection with Azure Storage, but this time we're allowed to specify additional parameters to control what is possible to access for a token owner. In Azure Storage, we could control things such as the connection protocol (HTTP or HTTPS), service (blob, table, queue, and file storage), read/write permissions, and lifetime of a token. We can generate a SAS token using the Azure CLI:

```
az storage account generate-sas --permissions rl \
    --resource-types sco \
    --services bf \
    --expiry 2023-08-14 \
    --account-name <storage-account-name> \
    --account-key <storage-account-key>
```

Such a command will generate a token that will look like this:

```
se=2023-08-14&sp=rl&sv=2021-06-08&ss=bf&srt=sco&sig=DwT1lOM…
SLqLvT3CoiNs%3D
```

As you can see, it's a query string that can be appended to the selected Azure Storage endpoint:

```
https://<storage-account-name>.blob.core.windows.net? se=2023-08-
14&sp=rl&sv=2021-06-08&ss=bf&srt=sco&sig=DwT1lOM…SLqLvT3CoiNs%3D
```

Depending on the selected permissions and services, you'll be able to perform different operations as long as the token is valid. Note that the used command has three parameters that define the permissions level:

- `--permissions`: Used to configure the access level for the selected service. Allowed values: (a)`dd` (c)`reate`, (d)`elete`, (f)`ilter_by_tags`, (i)`set_immutability_policy`, (l)`ist`, (p)`rocess`, (r)`ead`, (t)`ag`, (u)`pdate`, (w)`rite`, (x)`delete_previous_version`, (y)`permanent_delete`. If needed, you can combine them as a single value. Some of those permissions are applicable for certain services only (for instance, immutability policy works for Blob Storage only), hence may be ignored if a service doesn't support it.

- `--resource-types`: You can decide whether you're creating a token for (s)`ervice`, (c)`ontainer`, or (o)`bject`. Can be combined.

- `--services`: Defines which service is accessible with that token. You can define (t)`able`, (b)`lob`, (f)`ile`, or (q)`ueue`. Those values can be combined as well.

Thanks to the variety of options, you may create a token that will provide either quite a wide set of permissions (even the whole storage account) or only a tiny fragment (it's possible to create a token giving you only read access to an object such as a blob or a message on a queue). You can also set an expiry date using the `--expiry` parameter – thanks to that, a token will be automatically revoked (as opposed to access keys, which remain valid if you don't revoke them manually). This makes them a much better choice for integrating with applications.

> **Important note**
>
> A SAS token also has a disadvantage as it requires far more administrative tasks. You need to have a manual or an automated process of generating them, which can become quite complex in more advanced setups. In such scenarios, remember that those tokens can be generated from the CLI (using the Azure CLI and **Azure PowerShell**) or via a **REST API** – see `https://learn.microsoft.com/en-us/rest/api/storageservices/delegate-access-with-shared-access-signature`.

Let's now see the third option for making a connection with Azure Storage, which is an Azure AD token – the same token used with **managed identities** or RBAC in Azure.

Connecting using an Azure AD token

When working with Azure and interacting with Azure services, most of the time authentication and authorization process will be done using **Azure AD**. This is, however, applicable most of the time for interacting with the **control plane** of services – when the **data plane** is considered, some services don't support Azure AD-based authentication, so they cannot leverage the **Azure-based RBAC model**. Fortunately, Azure Storage supports the Azure AD authentication model, so you can use it for your applications, services, and scripts.

To authenticate with Azure AD, you will need to assign a role to the appropriate principal first and obtain an Azure AD token, which will be put in the `Authorization` header appended to each HTTP request made against Azure Storage. When using SDKs, that header will be automatically added based on classes or objects used for the selected programming language. For scripts, you'll need to add it manually. Here's an example using the cURL library:

```
curl --request POST https://<storage-account-name>.blob.core.windows.
net' \
--header 'Authorization: Bearer <access-token>' \
--header 'Content-Type: application/json
```

The preceding example would send a request to the Blob Storage endpoint with the Azure AD access token put in the `Authorization` header. Obtaining a token for such a scenario is another topic that we will not cover in this book. For our purpose, we could get it simply by using the Azure CLI:

```
az account get-access-token
```

It's the simplest way to get it as the only thing it requires is authenticating using either your account, service principal credentials, or a configured managed identity (both system- and user-assigned). To learn about other ways to automatically obtain a token, take a look at the Azure AD documentation: https://learn.microsoft.com/en-us/azure/active-directory/develop/v2-protocols.

Once you obtain a token, you need to assign a proper role to the selected principal. Remember that the control and data plane are separate beings, meaning a principal may be allowed to perform operations on the control-plane level (such as configuring networking, encryption, or failover settings), but disallowed from interacting with data stored in your storage account (tables, blobs, messages on a queue, and files). Some roles give you access to both the control and data plane, while others explicitly tell you that data operations are disallowed. To refresh your memory a little, go to *Chapter 1, Azure Fundamentals*, where we discussed RBAC and ABAC authorization in the *Authorization using RBAC and ABAC with a focus on role definitions and assignments* section.

For Azure Storage, you may find several inbuilt roles that are designed specifically for Azure AD access, such as the following:

- Reader and Data Access
- Storage Blob Data Contributor
- Storage Queue Data Reader
- Storage Table Data Contributor

Those are only a few of the available inbuilt roles, but as you can see, they are linked to individual Azure Storage services. Let's look at the JSON representation of one of those roles:

```
{
    "id": "/providers/Microsoft.Authorization/roleDefinitions/
```

```
ba92f5b4-2d11-453d-a403-e96b0029c9fe",
    "properties": {
        "roleName": "Storage Blob Data Contributor",
        "description": "Allows for read, write and delete access to
Azure Storage blob containers and data",
        "assignableScopes": [
            "/"
        ],
        "permissions": [
            {
                "actions": [...                    ],
                "notActions": [],
                "dataActions": [
                    ...                        ],
                "notDataActions": []
            }
        ]
    }
}
```

This role consists of the following actions (operations on the control-plane level) allowed by it:

```
"actions": [
                "Microsoft.Storage/storageAccounts/blobServices/
containers/delete",
                "Microsoft.Storage/storageAccounts/blobServices/
containers/read",
                "Microsoft.Storage/storageAccounts/blobServices/
containers/write",
                "Microsoft.Storage/storageAccounts/blobServices/
generateUserDelegationKey/action"
]
```

Additionally, it also defines a concept called "data actions" (operations on a data-plane level):

```
"dataActions": [
                "Microsoft.Storage/storageAccounts/blobServices/
containers/blobs/delete",
                "Microsoft.Storage/storageAccounts/blobServices/
containers/blobs/read",
                "Microsoft.Storage/storageAccounts/blobServices/
containers/blobs/write",
                "Microsoft.Storage/storageAccounts/blobServices/
containers/blobs/move/action",
                "Microsoft.Storage/storageAccounts/blobServices/
containers/blobs/add/action"]
```

When that role is assigned to a principal, it will be allowed to create, update, read, and delete blob containers, generate SAS tokens for them, and access Blob Storage data. On the other hand, that role doesn't grant access to other services such as tables or queues.

There's one more thing worth mentioning when talking about Azure AD authentication in Azure Storage. Note that while you may expect that clients will use that method of authentication, they will be also perfectly capable of using other ways of making a connection unless you disable them. This is especially important when modeling proper access for your storage accounts. Some roles in Azure may forbid a principal from accessing data. On the other hand, those roles (for example, **Storage Account Contributor**) will still allow a principal to access an access key (or generate an SAS token) and use it. This is why current best practices advise Azure Storage users to disable other authentication methods if using Azure AD. Here's how we can do that.

Disabling shared (access) key access

To disable access via access keys in your storage account, you can use the following command:

```
az storage account update \
    --name <storage-account-name> \
    --resource-group <resource-group-name> \
    --allow-shared-key-access false
```

Once it's executed, all connections using keys (both access key and SAS token) will start receiving a 403 Forbidden status. It's important to make some preparations before disabling connection via keys – if you have some services connecting with your storage account using *old* connection methods, first migrate them to the Azure AD connection before disabling access via keys. To learn more about proper operations and administrative tasks for that feature, consult the following article in the documentation: https://learn.microsoft.com/en-us/azure/storage/common/shared-key-authorization-prevent?tabs=azure-cli/.

Let's talk now about containers and blobs, which are objects available for Blob Storage only.

Containers and blobs

We talked about a storage account, which is an instance of Azure Storage and acts as a high-level container for other services, including Blob Storage. Blob Storage itself is a service dedicated to storing generic data – you can use it for binary files, text files, logs, backups, and much, much more. To start working with that service, you'll need to understand how it's structured. This is why we'll spend some time talking about containers and blobs.

Blob Storage containers

A container in Blob Storage is exactly what its name says to you – it's basically a container for data. What's unique about containers in Blob Storage is the fact that they only look like hierarchical filesystems. They are implemented as a flat hierarchy, which may be tricky in big data scenarios. However, for that kind of data architecture, you may use the hierarchical namespaces feature of Blob Storage, which is something that you need to opt in to.

To create a container, use the following command:

```
az storage container create -n <container-name> --account-name
<storage-account-name>
```

If your storage account allows you to connect using Azure AD only, you'll need to add one more parameter:

```
az storage container create -n <container-name> --account-name
<storage-account-name> --auth-mode login
```

Each container may or may not be available publicly (assuming the storage account has public access enabled). To configure that during the creation of a container, use the `--public-access` parameter:

```
az storage container create -n <container-name> --account-name
<storage-account-name> --public-access blob
```

Allowed values are `blob`, `container`, and `off`. If you select `blob`, public access will be granted for specific blobs only. This means that the client will be disallowed from listing the contents of a container and will have to access a specific blob. Container access closes that gap by giving a client access to the whole container and its blobs.

> **Important note**
>
> Remember that the `--public-access` parameter is applicable only if the storage account itself is available publicly. If you disable public access for the service, it doesn't matter which value is selected for the parameter. You can still use it, though, to avoid exposing all the blobs in a container for a client unless they have appropriate permissions.

As containers themselves serve little purpose, let's see how they work in conjunction with blobs.

Blob Storage blobs

A blob in Azure Storage is a generic file in any format. Using that Azure service, you can store a couple of huge files and thousands of tiny files in the same place. It doesn't care about the file format, its size, or its purpose – it's up to you how you use it later. A blob can be uploaded to a container using a couple of different methods – we'll discuss them in the last section of this chapter, *Uploading blobs to Blob Storage*.

Each blob needs to be assigned to a single container. This means that it's up to the access policies of a container to decide how blobs are accessed generically. When a general-purpose storage account is created, by default it won't allow you to configure blob-level permissions. As mentioned in the previous section, everything is configured on a container level. This will work in generic use cases (such as storage for backup and archiving of applications), but in advanced data scenarios (big data,

machine learning (ML), data lakes, and so on) it probably won't be enough. If you enable hierarchical namespaces on your storage account level, you'll be able to configure an **access control list** (ACL) on a blob level thanks to both Azure RBAC and the **POSIX**-like permissions model. Unfortunately, hierarchical namespaces aren't a topic planned for this book. However, if you'd like to learn more about them, read the following article from the documentation: `https://learn.microsoft.com/en-us/azure/storage/blobs/data-lake-storage-namespace`.

Before we proceed, there's one more thing related to a Blob Storage blob. Each blob uploaded to a container can have a different type defining its purpose. As for now, we have the following:

- **Block blobs**: The most common blobs with no special meaning
- **Append blobs**: Blobs optimized for append operations, making them an ideal choice for logs
- **Page blobs**: Used for storing OS data, data disks, and data persisted by Azure databases

The type of a blob can be set when the blob is created – we'll cover that parameter in the *Uploading blobs to Blob Storage* section.

As for now, you learned some new information about Azure Storage and its fundamentals. In the next section, we'll learn about access tiers, which is a topic closely related to Blob Storage blobs, as it allows us to configure the expected performance level of our Blob Storage service and affects the pricing of the whole storage account.

Configuring access tiers in Blob Storage

Blob Storage is a service that you can use to store any data, meaning there are not many various parameters that refer to the uploaded files in terms of their structure or characteristics. However, there are a few different use cases that can be covered by this service:

- Generic storage for applications
- Storage for backup files
- Storage for archived files
- Storage for logs

Note that some of those scenarios may expect different performance tiers as the way uploaded files are modified and used will be different. For instance, let's say you're using Azure Storage for storing backup files. Backups are files that in most cases are quite big, but what's more important is that most of the time, you just upload them and rarely use them. It's a perfect example of a storage solution called **cold storage**. With Azure Storage, you can develop a solution that can be treated as either *hot* or *cold* storage. We'll cover that topic by explaining what access tiers for Blob Storage are.

Hot and cold storage

The difference between hot and cold storage is quite simple – if your data is going to be accessed frequently (let's say, at least once each hour), you may consider it *hot*. There's no single metric that would tell you when data becomes *hot* and when it's *cold*. We need to decide that ourselves by looking at available metrics:

- Size of accessed files

- Number of performed operations

- How frequently data is accessed

Some common scenarios (such as storage for applications and storage for log files) will be most of the time considered *hot* paths. Such data may be accessed anytime, and the size of files will very often be less than 1 MB. When Azure Storage is considered, you need to compare pricing for working with both hot and cold data:

- 100k write operations (hot) cost $0.65

- 100k read operations (hot) cost $0.05

- 100k write operations (cold) cost $2.34

- 100k read operations (cold) cost $1.30

As you can see, when comparing read/write operations, hot data is much cheaper. However, if we compare the cost of storing data, we'll see that the hot tier will not be optimal:

- 1000 GBs (hot) cost 21$

- 1000 GBs (cold) cost 3.60$

This is why you need to take into consideration the way data will be used in Blob Storage. For small applications and services, it's unlikely you see the difference in cost. For bigger systems, however, the selected tier may greatly affect the pricing of the whole solution.

> **Important note**
> While access tiers will affect the pricing of Blob Storage, they can be configured for block blobs only.

In Azure, there's one more access tier between the hot and cold tiers called *cool*. Let's quickly define it before we start configuring tiers for our storage account.

Cool tier

The **cool tier** in Blob Storage is exactly between the hot and cold tiers. It's more expensive than the hot tier in terms of read/write operations, but cheaper than the cold tier. Of course, it's also less expensive than the hot tier when calculating data storage costs, but more expensive than the cold tier. When deciding between the cool and cold tiers, you may try looking at how long your data is going to be stored. In general, the cool tier is meant for infrequently accessed data that will be stored for no longer than 1 month. The cold tier can be used if you're going to store your data for much longer.

Let's now see how we can configure the access tier when creating an Azure Storage instance.

Configuring the access tier

When you are creating an Azure Storage instance, you can use the `--access-tier` parameter to define which access tier should be configured on your storage account level:

```
az storage account create --name <storage-name> \
   --resource-group <resource-group-name> \
   --location <location> \
   --sku Standard_LRS \
   --access-tier Hot
```

If you don't provide that parameter, it defaults to the *hot* tier. Besides standard values (hot/cool/cold), Azure Storage accepts *Premium* as a valid access tier. This is, however, reserved for premium storage accounts (`Premium_LRS`, `Premium_ZRS`).

It's also possible to configure the access tier on a blob level. We'll cover that in the next section.

Configuring the access tier on a blob level

Your blobs may base their access tiers on the storage account (or, in other words, inherit that setting from a storage account), but that's not always the case. Sometimes, you want to have a single storage account and just add some files that will be treated differently. To set the access tier for an already existing blob, you could use the following command:

```
az storage blob set-tier --account-key <storage-account-key> \
   --account-name <storage-account-name> \
   --container-name <container-name> \
   --name <blob-name> \
   --tier <tier-name>
```

Note that the preceding command uses the account key as the authentication method. Remember that it's perfectly fine to use other ways to authenticate (Azure AD login, SAS token, etc.).

The `--tier` parameter accepts different values depending on the type of blob:

- `P10`, `P15`, `P20`, `P30`, `P4`, `P40`, `P50`, `P6`, `P60`, `P70` (premium page blobs)
- `Hot`, `Cool`, `Cold`, `Archive` for block blobs

It's also possible to set a blob tier when performing upload operations. We'll cover that in the *Uploading blobs to Blob Storage* section. Before we discuss the next topic, let's talk about one more tier that we missed so far – *archive*.

Archive tier

Some data uploaded to Azure Storage will stay there for a long time. It may be a couple of months or even years. Cool and cold access tiers can be used in such cases to optimize cost, but that's not always optimal. Fortunately, Azure offers one more tier named *archive* to cover scenarios where you really want to archive some data.

The **archive tier** has two major differences when compared with other access tiers:

- It cannot be read and written to while it's archived
- To access file data, you need to first rehydrate it

The process of rehydration of an archived file can take up to several hours. This is why you shouldn't keep files that may be critical to your business (for example, recovery keys) in the archive tier. The benefit of that tier is the price for data storage, which is the lowest among all access tiers.

> **Important note**
> Remember that you need to keep your data in the archive tier for at least 180 days. Otherwise, you'll be charged some extra money as an early-deletion fee.

We described the process of setting up the access tier for a file in the *Configuring access tiers in Blob Storage* section. As you're now familiar with the basic concepts of Azure Storage and Blob Storage, it's time to proceed to the next part of this chapter, where we'll discuss the lifecycle and replication of objects in Azure Storage.

Configuring lifecycle and replication in Blob Storage

Each object stored in Blob Storage can have its own rules for lifecycle. What's more, the storage account enables you to configure replications for all objects stored. In this section, we'll focus on managing those concepts from the administrator's point of view. To get started, we'll revisit replication options to see what available operations there are to perform.

Replication of a storage account

When you create a storage account, you may decide the SKU used for it. The SKU parameter serves two purposes:

- Defines the selected performance tier
- Sets up the replication mode for the storage account

As with many services in Azure, Azure Storage is quite flexible, meaning it allows for reconfiguring some of its options after the creation of an instance. This also applies to replication mode, which can be changed anytime with the following command:

```
az storage account update --name <storage-account-name> --resource-
group <resource-group-name> --sku <sku-name>
```

When updating the SKU of your storage account, you need to remember one limitation – if you previously selected ZRS replication, it cannot be changed to LRS or GRS. The same applies to LRS/GRS replication – once a storage account is created, it cannot be changed to ZRS. It's caused by some infrastructure limitations of Azure, which prevent you from changing locally or geographically replicated accounts to zonal replication. Besides that limitation, you're free to change the SKU anytime.

> **Important note**
>
> One more thing worth remembering is the fact that changing from LRS to GRS replication will incur additional costs as it requires replicating your data to a secondary region. The cost will depend on the volume of data stored in the primary region.

Besides replication, Azure Storage allows us to configure the lifecycle of blobs uploaded to your storage account. Let's see how it works and how we can use it for our purpose.

Lifecycle of blobs in Blob Storage

We talked about access tiers, which allow you to decide whether blobs are meant for frequent access or are instead stored for some time and then removed. Some time ago, all the operations involving access tiers required a custom solution that was implemented on the client's side. Such a solution had lifecycle rules implemented, which were used to automatically move blobs from one tier to another. Fortunately, Azure Storage has that feature currently integrated internally, meaning we can configure lifecycle policies for automated management.

Each lifecycle policy is defined as a JSON document with the following structure:

```
{
  "rules": [
    {
```

```
     "name": "<rule-name>",
     "enabled": true,
     "type": "Lifecycle",
     "definition": <rule-definition>
  }


 ]
}
```

The definition of a lifecycle rule may contain actions, filters, and prefix matches pointing at more specific blobs. An `actions` object may look like this:

```
"actions": {
        "baseBlob": {
          "tierToCool": {
            "daysAfterModificationGreaterThan": 14
          },
          "tierToArchive": {
            "daysAfterModificationGreaterThan": 180,
            "daysAfterLastTierChangeGreaterThan": 7
          },
          "delete": {
            "daysAfterModificationGreaterThan": 365
          }
        }
}
```

As you can see, those defined actions would:

- Move the blob to the cool tier after 14 days since the last modification

- Archive a blob after 180 days

- Delete a blob after 365 days

To better understand the syntax (and see more examples), you can take a look at the documentation: `https://learn.microsoft.com/en-us/azure/storage/blobs/lifecycle-management-overview`. To use such a policy, you need to enable it in your Blob Storage. The first step is to enable tracking of the access time of a blob:

```
az storage account blob-service-properties update \
    --resource-group <resource-group-name> \
    --account-name <storage-account-name> \
    --enable-last-access-tracking true
```

This option enables us to use the `daysAfterModificationGreaterThan` parameter in the lifecycle rule. The second step is deploying a policy:

```
az storage account management-policy create \
    --account-name <storage-account-name> \
    --policy @policy.json \
    --resource-group <resource-group-name>
```

Note that `@policy.json` allows us to instruct the Azure CLI to load a lifecycle policy definition from the file. For instance, if you saved a policy in a file named `my-policy.json`, use `--policy @my-policy.json` to point to the file. Once the policy is deployed, it will start generating events containing information about modified files. Those events have a `Microsoft.Storage.LifecyclePolicyCompleted` type and can be found in either activity logs or topics created by Azure Event Grid.

After discussing the topic of replication and lifecycle in Blob Storage, we're ready to see how blobs can be uploaded to Blob Storage. Let's go to the last section of this chapter to learn about the upload process.

Uploading blobs to Blob Storage

As Blob Storage acts as a generic storage solution for files, there needs to be a way to upload files to created containers. Fortunately, there are several different ways to perform upload operations to a storage account – they can be used in a couple of different scenarios:

- Using an SDK will be helpful when working in a traditional development environment.
- The Azure CLI could be leveraged when writing automation scripts. The same applies to Azure PowerShell.
- You can also use additional tools such as **AzCopy** if you need to work with larger datasets.

In this section, we'll focus on the Azure CLI and **AzCopy** for examples of performing upload operations. Let's start with the former.

Using the Azure CLI to upload a file

Uploading a file using the Azure CLI can be performed using the following command:

```
az storage blob upload -f <path-to-file> -c <container-name> -n <blob-name>
```

However, in most cases, you'll also need to point to a specific storage account:

```
az storage blob upload -f <path-to-file> -c <container-name> -n <blob-name> --account-key <account-key> --account-name <storage-account-name>
```

Depending on the authentication method, you may need to adjust the parameters a little – if you obtain a SAS token with a URL, you could use the `--blob-url` parameter. For an Azure AD login, the only thing needed is to use the `--auth-mode Login` parameter.

Using the Azure CLI command, you may point to any local file available on your machine. Using this method is, however, limited to a single file only. If you want to upload several files, you need to use another command:

```
az storage blob upload-batch -d <container-name> -s <path-to-local-
directory>
```

The preceding example would upload all files from the local directory to the destination container. It's possible to use the `--pattern` parameter to filter files:

```
az storage blob upload-batch -d <container-name> -s <path-to-local-
directory> --pattern *.dat
```

This method is much better if you have multiple files that need to be uploaded.

> **Important note**
>
> The `--pattern` parameter is based on a Python function called `fnmatch`. You can find more information here for a better understanding of possible filtering options: `https://docs.python.org/3.7/library/fnmatch.html`.

Remember that, by default, each blob uploaded using those methods is considered a block blob in the hot tier. To change it, you can use the `az storage blob set-tier` command after performing the upload. During upload, you could use two additional parameters to save some time:

- `--tier`: Allows you to select an access tier (hot/cool/cold/archive)
- `--type`: Allows you to select a blob type (block/append/page)

Using the Azure CLI for uploads is a simple solution that will work in many scenarios. It may not, however, be sufficient for more advanced scenarios or bigger data volumes. To overcome those challenges, you could use `azcopy`, described in the next section.

Using AzCopy to upload a file

AzCopy is an additional tool that you can download and use in data migration scenarios. It can be used to manage data stored in your storage account, including containers and blobs. To create a container, you can simply use the following command:

```
azcopy make 'https://<storage-account-name>.blob.core.windows.
net/<container-name>'
```

Remember that you can connect with a storage account using different authentication options. If an Azure AD login is not available, you may use a SAS token:

```
azcopy make 'https://<storage-account-name>.blob.core.windows.
net/<container-name><SAS-token>'
```

Once the container is created, you can upload a file:

```
azcopy copy '<path-to-file>' 'https://<storage-account-name>.blob.
core.windows.net/<container-name>/<filename>'
```

The same is applicable to directory upload:

```
azcopy copy '<path-to-directory>' 'https://<storage-account-name>.
blob.core.windows.net/<container-name>' --recursive
```

Notice the `--recursive` parameter, which allows you to upload child directories as well. AzCopy is a much better option for copying large datasets as it can upload data concurrently, perform checksum validation to verify whether upload or copy operations were successful, and can also benchmark your storage account. To view more information, see the following article: `https://learn.microsoft.com/en-us/azure/storage/common/storage-use-azcopy-optimize`.

That's all about uploading blobs to Blob Storage. Let's proceed to the summary, where we check the learnings from this chapter and the next steps regarding your learning path.

Summary

With *Chapter 9*, we started another area useful for Azure administrators, which is storage. Information contained in this chapter will be helpful on many occasions, as Blob Storage is one of the most popular services used in Azure thanks to its simplicity, flexibility, and decent performance. You learned important topics such as storage accounts, containers, and blobs, including their access tiers, replication, and lifecycle rules. We also discussed different options for performing upload operations to Blob Storage.

In the next chapter, you'll learn about **Azure File Service**, which is another service offered by Azure Storage. This time, we'll use that Azure service to set up a file share that can be used by people inside your organization as a replacement for standard on-premises shares. We'll also discuss the **File Sync** feature, which can be helpful to automate the management of the service.

10

Azure Files and Azure File Sync

In *Chapter 9*, we started talking about **Azure Storage** by exploring **Blob Storage** as a generic storage solution for files. We also mentioned that Azure Storage offers additional capabilities by exposing various endpoints not only for blob management but tables, queues, and file shares as well. In this chapter, we're going to discover various features of **File Service**, which can easily be used as a replacement for common on-premises setups.

Upon completing this chapter, you'll be able to successfully configure and manage File Service. You'll also be able to automatically synchronize data stored within that service. In this chapter, we're going to cover the following main topics:

- Managing Azure Files (File Service)
- File share snapshots
- Azure File Sync

Technical requirements

For the exercises in this chapter, you'll need the following:

- The Azure CLI (`https://learn.microsoft.com/en-us/cli/azure/install-azure-cli`)
- A command line of any kind (either available in your operating system or your favorite one)

The Code in Action video for this book can be viewed at: `https://packt.link/GTX9F`

Managing Azure Files (File Service)

Azure Files (often called File Service or File Storage) is a managed solution that's part of Azure Storage. While Blob Storage, as described in *Chapter 9*, enables us to store various files, configure their life cycles, and replicate them accordingly, Azure Files is meant as an enterprise-grade file share solution that can be integrated with the end user machine as a replacement for on-premises shares. Such an approach allows you to simplify infrastructure setup and lower the cost of operations as you no longer need to manage infrastructure yourself.

Let's start our journey with Azure Files by describing possible access protocols.

Available access protocols

As Azure Files is a cloud-based file share, to be useful as a replacement for on-premises components, it needs to support a similar set of common protocols that are used in file-sharing scenarios. For now, this service supports the following access methods:

- **Server Message Block (SMB)**
- **Network File System (NFS)**
- REST API (HTTP)

Each of these protocols will be useful in different scenarios. For typical use cases, SMB and NFS will be the most common choices. For better control over the sharing process, the REST API may be an interesting choice as it allows you to control many different aspects of integration. Let's quickly characterize the pros and cons of each of these protocols.

SMB

The SMB protocol may be known to you as the Microsoft SMB Protocol as it's its common name for Windows operating systems implementation. Though it's popular in Windows-based infrastructure, this protocol is perfectly capable of working on Unix-based and other operating systems. Its main purpose is file sharing, but it also supports other operations, such as printing, change notifications, and locks. We'll use SMB-based shares in Azure Files for caching using **Azure File Sync**.

NFS

NFS serves a similar purpose to the SMB protocol and can be run on various operating systems as well (though it may be more popular in Unix-based systems). However, compared to SMB-based file shares in Azure Files, NFS-based Azure Files shares can be run on Linux only. The NFS protocol may be better suited for transferring small-to-medium-sized files (roughly less than 1 gigabyte), but in terms of performance, it is comparable to SMB in general. The biggest difference between these protocols may be case sensitivity – NFS is case-sensitive, which may be a game-changer in some scenarios (such as searching).

REST API (HTTP)

Azure Files offers a **REST API** called **FileREST API**, which can be used to integrate your applications and systems with the service. It can be used as a replacement for SMB and NFS protocols (for instance, because you have operating systems that don't support both) or an addition to cover gaps in SMB/NFS implementation. The FileREST API follows the same guidelines and requirements as any other **Azure API** we discussed previously. This means that you need to authenticate and authorize to be able to make any request. Authentication is implemented via **Azure AD**, while authorization is based on **Azure IAM (RBAC/ABAC)**.

When using the FileREST API, you can do the following:

- Perform operations on File Service
- Work with file shares
- Work with directories and files

Of course, File Service will be managed via the service's control plane, while shares, directories, and files are part of the data plane. This will affect the way we structure access and implement integration. Now, let's learn how to create an instance of File Service and use it as a mounted share on our computer.

Creating a File Service instance

To get started with the service, we need to create an instance of it. The process of creating a File Service instance is the same as other Azure Storage services. To create it, you need to create a storage account:

```
az group create -n <resource-group-name> -l <location>
az storage account create -g <resource-group-name> -n <storage-account-name>
```

Each storage account will have a File Service endpoint defined within the `primaryEndpoints` property:

```
https://<storage-account-name>.file.core.windows.net/
```

This endpoint will be our entry point to the service. However, creating an empty storage account is not enough to get started with File Service itself. To proceed, we need to create a share. Let's do that now.

Creating a File Service share

To work with shares exposed by File Service in the Azure CLI, we have three different groups of operations:

```
az storage file # For shares using SMB 3.0 protocol
az storage share # Generic
az storage share-rm # For access using Microsoft.Storage provider
```

These three methods have different use cases and, in some scenarios, can be used interchangeably. In this chapter, we'll cover all of them so that we can consider their differences and discuss to what cases they're applicable. Let's start with the second method of interacting with the service since SMB-related operations don't allow us to create a share and are rather meant for working with files.

Accessing File Service as a generic share

We'll start with creating a share on File Service using the following method:

```
az storage share create --account-name <storage-account-name> --name <share-name>
```

After a moment, your share will be ready to be used. Compared to **Blob Service**, file shares are meant to be integrated with local or remote machines for file sharing rather than storing generic blobs. This is why creating an empty share provides little to no business value. We'll need to mount it on our local computer or virtual machine to see its full capabilities. Before we reach that point, let's see how we can create a file share by interacting with the **Microsoft.Storage resource provider**.

Accessing File Service with a resource provider

To create a file share using the `Microsoft.Storage` resource provider, use the following method:

```
az storage share-rm create --storage-account <storage-account-name>
--name <share-name>
```

As you can see, this method of creating a share is very similar to the first one we used. However, using it gives you more control over the process of creating a share. For instance, you're able to decide which access tier should be set for a share (`Hot`, `Cool`, `Premium`, or `TransactionOptimized`). What's more, you can also set enabled protocols (SMB or NFS) and a quota (how much data can be stored on a share). You might be wondering what the case is for using the first method presented if it's so limited. Well, you can think about it as a way of working with a share itself rather than its infrastructure. In other words, you can use `az storage share-rm` operations to set up the service itself and then leverage `az storage share` to be closer to the data plane (so that you can close file handles or set a share's metadata). In general, however, you can use just one of those methods and never bother with the alternative. I prefer to work with the former as it gives me more control over the infrastructure I'm creating.

So far, we've talked about interacting with File Service at the control plane level – now, let's learn how we can work with data.

Accessing File Service with SMB

All the operations in this section will be using the `az storage file` command to interact with the service. While this group of operations doesn't allow you to manage a share itself, you can use it to interact with the stored data. For example, we could upload a file to a previously created share:

```
az storage file upload -s <share-name> --source <source-file-path>
--account-name <storage-account-name>
```

Once the upload is completed, the uploaded file will be immediately available for all the machines that have that share mounted.

> **Important note**
> Remember that the described group of operations works with SMB-enabled shares only.

To work with files using the Azure CLI, we have four different methods:

- `upload`
- `upload-batch`
- `download`
- `download-batch`

They can be used to interact with a file share, but they shouldn't be used as a typical way of accessing data stored within a share (doing so would defeat the purpose of a share – if you need to manage files programmatically, Blob Service is a much better choice). To manage files in a *normal* way, let's try to mount a share to both Windows and Linux machines.

Mounting a file share

In this section, we'll cover the topic of mounting a file share for two popular operating systems – Windows and Linux. If you have access to one (or both) of those systems locally, you can use your own computer to perform the exercises. As an alternative, you could provision a virtual machine in Azure and work with it to mount a share. Go back to *Chapter 5* to refresh your memory a little before we proceed.

Mounting a file share on Windows using an access key

When mounting a file share, you need to decide whether you want to authenticate using **Azure Active Directory** or an access key. Both methods will give you access to a share, but they are slightly different in terms of the access level they provide:

- An access key gives you admin-level access to a share
- Active Directory access depends on a role assigned to the principal that's used when mounting a share

To mount a share using an access key, you can use the following script:

```
$connectTestResult = Test-NetConnection -ComputerName <storage-
account-name>.file.core.windows.net -Port 445
if ($connectTestResult.TcpTestSucceeded) {
    cmd.exe /C "cmdkey /add:`" <storage-account-name>.file.core.
windows.net`" /user:`"localhost\<share-name>`" /pass:`"<access-key>"`"
    # Mount the drive
    New-PSDrive -Name <drive-letter> -PSProvider FileSystem -Root
"\\<storage-account-name>.file.core.windows.net\<share-name>" -Persist
} else {
    Write-Error -Message "Unable to reach the Azure storage account
via port 445."
}
```

As you can see, it's a PowerShell script, which means you can run it on a machine where you want to have the share mounted. Take note of a couple of details that need to be configured before running it:

- An access key must be provided when adding a share
- You need to select a drive letter that will be used for the mount

This script will also test connection with File Service using `port 445` and return an error if a connection cannot be established. In some cases, `port 445` may be blocked by your firewall or organization policies – if you cannot connect with a share, make sure it's opened.

After running the script, you should see a result similar to mine:

```
CMDKEY: Credential added successfully.

Name   Used (GB) Free (GB) Provider  Root
----   --------- --------- --------  ----
Z      0.00      5120.00   FileSystem \\<storage-account>.file.core...
```

A mounted share will also be immediately available in the filesystem of the operating system:

```
Z:\>dir
 Volume in drive Z has no label.
 Volume Serial Number is 3068-7F6A

 Directory of Z:\

08/04/2023  12:25 PM    <DIR>          .
08/04/2023  12:25 PM    <DIR>          ..
08/03/2023  09:21 PM            94,026 capture.gif
               1 File(s)         94,026 bytes
               2 Dir(s)  5,497,558,007,808 bytes free
```

From now on, we're able to interact with File Service as a local drive. This means that we can copy files onto it from multiple locations, and those files will be available for any machine that has that share mounted. Now, let's learn how the same share can be mounted using Azure Active Directory.

Mounting a file share on Windows using Active Directory

Mounting a file share using Active Directory is possible after making additional configuration changes to the on-premises machine (or a remote machine, which is domain-joined). As the process is quite detailed and lengthy, we're not going to describe it in this book – all the details are described on the documentation page at https://learn.microsoft.com/en-us/azure/storage/files/storage-files-identity-auth-active-directory-enable. However, let's discuss the whole idea of using File Service with a share authenticated via Active Directory.

Using a shared key, as described in the previous section, is a simple idea that is also very easy to configure. It has one big advantage – everyone using that authentication method becomes an administrator of that share. They can upload and delete any files and modify their configuration. What's more, we're sharing the access key, which needs to be saved locally to have persistent access. Access to that key can be secured, but in general, it adds some operational burden that you need to handle. This is why the Active Directory authentication mechanism is much better – it requires more configuration upfront but is easier to manage at scale.

When using File Service, you have three different options for authentication using Active Directory:

- **Active Directory domain controller** (both on-premises and hosted in the cloud)
- **Azure Active Directory Domain Services** (a **PaaS** version of the Active Directory domain controller)
- **Azure Active Directory Kerberos** (leverages **Kerberos** authentication and works for Azure Active Directory-joined clients)

Which option you choose will depend on your preferences and technical expectations. In some scenarios, using the first option may be the preferred way of integrating File Service, while in other companies that already use Domain Services, it may be natural to go that way.

Once you select the desired option, you need to enable Active Directory authentication for File Service using one of the following methods:

```
az storage account update --enable-files-aadds # For Domain Services
az storage account update --enable-files-aadkerb # Kerberos
az storage account update --enable-files-aads # Active Directory
```

Some of these methods need to be run after configuring Active Directory authentication (for example – before you enable authentication via Domain Services, you need to enable that feature at the tenant level), so make sure you've read detailed instructions on how to configure Active Directory authentication for File Service before you start playing with those commands.

Now, let's learn how to mount a share on a machine running Linux.

Mounting a file share on Linux

Mounting a file share on Linux is like mounting a file share on Windows using an access key. All you need to do is run the following script:

```
sudo mkdir /mnt/<mount-point>
if [ ! -d "/etc/smbcredentials" ]; then
sudo mkdir /etc/smbcredentials
fi
if [ ! -f "/etc/smbcredentials/<mount-name>.cred" ]; then
    sudo bash -c 'echo "username=/<mount-name>" >> /etc/
```

```
smbcredentials//<mount-name>.cred'
    sudo bash -c 'echo "password=<access-key>" >> /etc/
smbcredentials//<mount-name>.cred'
fi
sudo chmod 600 /etc/smbcredentials//<mount-name>.cred

sudo bash -c 'echo "//<storage-account-name>.file.core.windows.
net//<mount-name>./mnt//<mount-name>.cifs nofail,credentials=/
etc/smbcredentials//<mount-name>..cred,dir_mode=0777,file_
mode=0777,serverino,nosharesock,actimeo=30" >> /etc/fstab'
sudo mount -t cifs //<storage-account-name>.file.core.
windows.net//<mount-name>./mnt//<mount-name>.-o credentials=/
etc/smbcredentials//<mount-name>..cred,dir_mode=0777,file_
mode=0777,serverino,nosharesock,actimeo=30
```

The whole script can be described in the following steps:

1. Create a file for the SMB credentials that will store the access key for our file share.

2. Set file permissions to 600 (read/write for the owner only).

3. Append the mount configuration to the fstab file.

4. Mount a file share using the chosen mount point.

The general idea of this script is the same as the one we used for Windows. The main difference (besides the commands) is the fact that, on Windows, we selected a drive letter, while on Linux, we must define a mount point with our custom name mounted to /mnt/<mount-name>.

Now that we've learned how to mount a file share, it's time to learn how to undo that operation. Proceed to the next section to learn more.

Unmounting a file share

Each file share can be unmounted at any moment. The procedure is slightly different for Windows and Linux, as we need to use different commands to perform that operation. For Windows, you may either do that from the **GUI** (by right-clicking on the share icon and choosing **Disconnect**) or from the command line:

```
net use <drive-letter> /delete
```

Of course, you need to have permission to run that command – in some scenarios, running it with a local user account may fail due to insufficient rights.

On Linux, to unmount a file share, use this command:

```
sudo umount <mount-point>
```

However, remember that we permanently mounted our file share using the `fstab` file. This means that even if the unmount operation is run without an error and you see that the share was unmounted, it'll be automatically mounted once again after each reboot. To avoid that issue, you need to remove an entry from the `fstab` file.

For now, you will be introduced to the basics of File Service in Azure Storage so that you can perform basic operations. Let's proceed to the next topic regarding **file share snapshots** to see how we can improve the reliability of our file shares and backup data.

Working with file share snapshots

File shares are mostly part of your infrastructure, which is one of the critical components for business continuity. They're often involved in the day-to-day work of many people working in a company so that they can share data, collaborate, and send files. In some scenarios, file shares may be also part of the application's infrastructure, and issues when connecting with them may affect your end users as well. In this section, we'll cover the topic of snapshots, which can be configured for File Service.

A **snapshot**, in the context of a file share, is described as a state that was saved at a certain point in time. This means that different snapshots may contain different files (or files with different content). Snapshots for File Service are very similar to the backups you can perform for a database. They need to be configured, stored, and tested in a way that ensures their reliability and availability. One thing worth mentioning before we proceed is the protocol support for snapshots in Azure Storage. Unfortunately, this Azure service doesn't support file share snapshots when using NFS – the only way to use that feature is by configuring your file shares to use SMB. Now, let's see how we can work with a snapshot using the Azure CLI.

Creating a file share snapshot

In Azure, creating a snapshot of your file share hosted on Azure Storage is a matter of a single command. To create it, just use the following command:

```
az storage share snapshot -n <share-name> --account-name <storage-
account-name>
```

This command is the easiest way to create a snapshot at any given point in time. As a result, you'll get a response similar to mine:

```
{
    "date": "2023-08-04T17:41:34+00:00",
    "etag": "\"0x8DB9454C37C0D98\"",
    "last_modified": "2023-08-03T19:06:38+00:00",
    "request_id": "9466ef49-501a-002f-17fa-c6a56a000000",
    "snapshot": "2023-08-04T17:41:35.0000000Z",
    "version": "2022-11-02"
}
```

As you can see, each snapshot is decorated with metadata containing the date of creation, access date, version, and request identifier. The question now is, what happens after the snapshot is created? The answer is quite simple – the snapshot is accessible as it was a separate share created inside your storage account. You can access it by appending the value of the `snapshot` property that's returned by the `az storage share snapshot` command to the share URL:

```
# Share URL
https://<storage-account-name>.file.core.windows.net/<share-name>
# Share snapshot URL
https://<storage-account-name>.file.core.windows.net/<share-name>?snapshot=<snapshot>
```

In my case, I'd use `2023-08-04T17:41:35.0000000Z` as the value of the snapshot field in the query string. You can mount a share for the given snapshot by using the same method we used for mounting a share in the *Mounting a file share* section. However, there's a small difference between mounting a file share and mounting a snapshot:

- For Windows, you need to use the `Set-Location` cmdlet to set a working directory to a directory of a snapshot represented by GMT when the snapshot was taken

- For Linux, you need to specify the GMT of your snapshot as the value of the `snapshot` parameter:

```
sudo mount -t cifs //<storage-account-name>.file.core.windows.
net/<file-share-name> /mnt/<file-share-name>/snapshot1 -o
credentials=/etc/smbcredentials/<credentials>.cred,snapshot=@
GMT-<gmt-time>
```

The easiest way to convert the time of a snapshot to the desired value is by extracting parts of the needed information from the timestamp. The value needed by both the `Set-Location` and `mount` commands looks like this: `@GMT-year.month.day-hour.minutes.seconds`. If we take the value I got from File Service (`2023-08-04T17:41:35.0000000Z`), it turns out that the value of the snapshot parameter would be `@GMT-2023.08.04-17.41.35`. Such a value can be used for both Windows and Linux:

- For Windows: `Set-Location Z:\@GMT-2023.08.04-17.41.35`

- For Linux:

```
sudo mount -t cifs //aach1001.file.core.windows.
net/aach1001 /mnt/aach1001 -o credentials=/etc/
smbcredentials/aach1001.cred,dir_mode=0777,file_
mode=0777,serverino,nosharesock,actimeo=30,snapshot=@
GMT-2023.08.04-17.41.35
```

Of course, these commands are just examples based on my infrastructure. In your case, you'd need to convert them using the names provided for your storage account, file share name, credentials file (Linux), and snapshot's timestamp.

Snapshots are a great way to secure yourself from accidental deletion or modification of files. One thing you need to remember is the fact that they're not performed automatically – you need to do that manually or develop a process that will create them automatically. They also have one con – they are meant for file-level security only, meaning they won't secure you if you accidentally delete a whole share (though snapshots block you from deleting a share if they are not removed).

> **Important note**
>
> Remember that snapshots are not backups. Snapshots are generally meant for materializing differences between different states of a system or a machine. Backups, on the other hand, target disaster recovery scenarios with the possibility of restoring the complete state.

To implement a higher-level security mechanism, let's take a look at how to soft delete file shares.

Configuring soft delete

Soft delete is a feature that allows you to secure your resources from accidental deletion. It works by providing a time frame within which you can restore them. Resources that are *softly deleted* are often invisible – they're moved to a special container, where they stay until they're permanently deleted or automatically deleted after reaching a defined date. In File Service, you're able to configure soft delete for shares, so even if somebody deletes them (accidentally or not), you still have time to restore them if they contain important data. When using this feature, remember that it works for SMB shares only – NFS shares cannot use it. Let's see how this feature can be configured.

Enabling soft delete

As soft delete is not enabled automatically, you need to enable it for the storage account you've created:

```
az storage account file-service-properties update \
    --resource-group <resource-group-name> \
    --account-name <storage-account-name> \
    --enable-delete-retention true \
    --delete-retention-days <retention-days>
```

For the –delete-retention-days parameter, you can provide a value from *1* to *365* – that is, the maximum time until a share is permanently deleted is 1 year. Once soft delete is enabled, each file share that's deleted from that storage account will still be available, even if you remove it. Let's check whether it works. First, I'll list all the shares that are available for my storage account:

```
az storage share list --account-name aach1001 -o table

Name      Quota    Last Modified
--------  -------  ---------------
aach1001
aach1002
```

Now, I'm removing the first one:

```
az storage share delete -n aach1001 --account-name aach1001
```

If I list available shares, you'll notice that one share is no longer there:

```
az storage share list --account-name aach1001 -o table

Name        Quota     Last Modified
--------    -------   ---------------
aach1002
```

To see that share `aach1001` still exists, I'd need to use a separate command:

```
az storage share-rm list --storage-account aach1001 --include-deleted
-o table
```

As a result, I'll get a response telling me what which are available and which ones have been deleted:

```
Name        ResourceGroup   ShareQuota   Deleted
--------    -------------   ----------   --------
aach1001    aach10          5120
aach1002    aach10          5120         True
```

The removed share will be available to be restored for the number of days provided by the `--delete-retention-days` parameter (in my case, 7 days). In the next section, you'll learn how a share, with soft delete enabled, can be restored.

Restoring deleted share

To restore a deleted share, we can use a single Azure CLI command, which will bring it back and let us use it:

```
az storage share-rm restore -n <share-name> \
  --deleted-version <share-version> \
  -g <resource-group-name> \
  --storage-account <storage-account-name>
```

As you can see, there's one argument called `--deleted-version`, which might be interesting for us as we never discussed it before. It turns out that once a share is deleted (assuming soft delete is enabled), it gets a version representing a snapshot of data. You might be wondering what the purpose of that parameter is. The answer is simple – once a share is deleted, you're perfectly fine to create a new share with the same name. Once a share with the same name is deleted again, you'll see that the list of deleted shares contains more than one with the same name – the difference will be visible when we look at the `version` parameter.

This section should help you understand how to secure your File Service data using share snapshots and delete features. In the next section, we'll focus on the last topic on our agenda – using Azure File Sync to improve the performance of our file shares.

Working with Azure File Sync

Azure Files service allows you to have a file share, which simplifies infrastructure and configuration management. However, as it's a cloud-based solution, it also has its cons. It turns out that in bigger organizations, you may be affected by performance issues or need a longer time to synchronize data stored on your file shares. This comes from the fact that the ideal setup for file shares based on Azure Files is a one-to-one mapping between a share and storage account. Of course, in most scenarios, you're not looking to have an individual share for each employee – you're seeking a solution for sharing files with as many people as possible using a single share.

To overcome the challenge of when you have too many files or the access time is too long, Azure offers a feature called Azure File Sync, which can be used on machines running Windows Server. When Azure File Sync is enabled, your machine works as a cache for File Service data. Before we dive deeper into the configuration of that feature, let's talk about the prerequisites for it.

Planning for Azure File Sync

Before you enable Azure File Sync, you need to consider its various pros and cons. The first thing that's worth remembering is the fact that it works with SMB-based shares only. Unfortunately, you cannot use it for NFS shares, which may limit its usability in some scenarios. Second, you need a Windows-based machine, as Azure File Sync doesn't support Linux.

> **Important note**
>
> At the time of writing, we can use File Service shares as direct mounts on any machine, which is much closer to the PaaS/serverless type of infrastructure. With Azure File Sync, we're coming back to the **IaaS** approach, as it requires managing machines deployed in the cloud or on-premises environments.

The reason why Azure File Sync is coupled with specific details of operating systems comes from the fact that shares exposed by Azure Files don't have such an efficient change detection mechanism as Windows Server has. This is also the reason why Azure File Sync becomes so useful in certain scenarios – its in-built synchronization mechanism for file shares over SMB or FileREST has some scalability issues that are solved when using Azure File Sync.

Let's start by describing the main concepts of Azure File Sync.

The main concepts of Azure File Sync

Azure File Sync has two main concepts that are worth mentioning before we start to configure it:

- **Registered server**
- **Sync group**

Before you're able to define sync groups (which define relationships and allow you to link multiple storage accounts and servers), you need to create a registered server. A registered server is a single machine that has an Azure File Sync agent installed and can be used to synchronize data exposed by file shares.

Each sync group is deployed into another concept called **Storage Sync Services**. Storage Sync Services is the underlying concept of Azure File Sync and encapsulates and correlates sync groups and registered servers. All these concepts need to be deployed in a way that ensures optimal performance. We'll discuss this in the next section.

Performance considerations

When you're planning to deploy Azure File Sync, you need to consider two factors:

- Each server with an Azure File Sync agent can sync up to 30 file shares
- It's advised to have a single file share per storage account

While the first limitation is easy to follow (you need to calculate the number of servers needed, which can be done by dividing all your file shares by 30), the second one may be a little bit tricky in some scenarios. To solve that problem, you need to check the utilization of each file share to ensure that the ones with the most traffic are not deployed to the same storage account. If you skip that check, you may hit IOPS limits for File Service shares, meaning the end user will expect a downgraded user experience when using configured file shares.

One more thing to think about when starting with Azure File Sync is the initial synchronization operation. This operation is unique in terms of the CPU and memory utilization of a server that runs the Azure File Sync agent. It's advised to allocate more compute resources for such a machine until the initial synchronization process is completed. This can be done in Azure by scaling up your server, starting synchronization, and scaling down when it's finished. This not only speeds up the operation but also allows you to save some money as you don't need to have a much more powerful machine available all the time.

Besides pure performance considerations, let's also talk about storage availability for the synchronization process to happen.

Free space consideration

The answer to the question "*How much disk space do I need?*" depends on the number of files available in your file shares. As Azure File Sync works with Windows Server only, the way we calculate disk space is simplified as we only have one filesystem to think about (**NTFS**). NTFS allocates 4 KiB of disk space for each file, meaning that for X files, we need to have X * 4 KiB of disk space available. Unfortunately, that's not all we need. If our files are stored within directories, NTFS will allocate an additional 4 KiB per file and directory for sync operation metadata. Assuming we have X files and Y directories, an additional (X + Y) * 4 KiB of space will be occupied.

Azure File Sync itself has a thing called **heatstore** that takes 1.1 KiB per file (in our scenario, X * 1.1 KiB). Now, if we combine all these calculations, we'll get the following formula:

```
(X * 4) + ((X + Y) * 4) + (X * 1.1) = disk_space_occupied
4X + 4X + 4Y + 1.1X = disk_space_occupied
9.1X + 4Y = disk_space_occupied
```

Assuming we have 500k files and 100k directories, we'd have the following:

```
9.1 * 500,000 + 4 * 100,000 = disk_space_occupied
4,950,000 = disk_space_occupied (KiB)
4,95 = disk_space_occupied (GiB)
```

The result is 4.95 GiB of disk space occupied by Azure File Sync for the synchronization process. This could be extended by a **free space policy** as well, which would depend on the size of a disk. If you provision a disk with 500 GiB of disk space and apply a free space policy to ensure that it always has 10% of its disk space available, the result would be 4.95 GiB + 50 GiB = 54.95 GiB in total. This doesn't involve the size of your data. If the data that are presented in that scenario would take 450 GiB, the selected disk (500 GiB) would not be enough to support Azure File Sync operations.

Now, let's discuss how to deploy Azure File Sync.

Deploying Azure File Sync

Deploying Azure File Sync is a lengthy and detailed procedure, so we're not going to include it in this book. The best source, which provides step-by-step instructions, is described in the documentation at learn.microsoft.com/en-us/azure/storage/file-sync/file-sync-deployment-guide. However, we will highlight the steps that you must take to set this up so that you have a better picture of the whole process:

1. Ensure the availability of Azure File Sync in your region.

2. Create a file share.

3. Configure a storage account with the correct settings (SMB version >= 3.1.1, **NTLM v2 authentication**, and AES-128-GCM encryption).

4. Allow access to the storage account using access keys.

5. Deploy a machine running a supported version of Windows Server.

6. Prepare a machine to integrate with Azure File Sync, including network access to Azure Storage.

7. Deploy Storage Sync Service.

8. Install the Azure File Sync agent.

9. Register your machine with Storage Sync Service.

10. Create a sync group and cloud endpoint.

11. Create a server endpoint.

12. Configure firewall/network settings.

As you can see, several steps are needed to get Azure File Sync up and working. In more advanced scenarios, you may also configure the whole service and your machines as a cluster with a failover option so that you have high availability for the whole infrastructure. The need to have it configured that way will depend on your requirements – if deployed file shares are critical to your business, it'll be worth it to have Azure File Sync configured with availability in mind.

With that, we've reached the end of this chapter, where we configured Azure Files as a solution for cloud-based file shares. Let's summarize what we've learned and find out what awaits us in the next chapter.

Summary

In this chapter, you learned about Azure Files as the second service available in Azure Storage that we planned to cover in this book. We talked about concepts such as sharing files using this service and discussed the differences between direct mounts and advanced infrastructure while leveraging Azure File Sync for caching and improving the performance of the whole setup. We also tried to improve the reliability and security of the data that's stored in deployed file shares using snapshots and the soft delete feature.

Everything you learned in this chapter will help you build file shares in the cloud that can be utilized in scenarios where you want to transform your on-premises infrastructure into modern cloud-based components. This is a common task for Azure administrators that is performed in many companies nowadays.

The next chapter will mark the end of *Part 4* of this book, *Azure Storage for Administrators*. We'll cover more details related to security, automation, and transferring data to and from Azure Storage accounts.

11

Azure Storage Security and Additional Tooling

In the previous two chapters, we talked about Azure Storage with a focus on Blob and File Storage Services. Those chapters were meant to give you a general overview of those services' capabilities and configuration options. This chapter will summarize our findings and lessons learned and, additionally, give you more insights into security options for Azure Storage and what's possible to do and implement when challenged with automation tasks and data import/export activities.

Topics covered in this chapter may be considered advanced, as they require prior knowledge of **Blob Service** configuration (described in *Chapter 9*), **Azure AD** concepts (*Chapter 2*), and **managed identities** (*Chapter 2*). Let's see what's going to be described shortly:

- Configuring soft delete in Blob Storage
- Using Azure AD for authorization
- Using managed identities
- Considering various options for automation
- Using the Azure Import/Export service

Technical requirements

For the exercises in this chapter, you'll need the following:

- The Azure CLI (`https://learn.microsoft.com/en-us/cli/azure/install-azure-cli`)
- A command line of any kind (either the one available in your operating system or your favorite one)

The Code in Action video for this book can be viewed at: `https://packt.link/GTX9F`

Configuring soft delete in Blob Storage

Soft delete as a concept has already been briefly described in *Chapter 9* in the *Configuring soft delete* section. Let's quickly remind ourselves what it means to have soft delete configured for a service. Under normal circumstances, any time you delete data from a service (storage or database), it'll be permanently deleted unless it's part of a backup or snapshot of your data. While backups could be described as a kind of soft delete solution, they're rather meant for disaster recovery scenarios. Soft delete, on the other hand, is a simple feature that marks your data as *deleted* without it being deleted permanently. This allows you to restore data at any time without the need to recover a whole storage account or database.

Soft delete will work differently for different services, as it's a feature that is tightly coupled with its functionalities and capabilities. For instance, in **File Service**, you're allowed to enable soft delete for file shares, so you can restore it and the data stored on it if something bad happens. In Blob Storage, soft delete can be enabled for both containers and blobs, meaning you have granular control over that feature.

Let's now see how we can configure it for a storage account.

Enabling soft delete for containers

To enable soft delete for Blob Storage containers, we need to reconfigure our storage account first. To do that, we can use the following CLI command:

```
az storage account blob-service-properties update \
    --enable-container-delete-retention true \
    --container-delete-retention-days <retention-days> \
    --account-name <storage-account-name> \
    --resource-group <resource-group-name>
```

All you need is to provide proper values for the `--container-delete-retention-days`, `--account-name`, and `--resource-group` parameters. Of course, the same can be applied to a storage account when creating it – for example, using ARM templates or another **IaC** solution:

```
{
  "resources": [
      {
          "type": "Microsoft.Storage/storageAccounts/blobServices",
          "apiVersion": "2019-06-01",
          "name": "<storage-account-name>/default",
          "properties": {
              "containerDeleteRetentionPolicy": {
                  "enabled": true,
                  "days": <retention-days>
```

```
                }
            }
        }
    ]
}
```

As you can see, soft delete for containers is actually a property for the whole Blob Service, meaning you cannot enable it for individual containers. Once this setting is enabled, your containers will be marked for deletion for the number of days specified by the `<retention-days>` value.

We've successfully enabled soft delete for containers; now, we'll learn how we can do the same for blobs in those containers.

Enabling soft delete for blobs

When talking about soft delete for blobs in Azure Storage, we need to cover the topic of **blob versioning**, which is the way in which soft delete for that kind of data is implemented. When we were working with File Service or containers in Blob Storage, soft delete was preventing us from accidentally deleting a container for data (share in File Service, container in Blob Storage). As blobs themselves are not containers, they require a slightly different approach to give soft delete a necessary value.

In Azure Storage, blobs can be versioned, meaning you can have multiple versions of the same blob at the same time. As versions of a blob are snapshots of its data at a certain point in time, they work as a soft delete solution, as you always have previous versions of data available (until they're removed as well). As a result, blobs in Azure Storage can be secured by both *traditional* soft delete and versioning, meaning you can have a secure solution, improving the reliability of the stored data and making accidental deletions difficult.

Let's see how both soft delete and versioning work for blobs.

Configuring soft delete

To enable soft delete for blobs, we need to follow very similar instructions to the ones we used when doing the same for containers. All configurations can be performed using a single Azure CLI command:

```
az storage account blob-service-properties update \
    --enable-delete-retention true \
    --delete-retention-days <retention-days> \
    --account-name <storage-account-name> \
    --resource-group <resource-group-name> \
```

As you can see, the only difference here is the parameters used for the `az storage account blob-service-properties update` command. Once soft delete is enabled for blobs, they will be marked for deletion for the defined number of days. A very similar command can be used for enabling versioning, which we'll cover in the next section.

Configuring versioning

To enable versioning, you can use the following command:

```
az storage account blob-service-properties update \
    --resource-group <resource-group-name> \
    --account-name <storage-account-name> \
    --enable-versioning true
```

Once versioning is enabled, any time you perform a write operation on a blob, a new version will be created. Each version is an immutable object, so you cannot alter the previous state of your data. We'll talk more about that in the next section, covering the advantages of using soft delete and versioning for blobs.

Use cases for soft delete and versioning in Blob Storage

Using soft delete and versioning in Blob Storage is among the recommendations related to data protection in Azure. If you seek more reliable infrastructure for data, need to ensure consistency, and need to avoid solutions that may easily corrupt data, these features will become the bread and butter of each service deployed and managed by you. As both soft delete and versioning are properties managed via **Azure Resource Manager** (**ARM**), it's always a good idea to deploy a policy that will automatically audit and configure those settings. We'll talk more about **Azure Policy** and its possible use cases in *Chapter 12*.

However, when working with soft delete and versioning, you need to understand the possible use cases and challenges that may arise when they're implemented. Let's discuss them now before proceeding to the next topic in this chapter, related to using Azure AD for authentication and authorization in Azure Storage.

Soft delete technical details

When soft delete for blobs is enabled, each time a blob is deleted, it goes into a *deleted* state for the given number of days. If the file is within that retention period, you're allowed to perform the Undelete Blob operation, which can be performed using data plane operations in Azure Storage.

> **Important note**
> You can see the technical details of the Undelete Blob operation by reading its documentation at https://learn.microsoft.com/en-us/rest/api/storageservices/undelete-blob?tabs=azure-ad.

It's important to remember that while the retention period can be changed (let's say you started with 7 days and then switched to 21 days), updating it won't affect the files, which are already in a *soft-deleted* state. You'd need to restore those files and delete them once again to have an updated retention period in place for all of them.

What's more, each object (blob) that is deleted when soft delete is enabled becomes invisible until it's automatically removed from your storage account. It's possible to list these invisible files by running an appropriate command, such as the one from Azure CLI, presented as follows:

```
az storage blob list --include d
```

By using the `--include` parameter with the `(d)eleted` value, you'll be able to see all the files that were deleted and are still available for the storage account and container. Under normal circumstances (i.e., without soft delete enabled), this command would return no result. When soft delete is enabled, if the retention period has not been completed, the deleted files will be available for list operations and allowed to be restored.

Let's talk now about some technical details of versioning, which works slightly differently when compared with the soft delete feature.

Versioning technical details

The basic concept of blob versioning assumes that each time a blob is modified or deleted, it automatically creates a new version of itself. This approach allows you to introduce changes to the stored data in a safe way, as even if something goes wrong, you can still restore a previous version of a blob. Versioning could be considered a special case of soft delete, but in general, it's described as a separate feature of Blob Storage.

We mentioned in the *Configuring versioning* section that versioning needs to be enabled by yourself, meaning it's an opt-in feature. When versioning is configured, you may leverage the life cycle policy described in *Chapter 9* to automatically manage revisions of your file (for instance, delete them after a certain period of inactivity). This setup is especially helpful if you want to automatically manage stored data.

> **Important note**
> Remember that versions of a blob take up additional storage, which you'll need to pay for. In high-scale scenarios (or services that frequently modify data), it's important to have a mechanism for managing obsolete data.

To list the versions of a blob, you may use the following command:

```
az storage blob list --include v
```

In the previous section, we used d to indicate *deleted* blobs when listing them. For versioning, we're using v, which stands for *versions*. These values can be combined, so you could list both deleted blobs and their versions:

```
az storage blob list --include vd
```

In the end, both soft delete and versioning of a blob are features that are recommended by Microsoft to ensure data integrity and security. It means that they can be enabled simultaneously without the risk that they will interfere with each other.

As we've discussed topics related to data protection in Blob Storage, let's switch our focus to the details of using Azure AD authentication and authorization when interacting with that service.

Using Azure AD for authorization

When interacting with Azure Storage, you may use three different options when it comes to authenticating and authorizing each request:

- Access key
- Shared access token
- Azure AD token

While the former two are the native ways of connecting with Azure Storage and are the simplest options, Azure AD authentication and authorization is a feature that gives you the most flexibility and improved security. Let's discuss it further to have a better understanding of its capabilities.

Azure AD authorization benefits

Both access keys and shared access tokens are simple mechanisms for securing access to Azure Storage. The access flow for them looks like this, starting with the access key:

1. Obtain the access key from your Azure Storage account.
2. Share the key with a client.

Now, each client we share a key with can use it to connect to our storage account. What's more, it gives them full access to all services (blob, file, queue, and table). If a key leaks, we need to revoke it, which forces us to generate a new key and share it with all the clients once again. This setup, even if simple in the beginning, will become cumbersome in situations where you have tens of different clients using the same key.

An improvement would be to use a shared access token:

1. Generate a token with the proper lifetime, permissions, and selected services.
2. Share the token with a client.

By using this approach, we're able to generate a token per client. What's more, tokens give you granular control over permissions (read/create/delete) and services (blob/file/queue/table). A token can also be configured with a lifetime, meaning we can generate it for a certain amount of time (let's say one hour) and don't need to revoke it manually. The downside of this approach is the fact that the validation of a token is based on an access key. This means that revoking an access token invalidates tokens generated previously. Still, it's a better option when compared with sharing an access key explicitly.

The last option is using an Azure AD token for access. Here, the flow is slightly different – when we want to give access to a storage account or part of it (for instance, a container in Blob Storage), we need to assign a role using the **Identity and Access Management (IAM)** mechanism integrated into Azure. Then, each client can authenticate using Azure Active Directory and authorize based on a set of permissions defined in a role they have been given. The advantage of this approach is the fact that we manage access to the control and data planes of services using the same mechanism. This also allows us to enforce additional means of security (such as multi-factor authentication), though this approach may not always be applicable (for instance, in scenarios that make user interaction impossible, so you cannot apply additional factors when authenticating due to technical limitations).

Let's now see how authorization is solved when using Azure AD as our method of securing access.

Data plane and data actions in role-based access control

When working with **Role-Based Access Control (RBAC)** in Azure, you use roles that give a principal access to certain actions. These actions can be described as permissions that tell you what you can and cannot do. The structure of each role can be described with the following JSON object:

```
{
    "assignableScopes": [
     "/"
    ],
    "description": "<description>",
    "id": "<id>",
    "name": "<name>",
    "permissions": [
      {
        "actions": [],
        "dataActions": [],
        "notActions": [],
        "notDataActions": []
      }
    ],
    "roleName": "<role-name>",
    "roleType": "<role-type>",
    "type": "Microsoft.Authorization/roleDefinitions"
}
```

The most important things for us now are `permissions`, which consist of four arrays:

- `actions` – what you can do (**control plane**)

- `dataActions` – what you can do (**data plane**)

- `notActions` – what you cannot do (**control plane**)

- `notDataActions` – what you cannot do (**data plane**)

The important thing to remember here is that `notActions` and `notDataActions` take precedence – if they are defined, they override the `actions` and `dataActions` permissions defined for a role. Now, if we want to use Azure AD for authorization when interacting with Azure Storage, we need to understand the distinction between permissions assigned for the control plane and for the data plane. In short, control plane actions refer to actions managed via ARM and are often called *operational* actions. Data plane actions refer to interacting with data managed on a resource level. To better understand this, let's introduce some examples:

- Adding a disk to a virtual machine – control plane action

- Writing data to a disk – data plane action

- Configuring a virtual network for Azure Storage – control plane action

- Deleting a blob from Blob Storage – data plane action

As various operations refer to different planes, you need to carefully craft an appropriate access model when using RBAC and Azure AD. This model is much more difficult in the initial implementation when compared with access keys and shared access tokens, as it offers a much more flexible and advanced model of providing access to data stored in your storage accounts.

Let's now discuss example roles that are available in Azure for interacting with the data plane to see what they offer you as an Azure administrator.

Examples of roles in Azure for Azure Storage

Azure offers you plenty of different roles that relate to Azure Storage and cover various use cases. These roles include, but are not limited to, the following ones:

- Storage Account Backup Contributor

- Storage Account Contributor

- Storage Account Key Operator Service Role

- Storage Blob Data Contributor

We'll look at their definitions to see whether they can be used for the control plane only, the data plane only, or both planes, starting with the Storage Account Backup Contributor.

Storage Account Backup Contributor

The definition of this role looks as follows:

```
"permissions": [
        {
        "actions": [
            "Microsoft.Authorization/*/read",
            "Microsoft.Authorization/locks/read",
            ...,
            "Microsoft.Features/features/read",
            "Microsoft.Features/providers/features/read",
            "Microsoft.Resources/subscriptions/resourceGroups/read",
            "Microsoft.Storage/operations/read",
            "Microsoft.Storage/storageAccounts/
objectReplicationPolicies/delete",
            ...
            "Microsoft.Storage/storageAccounts/blobServices/containers/
read",
            "Microsoft.Storage/storageAccounts/blobServices/containers/
write",
            "Microsoft.Storage/storageAccounts/blobServices/read",
            "Microsoft.Storage/storageAccounts/blobServices/write",
            "Microsoft.Storage/storageAccounts/read",
            "Microsoft.Storage/storageAccounts/restoreBlobRanges/action"
        ],
        "dataActions": [],
        "notActions": [],
        "notDataActions": []
        }
    ]
```

As you can see, it gives access to control plane operations only, but on the other hand, it doesn't limit a principal from executing them (in case it had those permissions granted by another role). This means that a principal with that role can read a storage account's replication policies and see and modify containers in Blob Storage but cannot interact with them. It's a perfect role when implementing backups for virtual machines or databases, so an engineer can restore them if needed but is unable to read data they may not have access to.

To make a comparison, let's now check the Storage Blob Data Contributor role.

Storage Blob Data Contributor

As the name suggests, this role aims to manage data and should be defined using data plane permissions. To confirm this, we'll check its definition:

```
"permissions": [
      {
         "actions": [
            "Microsoft.Storage/storageAccounts/blobServices/containers/
delete",
            "Microsoft.Storage/storageAccounts/blobServices/containers/
read",
            "Microsoft.Storage/storageAccounts/blobServices/containers/
write",
            "Microsoft.Storage/storageAccounts/blobServices/
generateUserDelegationKey/action"
         ],
         "dataActions": [
            "Microsoft.Storage/storageAccounts/blobServices/containers/
blobs/delete",

            ...,
            "Microsoft.Storage/storageAccounts/blobServices/containers/
blobs/add/action"
         ],
         "notActions": [],
         "notDataActions": []
      }
   ]
```

If you take a closer look at the role definition, you'll see that the Storage Blob Data Contributor role defines both `actions` and `dataActions`. It allows a principal to perform the following operations:

- Manage blob containers
- Generate shared access tokens for Blob Storage
- Manage blobs

The tricky thing here is the fact that managing containers is defined via control plane permissions. From the perspective of Azure Storage, containers are a resource that can be managed via ARM (meaning you can create them using IaC solutions such as ARM Templates, Azure Bicep, or Terraform). Blobs, on the other hand, are considered *data*, meaning you need to interact with the data plane of Azure Storage to manage them.

Let's now see how we can use Azure AD to authorize our actions when using Azure CLI.

Using Azure AD in Azure CLI

As there are multiple ways to authenticate and authorize operations performed against Azure Storage, when using Azure CLI, you need to explicitly indicate which option you'd like to choose. To do this, we need to use the `--auth-mode` parameter. For example, if you'd like to upload a blob, you could use the following command:

```
az storage blob upload --auth-mode <login|key>
```

As you can see, this parameter accepts one of two possible values: `login` or `key`. Using `login` allows a command to leverage the credentials available via Azure CLI, so it'll use a token obtained from Azure AD at the time you signed into the Azure tenant. Using `key` is a legacy option that automatically queries the given storage account for access keys.

> **Important note**
>
> As the `key` option needs to query a storage account for an access key, you need to have the necessary permissions for the account used when logging in with Azure CLI. If your principal doesn't have those, you won't be able to use this option. In such a scenario, you need to obtain and explicitly pass either an access token or a shared access token (SAS token) using the `--account-key` or `--sas-token` parameter.

This way of controlling the authentication mechanism is available for all operations that interact with Azure Storage. Remember that you can always start with using access keys/tokens and then switch to using Azure AD once you configure all the services in a way that can leverage that capability.

One of the ways of interacting with Azure Storage and leveraging Azure AD is by using managed identities. We'll discuss this in the next part of this chapter.

Using managed identities

When deploying services to Azure, you can utilize a variety of different resources that will eventually interact with each other. You can have a virtual machine hosting an application connecting to a database, data orchestrators interacting with storage services, and many, many other possibilities. When designing such solutions, one often thinks about authentication and authorization mechanisms that will be used to determine what one service can and cannot do when connecting to another one. Most of the time, this can be solved by using concepts such as connection strings, access policies, or an in-built RBAC mechanism. This, however, is not always an ideal way of handling that challenge. In this section, we'll talk more about using managed identities when connecting with Azure Storage to see how they make the whole setup simple.

Definition of managed identity

A managed identity in Azure is a concept for assigning an identity to a service that normally cannot have one. You can think of it as making your resource (such as a virtual machine, database, or queue) a user. Under normal circumstances (i.e., using the default configuration after provisioning a resource), resources in Azure don't have representation in an Azure Active Directory tenant. Of course, you can create a service principal and authenticate using its login and password (or certificate), but that's far from assigning an identity to a resource. Managed identities work differently – they enable your resources to request a token from Azure AD by provisioning a special endpoint to do so.

> **Important note**
> We're not going to dive into the technical implementation of managed identities in Azure. However, if this topic seems interesting to you, take a look at the following link to learn more about the whole concept: `https://learn.microsoft.com/en-us/azure/active-directory/managed-identities-azure-resources/how-managed-identities-work-vm`.

Managed identities can be either system- or user-assigned. Let's describe them for a better understanding.

System-assigned managed identity

A **system-assigned managed identity** is a unique identity that can be assigned to a single resource only. It is created automatically once you enable this kind of identity on a resource. Each identity of this type has a unique identifier that points to its object in the Azure AD tenant.

User-assigned managed identity

A **user-assigned managed identity** is a separate identity that can be assigned to more than a single resource. It's very useful when building an infrastructure that is replicated or multiplied – you can create a managed identity once, give it the necessary permissions, and then assign it to multiple resources so they can have the same roles assigned.

Let's now discuss how managed identities can help us when interacting with Azure Storage.

Incorporating a managed identity into an application

As Azure Storage supports Azure AD authentication, we can simplify an application's setup and improve its security by using a managed identity instead of an access key or shared access token. The standard route of configuring access (using a non-Azure AD approach) would look like the following:

1. Create an Azure Storage instance.

2. Decide how the principal will connect with it from the following options:

    - Assign it a role that allows it to read the access key

    - Generate an SAS token

    - Obtain an access key and share it with the principal

3. Connect with a storage account using one of the configured methods:

    - Use the `--auth-model login` parameter

    - Use the `--sas-token` parameter

    - Use the `--account-key` parameter

Now, let's compare the configuration when a managed identity is used:

1. Create an Azure Storage instance.
2. Configure a **Managed Instance** on a supported resource (such as a virtual machine, Azure App Service, or Azure SQL Database).
3. Assign the principal represented by the managed identity the necessary permissions to access Azure Storage.

The whole setup is much simpler and is easier to manage and control. Remember, however, that not all Azure resources support managed identities; hence, the connection with Azure Storage needs to be performed using either access keys or SAS tokens.

We've talked a little bit about using managed identities in terms of giving access to Azure Storage. We'll now switch our focus to talking about automation options and summarize our current knowledge.

Considering various options for automation

Azure Storage, as a generic solution for building solutions that need scalable and reliable storage, can be easily automated using either native or external tools. In this section, we'll talk about scenarios that could possibly be automated and how to approach this. Let's start with managing data stored in Blob Service.

Automated cleanup of data

One of the biggest challenges when working with data-based infrastructure is providing a way to automatically clean up data that is no longer needed. This is often a requirement in systems that must follow legal requirements regarding how long users' data is stored. In Azure Storage, if you choose to use Blob Storage as your storage service, you can leverage life cycle management, which will help you move files between tiers (hot -> cool -> archive) and delete them after a certain period of inactivity.

SAS token handling

If you decide to use SAS tokens as your authorization mechanism, you'll need to incorporate some kind of service that will automatically generate those tokens based on a given set of rules. This is helpful if you need to generate tokens dynamically (meaning that it's more suited in the case of high-scale scenarios, where the number of generated tokens is too big to be handled manually).

You can generate a token using various different methods:

- Azure CLI (for instance, using the `az storage account generate-sas` command)
- Generating a token on the fly (see `https://learn.microsoft.com/en-us/rest/api/storageservices/create-service-sas`)
- Generating a token programmatically (for instance, using C# – see `https://learn.microsoft.com/en-us/azure/storage/blobs/sas-service-create-dotnet`)

Each of the listed methods can be used to generate the same SAS token. Which one is the best for your scenario depends on your technology stack and individual skills.

Stored access policies

To provide an additional level of security when using SAS tokens, Azure Storage allows you to use a feature called a **stored access policy**. Stored access policies allow you to define a set of permissions and access levels in one place (policy) and then use the policy to generate SAS tokens. The benefit of such an approach is the much easier management of access for different service clients. In such a scenario, instead of defining permissions for tokens individually, you can just select a policy. What's more, using policies will also help you in revoking access, as once a policy is revoked, all the tokens generated by it are revoked as well.

You can use a policy when generating a token as follows:

```
az storage container generate-sas \
   --account-key <account-key> \
   --account-name <account-name> \
   --name <container-name> \
   --policy-name <policy-name>
```

As you can see, instead of providing parameters such as the expiry of a token or permissions, you just pass the name of a policy. Policies themselves are created in a separate step that can be performed using Azure Portal, Azure PowerShell, Azure CLI, or even a REST API.

For more information on how to create a policy using Azure CLI, take a look at this link: `https://learn.microsoft.com/en-us/cli/azure/storage/container/policy?view=azure-cli-latest`.

Rotating access keys

One of the good practices of Azure Storage is to implement a mechanism that will automatically rotate access keys used for the account. It's important to perform this operation on a certain schedule as access keys grant full access to the storage account, and if they leak, they can be used to perform any operation on the data plane.

> **Important note**
> Remember that you can enable authorization using an access key. In such a scenario, there's no need to rotate access keys as they cannot be used to access your instance of Azure Storage.

To rotate a key, there are multiple possibilities:

- Azure Portal
- PowerShell (using `New-AzStorageAccountKey`)
- Azure CLI (using `az storage account keys renew`)

If you have only a couple of keys, building an automated solution may be a little bit of an overkill. However, if you have tens or hundreds of them, the best way to manage your infrastructure is to incorporate simple automation via scripts and the aforementioned commands.

It's also possible to set up an expiration policy for access keys, meaning they can be marked as expired and monitored. You can configure this policy on an account level using the following command:

```
az storage account update \
   --name <storage-account-name> \
   --resource-group <resource-group-name> \
   --key-exp-days <days-to-expire>
```

To monitor whether any of the keys are expired, you could leverage the in-built policy available in Azure. We'll talk more about Azure Policy in *Chapter 12*.

Let's now discuss the last topic of this chapter – the Azure Import/Export service, which is an additional service enabling you to swiftly import or export large volumes of data in Azure.

Using the Azure Import/Export service

When deciding to migrate data to or from Azure, you always need to consider the volume of files you need to import or export. While incoming traffic (inbound) is free in Azure, outbound connectivity is not. This means that transferring large volumes of data from an Azure data center may be a costly operation unless it's planned accordingly.

> **Important note**
> The price for each GB of data downloaded from an Azure data center depends on various factors. See the following documentation for a better understanding of the topic: `https://azure.microsoft.com/en-us/pricing/details/bandwidth/`.

Besides pricing, migrating large volumes of data gives us one more thing to consider – the time needed to complete an operation. If we're talking about transferring hundreds of terabytes or even petabytes, you need to ensure that your network can handle the load in an acceptable time. As you're not always in charge of the network infrastructure outside of your company, it may be better to use another option for data migration. That option in Azure could be Azure Import/Export. Let's explain how it works.

Azure Import/Export technical details

In short, Azure Import/Export works by shipping physical disks from your company to an Azure data center. This may be a little bit surprising, but this approach has the following benefits:

- You don't need an outbound/inbound internet connection to migrate data
- You don't need to worry about throughput
- You don't need to perform an analysis of the data to ensure that it doesn't get corrupted by transferring it over a network

The process of shipping a disk looks like the following:

1. Prepare the hard drives using the Azure Import/Export client tool.
2. Encrypt the disks with BitLocker.
3. Create an import job in the Azure portal.
4. Ship the drive(s) to an Azure data center.
5. Wait for the disks to be configured.
6. Wait for the job to complete the transfer of data to/from Azure Storage.
7. Wait for the disks to be returned.

While this process may look a little bit tricky in terms of delivery time, it may still be a better option than uploading or downloading all the files over a network.

> **Important note**
> The time needed for the disks to arrive at the data center and come back to your company depends on the distance between the physical locations. If you make a shipment within US or European borders, the whole process will probably be much quicker when compared to shipping between continents.

Let's talk now about the requirements of the Azure Import/Export service.

Azure Import/Export requirements

As of now, the Azure Import/Export service requires you to use a Windows machine, which will be used to prepare the disks. This requirement is implied considering the `WAImportExport` tool is used for the preparation process. On the other end (Azure), you can import or export data using general-purpose storage accounts (both V1 and V2) and Blob Storage accounts. Note that for the export part, you're allowed to load Blob Service data only (without files using the Archive tier). Unfortunately, it's impossible to export data stored inside File Service shares.

Regarding the technical requirements for the hardware, you can use both SSD and HDD disks that support SATA II (HDD) or SATA III (HDD, SSD). You cannot use USB disks or disks with USB adaptors.

Preparing disks and configuring the job

As the process of configuring the Azure Import/Export service and shipping the disks can be quite lengthy, we're not going to cover it in this chapter as there are great tutorials in Azure's documentation that cover this topic. You can find them at the following links:

- Blob Storage import: `https://learn.microsoft.com/en-us/azure/import-export/storage-import-export-data-to-blobs?tabs=azure-cli`

- Azure Files import: `https://learn.microsoft.com/en-us/azure/import-export/storage-import-export-data-to-files?tabs=azure-portal-preview`

- Blob Storage export: `https://learn.microsoft.com/en-us/azure/import-export/storage-import-export-data-from-blobs?tabs=azure-portal-preview`

No matter which path you follow, you'll need to perform the following steps:

1. Create a job in Azure Import/Export.
2. Prepare the drives (for the import option).
3. Ship the disks.
4. Verify the data.

Remember that using Azure Import/Export requires using an external company that will transport your data physically. This means that you should always have a backup of the data (in case the disks get lost or stolen) and make sure that the whole process is performed according to your internal procedures (security/compliance).

That's all for *Chapter 11*! Let's summarize what we've learned and see what awaits in *Chapter 12*.

Summary

This chapter was focused on extending your knowledge regarding Azure Storage and refining it based on the topics we covered initially in *Chapters 9* and *10*. We talked about soft delete and versioning of blobs in Blob Storage and discussed in detail how different authorization methods for Azure Storage may work in various scenarios. We also looked at managed identities in the context of Azure Storage, so you can configure services to interact with tables, blobs, or queues using an identity defined in Azure AD. In the remaining parts, we revisited automation options for Azure Storage and importing/exporting data using physical disks that can be shipped to an Azure data center.

Lessons from this chapter will help you work with Azure Storage in advanced scenarios, which include improving the reliability of data stored in the service, improving security, and implementing automation. As Azure Storage is one of the most popular services in Azure, becoming proficient in it will help you become a better Azure administrator.

The next chapter marks the beginning of the last part of the book, called *Governance and Monitoring*. To get started, we'll discuss Azure Policy, which is a feature of Azure Cloud that is helpful in auditing infrastructure rules and enforcing certain configurations.

Part 5: Governance and Monitoring

In *Part 5*, you'll read about more advanced topics related to the administration of Azure infrastructure. This part includes services and features that can help you govern your infrastructure and monitor it on various levels.

This part has the following chapters:

- *Chapter 12, Using Azure Policy*
- *Chapter 13, Azure Monitor and Alerts*
- *Chapter 14, Log Analytics*
- *Chapter 15, Exploring Network Watcher*

12

Using Azure Policy

In the previous chapters, we talked about various Azure services, their capabilities, automation options, and both basic and advanced configuration. We covered a variety of different resources – starting with **Azure Virtual Machines** and **Virtual Network** to **Azure Load Balancer** and **Azure Disks** before reaching **Azure Storage**, **File Service**, and **Blob Storage**. With this chapter, we'll be starting the last part of this book, *Governance and Monitoring*, which will be related in many ways to the topics we covered previously.

Our journey regarding governance and monitoring will begin with Azure Policy – a native feature of Azure that allows you to describe policies and rules guarding the proper configuration of your cloud resources. In this chapter, we'll cover the following topics:

- The basics of Azure Policy

- Deploying policies

- Creating custom policies

- The difference between policies and initiatives

- Discussing various policies by example

Technical requirements

For the exercises in this chapter, you'll need the following:

- The Azure CLI (https://learn.microsoft.com/en-us/cli/azure/install-azure-cli)

- A command line of any kind (either available in your operating system or your favorite one)

The Code in Action video for this book can be viewed at: https://packt.link/GTX9F

The basics of Azure Policy

In this section, we'll describe how Azure Policy works. We'll focus on how it's implemented and linked with **Azure Resource Manager**, what we can configure, and how to ensure that the implemented rules are applied correctly. Let's start by discussing how Azure Policy relates to properties exposed by resources via Azure Resource Manager.

Azure Resource Manager and Azure Policy

As mentioned in *Chapter 2, Basics of Infrastructure-as-Code*, each resource in Azure is described by a set of fields, which are individual for each type of service. For example, let's compare the configuration of a resource group with a storage account. In the following code snippet, we have a description of a resource group:

```
{
    "type": "Microsoft.Resources/resourceGroups",
    "apiVersion": "2022-09-01",
    "name": "<resource-group-name>",
    "location": "<resource-group-location>"
}
```

As you can see, a resource group (represented here as a JSON object, which can be used for deployment using ARM templates) consists of four fields:

- `type`, which defines what kind of resource it is
- `apiVersion`, which describes which version of the underlying API of a resource provider should be used when deploying that resource
- `name`, which is a unique identifier of a resource group inside a subscription
- `location`, which tells Azure Resource Manager to which region that resource should be deployed

For comparison, let's discuss a similar description based on an Azure Storage instance's configuration:

```
{
    "type": "Microsoft.Storage/storageAccounts",
    "apiVersion": "2023-01-01",
    "name": "<storage-account-name>",
    "location": "<storage-account-location>",
    "sku": {
        "name": "Standard_RAGRS",
        "tier": "Standard"
    },
    "kind": "StorageV2",
    "properties": {
```

```
            "accessTier": "Hot"
        }
    }
}
```

As you can see, the Azure Storage definition consists of similar fields as the one presented for the resource group. It contains additional fields as well, which are placed in the `properties` field. Even though both resources are different in terms of full schema, they can be managed via Azure Policy without additional configuration or features.

Now, let's look at the very basic definition of Azure Policy, which would block the deployment of resources that are configured to be deployed outside of the East US 2 region:

```
{
    "properties": {
        "displayName": "Allowed locations",
        "description": "Policy to allow only specific locations",
        "mode": "Indexed",
        "policyRule": {
            "if": {
                "not": {
                    "field": "location",
                    "in": [ "eastus2" ]
                }
            },
            "then": {
                "effect": "deny"
            }
        }
    }
}
```

If you compare the definition of a policy with ARM templates, you'll probably notice some similarities. Azure Policy policies are defined as JSON objects with defined schema and allow you to traverse properties of fields and objects exposed by Azure resources via Azure Resource Manager. In the preceding example, the `policyRule` property defines that if the `location` field is not within an array of allowed locations, then the effect of such a policy is to `deny` such a deployment.

> **Important note**
> A policy that denies applying a change to a resource will be triggered for both create and update operations.

Now, let's learn how a policy can be deployed using the Azure CLI.

Deploying policies

In Azure, when you want to control how deployed resources are configured and managed, you have one option if you want to do that natively – you need to query the Azure Resource Manager API to fetch information about instances of services you're interested in. In smaller environments, this will suffice; however, if you're managing hundreds or thousands of different resources, executing tens of queries every day will become cumbersome and difficult. This is why Azure offers **Azure Policy** – a native way to audit and remediate resources that are not compliant with a set of rules established by you or your organization.

Let's see an example of deploying a policy using the Azure CLI.

Deploying a policy using the Azure CLI

It's possible to deploy a policy using a variety of different methods (the Azure portal, ARM templates, SDKs, and so on), but for this chapter, we'll use the **Azure CLI** since it's the most generic way of performing that operation. Each time you want to deploy a new policy, you can use the following command:

```
az policy assignment create --name '<assignment-name>'\
   --display-name '<display-name>' \
   --scope '<scope>' \
   --policy '<policy-definition-id>'
```

As you can see, you have a couple of parameters that need to be defined before a policy is deployed:

- The name of a policy assignment
- The display name
- The scope (subscription/resource group/management group)
- The identifier of the policy (whether it's a custom or inbuilt policy)

You can easily find the identifier you're looking for by querying all the policies that are available to you:

```
az policy definition list
```

The problem with this command is that it returns all the policies as JSON objects, which makes finding the correct one almost impossible. To simplify this operation, you can use a query:

```
az policy definition list --query "[].{Name:name,
DisplayName:displayName}" -o table
```

As a result, you'll get a table containing only the name of a policy and its display name for the sake of clarity. An individual row of such a table will look like this:

```
0da106f2-4ca3-48e8-bc85-c638fe6aea8f  Function apps should use managed
identity
```

Before you make your first assignment, remember that the display name of a policy and the display name of an assignment are not the same things – while the former allows you to quickly understand the purpose of a policy, the latter is meant for you, as an administrator, to easily understand why an assignment was created.

> **Important note**
>
> If you create or want to use policies that are scoped to a management group, you'll need to use the `--management-group` parameter when listing definitions.

Now that we understand the basics, let's deploy our first policy. For the first deployment, I chose something related to Azure Storage – a policy named *Configure secure transfer of data on a storage account*. This policy ensures that storage accounts accept connections using HTTPS only. The policy is identified by its identifier:

```
/providers/Microsoft.Authorization/policyDefinitions/f81e3117-0093-
4b17-8a60-82363134f0eb
```

Here, the last part of that identifier is the name of a policy we're looking for. Now, to create an assignment, we can use the following command:

```
az policy assignment create \
  --policy f81e3117-0093-4b17-8a60-82363134f0eb \
  --mi-system-assigned \
  --location westeurope \
  --scope "/subscriptions/<subscription-id>/resourceGroups/<resource-
group-name>"
```

The example for the policy assignment requires some explanation before we go any further. As you can see, we're providing the last part of the identifier of a policy as the policy used for assignment. What's more, we're using the `--mi-system-assigned` parameter here – this is required because the policy defines a *modify* effect, which requires a principal to be assigned to make sure the policy can modify resources.

> **Important note**
>
> You don't need to check the policy's definition to learn what kind of effect is defined inside it. If you try to create a policy assignment without assigning a managed identity, Azure will return an error stating that an identity is needed because of the type of effect defined (in our scenario, this is modify).

We're also defining a location (this is needed for deployment as assignments are the same resources as any other instance of a service in Azure). In the end, we're defining a scope – a container for which a policy is applicable.

After running the preceding command, let's look at how we can verify if it has any effect or not:

```
az policy assignment non-compliance-message list \
  -n <policy-assignment-name> \
  --scope <scope>
```

Using this command, you can list all the messages that will be returned by policies that have been assigned for the given scope, assuming there are some irregularities in your resources. If the policies within the scope consider your resources as compliant, the command will return no response. For example, here's the result of an assignment in my resource group that contains a single storage account:

Figure 12.1 – The result of assigning a policy at the resource group level

As you can see, my storage account is considered compliant. This can happen for two reasons:

- The resource itself was compliant from the very beginning with the rules defined by the policy
- The policy applied the *modify* effect and aligned the resource so that it's compliant with the defined rules

To understand how policies in Azure work, let's quickly discuss when policies are evaluated. This will be helpful when you build policy-based solutions since policy evaluation is never immediate.

Evaluating a policy

Policies in Azure are not evaluated constantly. This means that there's always a time before a policy enforces defined rules. There are a couple of different triggers that start evaluating a policy – some of which may be a little bit tricky to understand:

- When a policy is assigned to a new scope, the evaluation will begin within 5 minutes. Note that it's not guaranteed that you'll get the result within that time frame – the outcome depends on the scale of the resources that the policy needs to scan.

- When the policy is updated for the given scope (this trigger follows the same rules as the one we apply when a policy is just assigned).

- When you deploy or update a resource within the assignment scope (this triggers a scan of that individual resource, which should be completed within 15 minutes).

- When you move a subscription within a management group structure.

- Standard evaluation is performed once every 24 hours.

- When you perform an on-demand scan.

As you can see, it's not always guaranteed that you'll get the results of an Azure Policy scan immediately when a change is made. This is why this service is great for standard governance and basic monitoring of resources, but for more sophisticated scenarios, you may need to either use a third-party tool or build a custom solution based on, for instance, Azure Event Grid.

Now, let's see the effect of a policy that detects that a resource was changed and is no longer compliant with the defined rules.

Reading Azure Policy activity logs

Each time a policy applies a change to your resources, the operation will be noted in the activity log available for each Azure resource. An event generated by Azure Policy may look like this:

```
"properties": {
        "policies": "[{\"policyDefinitionId\":\"/providers/Microsoft.
Authorization/policyDefinitions/f81e3117-0093-4b17-8a60-82363134f0eb\"
,\"policyDefinitionName\":\"f81e3117-0093-4b17-8a60-82363134f0eb\",\"p
olicyDefinitionDisplayName\":\"Configure secure transfer of data on a
storage account
\",\"policyDefinitionEffect\":\"Modify\",\"policyAssignmentId\":\
"/subscriptions/…/resourceGroups/aach11/providers/Microsoft.
Authorization/policyAssignments/
ZOnOpmtwSmGdtALcIHjH4g\",\"policyAssignmentName\":\
"ZOnOpmtwSmGdtALcIHjH4g\",\"policyAssignmentScope\":\
"/subscriptions/…/resourceGroups/
aach11\",\"policyExemptionIds\":[]}]",
        "fields": "[{\"operation\":\"AddOrReplace\",\
"field\":\"Microsoft.Storage/storageAccounts/
supportsHttpsTrafficOnly\",\"condition\":\
"[greaterOrEquals(requestContext().apiVersion, '2019-04-01')]\"}]",
        "eventCategory": "Policy",
        "entity": "/subscriptions/…/resourceGroups/…/providers/
Microsoft.Storage/storageAccounts/…",
        "message": "Microsoft.Authorization/policies/modify/action",
}
```

I removed some fields for clarity and to focus on the most important part of the event. As you can see, it contains information about the policy that triggered it, what field was changed, and which storage account was affected. As the policy focuses on modifying if an account is available via HTTPS only, we can see that the property being changed is named `supportsHttpsTrafficOnly`. To learn about the available fields and their values, look at the Azure Resource Manager reference for Azure resources: `https://learn.microsoft.com/en-us/azure/templates/`.

> **Important note**
>
> In *Chapter 2*, we talked about **Infrastructure as Code** (**IaC**) and ARM templates. This is why you, as an Azure administrator, should have at least a basic understanding of this topic. When working with Azure Policy, lots of concepts and fields are the same things as the ones defined in ARM templates or Bicep files. By learning one thing, you're able to reuse your knowledge across different Azure areas.

Now that we've discussed the basics of deployment of Azure Policy, let's see how a custom policy can be created.

Creating custom policies

Even though you have access to many interesting inbuilt policies in Azure, sometimes, you need to write your very own to cover customized scenarios from your organization. Fortunately, Azure offers a simple way to author a custom policy using a predefined syntax. In this section, we'll focus on writing a basic policy to cover our needs.

Understanding the syntax

Azure Policy has a pretty simple syntax and is similar to that for ARM templates, which we discussed previously. Here's a code snippet that contains boilerplate code:

```
{
    "properties": {
        "displayName": "<displayName>",
        "description": "<description>",
        "mode": "<mode>",
        "parameters": {
                <parameters>
        },
        "policyRule": {
            "if": {
                <rule>
            },
            "then": {
```

```
                "effect": "<effect>"
            }
        }
    }
}
```

The most important fields for now are mode, parameters, and policyRule. Let's discuss them in detail.

Policy modes

Azure Policy has two modes – all and indexed. The first one is self-explanatory – a policy with such a mode will evaluate all resources, including resource groups and subscriptions. Indexed mode is a special mode that only covers resources and support tags and locations. As such, resources are only a small part of what Azure offers (these resources are mostly child/extension resources of other services), so it's advised to go for all mode all the time.

Policy parameters

Each policy may have a list of parameters that should be used when you're creating an assignment. Parameters are useful when you're customizing your policies or defining different effects, depending on the scope (so you don't need to duplicate definitions just because you want to have a different effect generated by your policy).

A parameter may look like this:

```
"parameters": {
    "allowedSKUs": {
        "type": "array",
        "metadata": {
            "description": "The list of allowed SKUs for storage
account.",
            "displayName": "Allowed SKUs",
        },
        "defaultValue": [ "Standard_LRS" ],
        "allowedValues": [
            "Standard_LRS",
            "Standard_GRS",
            "Standard_RAGRS"
        ]
    }
}
```

With the use of such a parameter, we can limit options when it comes to selecting an available SKU for storage accounts within the policy's assignment scope. Parameters in Azure Policy allow for some additional means of validation and improved user experience by using strong types and match expressions. You can find a detailed explanation at `https://learn.microsoft.com/en-us/azure/governance/policy/concepts/definition-structure#sample-parameters`.

Policy rules

Each policy consists of one or more rules. A rule is an instruction that tells a policy what to do and how to validate a resource. Its basic schema looks like this:

```
{
    "if": {
        <condition>
    },
    "then": {
        "effect": "deny | audit | modify | append | auditIfNotExists |
deployIfNotExists | disabled"
    }
}
```

In short, a policy checks if a condition that's defined within a rule has been satisfied. If it is, then it applies a defined effect, which may either affect the deployment's operation (by denying it), alter a resource (`modify`/`append`/`deploy`), or just note the difference (`audit`).

> **Important note**
>
> Using `modify`/`append` effects (called remediation effects) may be difficult in environments managed by IaC tools (especially Terraform). Make sure you understand the impact of such policies on infrastructure managed by other teams before deploying those effects.

Now, let's learn how to combine our findings and build a simple custom policy in Azure.

Building and deploying custom policy

For the sake of this exercise, we'll build a policy that will deny the deployment of Azure Storage accounts that have access via access keys enabled. To get started, we need to find the name of that property in the schema of the service. There are multiple ways to do this, but the easiest way is to find aliases available for the `Microsoft.Storage` provider:

```
az provider show --namespace Microsoft.Storage --expand
"resourceTypes/aliases" --query "resourceTypes[].aliases[].name"
```

As a result, you'll receive many different aliases representing different settings of Azure Storage. In our case, we're interested in the following one:

```
Microsoft.Storage/storageAccounts/allowSharedKeyAccess
```

Now, we can start building a policy.

Defining a rule

We'll start by defining a rule for our policy. We want to deny all the deployments that may have access via a shared (access) key. To do so, we can use the following rule:

```
"if": {
    "allOf": [
        {
            "field": "type",
            "equals": "Microsoft.Storage/storageAccounts"
        },
        {
            "field": "Microsoft.Storage/storageAccounts/
allowSharedKeyAccess ",
            "notEquals": "false"
        }
    ]
},
"then": {
    "effect": "deny"
}
```

To simplify things, we'll skip providing a parameter – you can, however, do that by yourself by changing the value of the effect parameter:

```
"effect": "deny"
```

You can change it to the following syntax:

```
"effect": "[parameters('effectType')]"
```

The whole definition of our policy (without a parameter) will look like this:

```
{
    "properties": {
        "displayName": "Deny storage accounts using access keys",
        "description": "Deny storage accounts using access keys.",
        "mode": "all",
        "policyRule": {
```

```
        "if": {
            "allOf": [
                {
                    "field": "type",
                    "equals": "Microsoft.Storage/storageAccounts"
                },
                {
                    "field": "Microsoft.Storage/storageAccounts/
    allowSharedKeyAccess ",
                    "notEquals": "false"
                }
            ]
        },
        "then": {
            "effect": "deny"
        }
    }
}
```

Save it as a file named `custom-policy.json`. In the next section, we'll deploy our policy using the Azure CLI.

Deploying a custom policy

To deploy a custom policy, we need to create a custom definition first. Creating a custom definition using the Azure CLI requires passing parameters, mode, name, description, and rules as separate parameters. To do so, extract the `policyRule` parameter from the last code snippet in the previous section and save it in the `rule.json` file. Then, run the following command in your terminal:

```
az policy definition create -n DenyAccessKeyStorageAccountCustom \
  -m All \
  --rules @rule.json
```

This command will create a new policy definition with `All` mode and use rules defined in the provided `@rule.json` file. From now on, our custom definition can be used in your Azure environment and assigned to appropriate scopes.

> **Important note**
>
> As policies are JSON documents, they can be part of your infrastructure automation. You can push them to any version control system and review and automatically deploy them if needed.

With that, we've talked a lot about policies, their syntax, and deployments. Now, let's enhance our knowledge by discussing the differences between policies and initiatives.

Simplifying the deployment of policies using initiatives

In more advanced scenarios where you consider governance and compliance regarding cloud environments, you'll have to deploy tens of different policies. Some of these will be required by your organization; others may be enforced by external auditors. The problem with such a setup is that it requires lots of manual work or a complex automation system that can deploy those policies in the correct order and at an acceptable time. To overcome that challenge, Azure offers the concept of initiatives, which is several policies grouped as a single unit of deployment. In this section, we'll talk about the pros and cons of this solution.

The idea behind initiatives

Let's consider the following scenario – you have a bunch of policies that relate to Azure Storage. Some of them enforce certain configurations (HTTPS, disable access keys, enforce network rules, and so on), and some are used for auditing. You may also have policies that will remediate some settings. In most cases, such policies will be deployed for each selected scope without much customization. To simplify your work, you may organize those policies as a single group – initiative.

Initiatives have very similar syntax to the policies themselves – the only difference is that instead of defining rules, they define the identifiers of definitions of policies, which are part of an initiative – see `https://learn.microsoft.com/en-us/azure/governance/policy/concepts/initiative-definition-structure` for more information.

When to use initiatives

The value of initiatives depends on the scale of the environment you're working with. As an initiative is another object that needs to be maintained, it doesn't make much sense to start working with Azure Policy by defining initiatives that will never be used more than once. There's no single threshold that will tell you when an initiative is a better choice than assigning several policies at once – common sense should be applied when working with that capability so as not to overcomplicate your environment. However, remember that even in simpler environments, you may leverage initiatives to avoid repeating yourself when you need to deploy the same set of policies across only a few subscriptions or management groups.

> **Important note**
>
> Initiatives also don't make sense if you don't work with similar landing zones or areas. If your Azure environment doesn't share common traits, it's better to craft specialized policies or review each assignment individually. Having too many policies assigned to a given scope may introduce difficulties to development because, at some point, other teams may be blocked by them, even though they work in an area that has different limitations and requirements.

For the last topic of this chapter, we'll cover some examples of policies to see what they can offer to us.

Reviewing example policies

To better understand Azure Policy and its features, let's discuss some examples of policies that are already available to us. This will help you build your own policies if needed and organize your findings from this chapter.

Policy – secrets should not be active for longer than the specified number of days

This policy is related to Azure Key Vault and is meant to be used as a security mechanism to avoid storing secrets that may be valid longer than necessary. It defines the following rule:

```
"policyRule": {
    "if": {
      "allOf": [
        {
          "field": "type",
          "equals": "Microsoft.KeyVault.Data/vaults/secrets"
        },
        {
          "value": "[utcNow()]",
          "greater": "[addDays(if(empty(field('Microsoft.KeyVault.
Data/vaults/secrets/attributes.notBefore')), field('Microsoft.
KeyVault.Data/vaults/secrets/attributes.createdOn'), field('Microsoft.
KeyVault.Data/vaults/secrets/attributes.notBefore')),
parameters('maximumValidityInDays'))]"
        }
      ]
    },
    "then": {
      "effect": "[parameters('effect')]"
    }
}
```

As you can see, it defines quite a sophisticated condition that checks whether the timestamp generated by utcNow(), compared with the timestamp of a secret, is not greater than the number of days passed by the 'maximumValidityInDays' parameter.

Policy – allowed virtual machine size SKUs

This simple policy limits deployment possibilities for the SKUs of Azure Virtual Machines. Its rule is similar to the one we created when building a custom policy:

```
"if": {
    "allOf": [
        {
            "field": "type",
            "equals": "Microsoft.Compute/virtualMachines"
        },
        {
            "not": {
                "field": "Microsoft.Compute/virtualMachines/sku.name",
                "in": "[parameters('listOfAllowedSKUs')]"
            }
        }
    ]
},
"then": {
    "effect": "Deny"
}
}
```

The logic here is simple – the policy denies any deployment that doesn't contain the SKU of a virtual machine and would be included in the array of SKUs passed to the policy.

Policy – assign a built-in user-assigned managed identity to Virtual Machine Scale Sets

This is an advanced policy that creates deployments using ARM templates to automatically assign a user-assigned identity to scale sets within the configured scope. It's a nested policy that checks if the validated resource is a scale set and then checks if there's an identity assigned to it. As its definition is quite large, it would be difficult to enclose it in this book. If you're interested in learning more, look for the following definition identifier in your Azure environment: /providers/Microsoft. Authorization/policyDefinitions/516187d4-ef64-4a1b-ad6b-a7348502976c.

That's all for *Chapter 12*. Let's summarize what we've learned and see what awaits in the next chapter.

Summary

In this chapter, we started talking about governance and compliance in Azure. We discovered Azure Policy – a service that's meant to simplify the management of Azure resources by providing functionality to audit, modify, or deny deployments that do not follow defined rules. We also saw that, besides having a rich catalog of inbuilt policies, Azure offers a way to deploy a custom policy. We talked about the differences between initiatives and policies as well and looked at some examples of policies to better understand their syntax and capabilities.

Becoming fluent with Azure Policy is the key to becoming a better Azure administrator. In practically all cases, when you're tasked with managing an Azure environment, you'll need to use Azure Policy to help you keep cloud resources in line, ensure the compliance of deployed services, and enforce internal rules of your organization without lots of effort.

In the next chapter, we'll talk about Azure Monitor – an umbrella service that can be used to gather logs from other services and build a dashboard for monitoring the usage, health, and performance of deployed Azure resources.

13

Azure Monitor and Alerts

After covering **Azure Policy** in the previous chapter, it's time to see how we can monitor services in Azure and alert people who are responsible for infrastructure if something goes wrong. While it's possible to deploy a custom solution for monitoring using third-party services and hosting them using **Azure Virtual Machines**, using a native service has the advantage of being suited for a particular environment. In our case, that native service will be **Azure Monitor**.

Components, which we're going to cover in this chapter, will help you build an initial setup for monitoring your infrastructure and lay the foundation for more advanced topics, such as alerting and auditing. Some of the concepts we'll describe (such as diagnostic settings) are also connected to Azure Policy, which we discussed in the previous chapter.

In this chapter, we'll cover a couple of different topics:

- An overview of Azure Monitor
- Understanding logs
- Understanding data types and events
- Querying the activity log
- Implementing custom alerts for Azure infrastructure

Technical requirements

For the exercises in this chapter, you'll need the following:

- The Azure CLI (`https://learn.microsoft.com/en-us/cli/azure/install-azure-cli`)
- A command line of any kind (either available in your operating system or your favorite one)

The Code in Action video for this book can be viewed at: `https://packt.link/GTX9F`

Chapter materials

To get a better understanding of the concepts presented in this chapter, you may want to check out the following articles:

- https://learn.microsoft.com/en-us/azure/azure-monitor/visualize/workbooks-time

- https://learn.microsoft.com/en-us/azure/data-explorer/kusto/query/tutorials/learn-common-operators

These articles will help you get the most out of the basics needed to operate on logs in a Log Analytics workspace.

Getting started – an overview of Azure Monitor

Azure Monitor is a special kind of resource in Azure that doesn't need to be deployed. In other words, it's enabled from when you start creating your first subscription and access your Azure environment. By default, Azure Monitor doesn't incur any costs – it's just there to help you aggregate data about your resources and serve basic information about their performance, reliability, and availability. If you want to dive deeper into the service and leverage more advanced scenarios, Azure Monitor offers a bunch of additional capabilities, such as visualization and analysis tools or even **AI-enhanced operations** (**AIOps**).

> **Important note**
> Under the hood, Azure Monitor is a time series database for storing numeric data from resources deployed within your subscriptions. Depending on the complexity of your scenario, it may either stay like this or be extended with additional capabilities.

In this part of this chapter, we'll discuss the available functionalities of Azure Monitor and their use cases – starting with possible monitoring scenarios.

Monitoring scenarios

When using Azure Monitor, you can think about building a monitoring platform from many different workloads available in the cloud. Here are some examples:

- Native Azure resources

- Applications

- IaaS (virtual machines, network, and so on)

- Cloud-native solutions (containers, managed Kubernetes clusters, and so on)

Depending on your needs, you could configure Azure Monitor to work with different workloads and collect different data via its extensions and plugins.

> **Important note**
>
> Azure Monitor acts as an umbrella resource for all your monitoring/log collection activities. This means that you don't configure it directly to work with a particular workload. Instead, you enable various features or leverage additional resources that integrate with Azure Monitor to cover the whole landscape of your services.

Now, let's talk about monitoring native Azure resources, which is the most basic scenario for most cloud environments.

Monitoring native Azure resources

Most resources in Azure allow you to collect data called *metrics*. **Metrics** are different categories of data that are published by an instance of an Azure service. This means that different services publish different data. For example, a virtual machine may publish a metric called *CPU time*, while its disk will publish a *data writes/sec* metric instead.

Metrics are available from the very start for each deployed instance of a service and allow you to understand its basic performance. However, these metrics don't cover operations performed at the resource level. To check who (or what) made a change to a resource, you need to check the **activity log**, which will be described in detail later in this chapter in the *Querying the activity log* section.

As some Azure resources may host your applications, it may be beneficial to see what Azure Monitor has to offer in that area. We'll discuss this in the next section.

Monitoring applications

In Azure, it's possible to monitor applications using **Azure Application Insights**. Application Insights is a service that is tightly coupled with Azure Monitor. Thanks to this, you can simplify the process of building dashboards and querying data from your applications – everything is available in the same place, so people responsible for monitoring and maintenance can quickly query data to find the root cause of an issue.

Application Insights is deployed as a separate service, meaning you need to provision at least one instance of it to allow your applications to log data.

> **Important note**
>
> Most architectures in Azure assume that there's one instance of Application Insights per application. This allows you to easily control spending and leverage the free tier for data ingestion, which is granted for each Application Insights instance each month.

Application Insights offer additional capabilities that are not available in Azure Monitor:

- Live Metrics

- Integration with Azure DevOps and GitHub

- Smart detection, which detects anomalies in the data

- Application Map

- Aggregated views for performance and dependency tracking

There's one more unique trait of Application Insights – to connect with it, you need to obtain a secret called an instrumentation key. **Instrumentation keys** are values that are generated individually for each instance of that service, meaning most of the time, each application will log data to a different Application Insights resource.

With that, we've mostly talked about **PaaS** services and applications deployed in Azure. Let's see what Azure Monitor has to offer when **IaaS** is considered.

Monitoring IaaS and networks

IaaS components such as Azure Virtual Machines, Load Balancer, and virtual networks are much more difficult to monitor than managed cloud resources or applications as data published by them is much more difficult to understand. This comes from the fact that those resources publish lots of low-level data, such as **performance counters**, **traffic logs**, and **event traces**, so to understand the big picture, you need to understand some tiny details presented by them.

In terms of Azure Virtual Machines, Azure Monitor offers a dedicated agent that you need to install on each machine and configure. Those agents are used to collect and send data to Azure Monitor for further analysis. Based on that data, you may set up alerts that will be triggered when your virtual machines start working improperly.

For networks, Azure Monitor can be configured with additional services called **Network Watcher** and **Network Insights**. Both services will be described in detail in the last chapter of this book.

Monitoring cloud-native solutions

With the rise of cloud-native solutions and products in recent years, it's important to find a monitoring solution for them that is not only reliable but also plays well with their configuration and features. While the cloud-native toolset is extremely diversified, containing both free and paid products, Azure offers additional capabilities for Azure Monitor that can be used to monitor services such as Kubernetes and containers using managed Prometheus and Grafana. Besides those services, you can also leverage container insights available in Azure Monitor, which give you basic information about your clusters and workloads running on them.

You should now have a basic understanding of what Azure Monitor is and its main features. Let's dive deeper into this topic by discussing different types of logs.

Understanding logs in Azure Monitor

Azure Monitor can collect data from different services in different formats. Each service can publish data as a metric, log, event, or change. Depending on the type of published data, a different kind of log is leveraged to present aggregated results. In this section, we'll discuss the differences between different types of logs and what kind of data can be found inside them. We'll start by learning about platform logs.

Platform logs

Platform logs is a generic name for more detailed logs generated by Azure services. Depending on the considered layer (the place where the log is generated), we can talk about the following platform logs:

- Resource logs (generated at the resource level)
- Activity logs (generated at the subscription level)
- Microsoft Entra ID logs (generated at the tenant level)

If you look closely at the described platform logs, you'll see that platform logs are linked to similar scopes as **Azure Resource Manager** deployments. While activity logs and **Microsoft Entra ID logs** are just inbuilt features of the layers, resource logs require additional configuration. We'll discuss this in the *Resource logs* section in a moment.

Activity logs

Activity logs are logs generated at the subscription level and are presented for an individual resource. Each Azure resource allows you to query their activity logs – the only difference will be the scope for such a query (you can check the activity logs at the resource, resource group, or subscription level). Activity logs are mostly meant for storing events related to Azure Resource Manager changes (such as creating, modifying, or removing a resource).

As activity logs often store important information about changes that are performed at the resource level, it's worth considering exporting that log to Azure Event Hub or Azure Storage. The former may be used as a data pipeline for processing entries available in the logs when they're created. The latter could be a great idea for storing logs for auditing purposes.

> **Important note**
> You cannot modify entries that are added by Azure to an activity log. What's more, those entries will be removed after 90 days.

Now, let's talk about the last type of log – resource logs, which are the most important logs from an individual resource point of view.

Resource logs

Resource logs are special kinds of platform logs that are scoped to a single resource and give you insights into their performance and reliability. The difference between resource logs and activity logs is that resource logs are not collected by default. You need to explicitly enable them by switching on diagnostic settings. Let's discuss this topic in detail.

Diagnostic settings are an additional capability of most Azure resources that allow you to collect diagnostic data published by a service and send it to a Log Analytics workspace (or other supported destinations, such as a storage account or Azure Event Hub). Diagnostic settings may be enforced by Azure Policy, as described in *Chapter 12*, which is a good idea for an initial set of policies enabled in your environment.

On the other hand, remember that Azure services may publish lots of diagnostic data, depending on their utilization. With that in mind, make sure that you understand the implications of such behavior. While it may be tempting to enable those logs for each resource deployed in your environment, you need to have a way to utilize them to make that setup work for you.

> **Important note**
>
> Some cloud environments with strict requirements for compliance and security may require Azure resources to have diagnostic settings enabled by default for each deployed resource. This is a tradeoff that needs to be accepted to make sure you're compliant with external regulations.

Let's see how diagnostics settings can be enabled by example. To do that, we'll use Azure Storage and the Azure CLI.

Enabling diagnostics settings

To enable diagnostic settings, we need a resource. Let's create a storage account that we'll use later and reconfigure:

```
az group create -n <resource-group-name> -l <location>
az storage account create -n <storage-account-name> /
  -l <location>
  -g <resource-group-name>
```

After running these commands, you should have a resource group with an empty storage account created inside it. Let's create a Log Analytics workspace so that we can store data:

```
az group create -n <resource-group-name-2> -l <location>
az monitor log-analytics workspace create \
```

```
-g <resource-group-name-2> \
-n <workspace-name>
```

Note that we're using a separate resource group for the workspace – it's a common approach to separate infrastructure logs from the infrastructure itself to simplify management.

> **Important note**
>
> You can use a dedicated resource group (or even a subscription) to ingest resource logs. In that scenario, you must create a set of Log Analytics workspaces upfront and enforce using them with Azure Policy or IaC.

After a moment, a Log Analytics workspace should be created. Now, we're ready to use it as a destination for resource logs. To do so, we need to configure diagnostic settings for our storage account – first, we must obtain the full identifier of the account:

```
az storage account show -n <storage-account-name> \
  -g <resource-group-name> \
  --query id
```

We also need the identifier of the workspace we created. You can obtain it with a similar command to what we used for the storage account:

```
az monitor log-analytics workspace show -n <storage-account-name> \
  -g <resource-group-name> \
  --query id
```

Then, we can use those identifiers so that we can collect resource logs:

```
az monitor diagnostic-settings create --resource "<resource-id>" \
  --workspace "<workspace-id>" \
  --name <settings-name> \
  --metrics "[{category:Transaction,enabled:true}]"
```

There's one parameter that requires additional explanation: `--metrics`. This parameter tells diagnostic settings which metric should be published to the selected destination. In our case, we're selecting `Transaction`, which is a generic metric that's published at the storage account level. Specific services available for a storage account (such as Blob Storage or File Service) publish additional metrics unique to them. For example, we can enable the diagnostic settings of Blob Storage with the following command:

```
az monitor diagnostic-settings create \
  --resource "<resource-id>/blobServices/default" \
  --workspace "<workspace-id>" \
  --name <settings-name> \
```

```
--metrics "[{category:Transaction,enabled:true}]" \
--logs "[{category:StorageRead,enabled:true}]"
```

Two changes were made here:

- We appended /blobServices/default to indicate that we want to enable diagnostic settings for Blob Storage

- We used the --logs parameter to collect additional information published by the service (in this case, storage reads)

If you want to learn what metrics are published by different services, consult the Azure documentation, which contains detailed information about each of them: https://learn.microsoft.com/en-us/azure/azure-monitor/reference/supported-metrics/metrics-index.

After connecting a storage account with our Log Analytics workspace, we can try to query it for collected data. Let's see how we can do that.

Querying Log Analytics

To query Log Analytics for logs, we need to access the workspace where they're being sent. The easiest way to do that is to go to the Azure portal, find the workspace we created, and select the **Logs** blade from the menu:

Figure 13.1 – Accessing logs in a Log Analytics workspace

When you access the **Logs** view, you'll see a query window, where you can put a query written in a language called **Kusto**.

> **Important note**
> Kusto will be described in more detail in *Chapter 14*. However, if you want to learn more about Kusto right now, take a look at the following article: https://learn.microsoft.com/en-us/azure/data-explorer/kusto/query/.

One of the simplest queries we can write fetches all the logs generated by Blob Storage from our storage account:

```
StorageBlobLogs
| where _ResourceId == "<storage-account-resource-id>"
```

This query consists of two sections:

- The table we're querying from – `StorageBlobLogs`

- The filter – `where _ResourceId == "<storage-account-resource-id>"`

As a result, Log Analytics would return all the logs from the default time range (which is 24 hours). To change this, we can explicitly set it in our query:

```
StorageBlobLogs
| where _ResourceId == "<storage-account-resource-id>"
| where TimeGenerated > ago(1d)
```

As you can see, in our case, this query will fetch data for the storage account with the assumption that data was generated more than 1 day ago.

Kusto is a powerful language that can help you analyze and find important information about your resources and their performance. Unfortunately, we don't have space in this book to cover all the details of that language. To improve your knowledge and understanding of it, look at great tutorials for Kusto available in the *Chapter materials* section at the beginning of this chapter. As we covered all the topics necessary to go further, let's switch our focus to types of data and log events available in Azure Monitor.

Understanding data types and events in Azure Monitor

When you query logs in Azure Monitor (or, specifically, a Log Analytics workspace), you may realize that the logs themselves are presented as objects containing various properties. These properties are later presented as columns containing data represented by different data types. Inside these logs, you may find the following types:

- Strings

- Numbers

- Logical values

- Objects

Depending on the data source, the available columns and types will differ. For example, you can compare collected data to documents from NoSQL databases. Under the hood, data sent to a Log Analytics workspace is stored in separate tables, which may but don't have to share the same schema.

Tables can be created by you at any time – this approach is used when defining custom logs, which we'll describe in the next section.

Using custom logs

When you want to create a new log table for Azure Log Analytics, you need to define whether that table will be **Data Collection Rules (DCR)-** or **Log Analytics agent (MMA)**-based. The difference between those terms is expansive as DCR-based logs require you to define a custom rule on which the data collection process will be based, while MMA-based logs require a sample of the log data and are meant for data collection from Windows and Linux machines. In the next section, we'll define the DCR-based process.

Defining the DCR-based collection process

Each DCR consists of three sections, which define the data collection process:

- **Stream declaration**
- **Destinations**
- **Data flows**

Each of these sections has a purpose; we'll try to understand this in this section. Let's start with stream declarations, which are defined as follows:

```
"streamDeclarations": {
    "Custom-RawData": {
        "columns": [
            {
                "name": "MachineId",
                "type": "string"
            },
            {
                "name": "SoftwareVersion",
                "type": "string"
            },
            {
                "name": "AdditionalContext",
                "type": "string"
            }
        ]
    }
}
```

Our DCR will define a single declaration, where we're introducing three fields – `MachineId`, `SoftwareVersion`, and `AdditionalContext`. These fields may be used in data flows defined as follows:

```
"dataFlows": [
    {
        "streams": [
            "Custom-RawData"
        ],
        "destinations": [
            "LogAnalytics"
        ],
        "transformKql": "source | extend jsonContext = parse_
json(AdditionalContext) | project MachineId, SofwareVersion,
AdditionalContext = jsonContext, ExtendedColumn=tostring(jsonContext.
ProcessedData)",
        "outputStream": "App1-AdditionalDataTable"
    }
]
```

Our data flow will take a defined stream and output it to the `App1-AdditionalDataTable` custom table. Additionally, it will perform a transformation using the Kusto language by projecting fields from a stream and parsing JSON, which would be contained in the `AdditionalContext` field of the incoming stream.

The last part of our DCR defines destinations, which we could define as follows:

```
"destinations": {
    "logAnalytics": [
        {
            "workspaceResourceId": "<log-analytics-workspace-id>",
            "name": "LogAnalytics"
        }
    ]
}
```

Here, the only thing we need to pass is the identifier of our Log Analytics workspace. Once our DCR is ready, we can combine the values as follows:

```
{
    "properties": {
        "dataCollectionEndpointId": "/subscriptions/.../
resourceGroups/.../providers/Microsoft.Insights/
dataCollectionEndpoints/...",
        "streamDeclarations": {
            ...
```

```
        },
        "destinations": {
            . . .
        },
        "dataFlows": [
            . . .
        ]
    }
}
```

Then, you can deploy that DCR using the Azure CLI, the REST API, or Azure PowerShell (see `https://learn.microsoft.com/en-us/azure/azure-monitor/logs/logs-ingestion-api-overview` for reference).

Defining a DCR is an advanced topic, but it's worth remembering as it allows you to customize data that's ingested in Azure Monitor and transform it on the fly. This helps automate log aggregation and monitoring scenarios.

In the next section, you'll learn how to utilize activity logs by creating queries with the Azure CLI.

Querying activity logs

Activity logs help you understand changes and operations made at the resource level so that you can verify the author of any modification or auditing operations. Browsing that log in the Azure portal is handy in simpler scenarios but will become cumbersome when you're trying to find a specific entry that is buried among similar logged items. In this section, we'll learn how to query the activity log using the Azure CLI, which will simplify your day-to-day activities. Let's see some examples to get a better understanding of this topic.

Using the Azure CLI to query activity logs

To query an activity log in the Azure CLI, we'll use the following group of commands:

```
az monitor activity-log list
```

The log can be queried by scoping results to either a resource group or resource identifier. The latter is useful if you want to further limit results returned by the command. For example, if you'd like to see logs for a resource group for the last 24 hours, you could use the following command:

```
az monitor activity-log list \
    -g <resource-group-name> \
    --start-time <start-time> \
    --offset 1d
```

If you want to specify the date only, you should use the following syntax:

```
az monitor activity-log list \
  -g <resource-group-name> \
  --start-time "yyyy-mm-dd" \
  --offset 1d
```

For the date and time, we need to add one more part to the parameter value:

```
az monitor activity-log list \
  -g <resource-group-name> \
  --start-time "yyyy-mm-dd hh:mm:ss.xxxxx" \
  --offset 1d
```

Note that the --offset part of the command will work differently in conjunction with the --start-time and --end-time parameters. In our example, the offset will cause the query to search for entries within the following range:

```
start-time <= timestamp_of_log_entry <= start-time + offset
```

This allows us to search for logs *from* a certain point in time. To search for logs *up to* that point, we need to use the --end-time parameter:

```
az monitor activity-log list \
  -g <resource-group-name> \
  --end-time "yyyy-mm-dd hh:mm:ss.xxxxx" \
  --offset 1d
```

The result of running these commands will differ based on the resource group that's selected for the query target.

> **Important note**
> The selected offset can be changed on your side if your resource group doesn't contain entries generated within the last 24 hours.

The entries in activity logs may be a little bit difficult to read in a terminal as they are presented as JSON objects containing lots of information. While we could use the –query parameter to limit returned data, that approach is useful for ad hoc queries rather than detailed log investigations. To have a better view, we could format the result as **Tab Separated Values** (**TSV**) and then import them to a tool that can understand the format (such as Excel):

```
az monitor activity-log list
  -g <resource-group-name> \
  --end-time "yyyy-mm-dd hh:mm:ss.xxxxx" \
```

```
--offset 1d \
-o tsv > output.tsv
```

This approach is much easier to handle if you want to filter data or create a report for further investigation.

Now, let's learn how to find events that are correlated with each other.

Using the Azure CLI to find correlated events

Some events reported in activity logs are considered **correlated events**. This means that they share a common context that can be used to see how they relate to each other. Each event logged in the activity log possesses a `correlationId` field, which may relate to other events. To list all the correlation IDs, you could use the following command:

```
az monitor activity-log list \
  -g <resource-group-name> \
  --end-time "yyyy-mm-dd hh:mm:ss.xxxxx" \
  --offset 1d
  --query [].correlationId
```

You should receive a list of identifiers, which could look like this:

```
[
    "f2d0ed95-09f4-4727-baa5-171f6f2d0f89",
    "f2d0ed95-09f4-4727-baa5-171f6f2d0f89",
    "d7551f07-79f3-44e2-b14d-4c22a29a2dec",
    "d7551f07-79f3-44e2-b14d-4c22a29a2dec",
    "79d6738f-fd22-4626-a14f-70bcb4e765e2",
    "79d6738f-fd22-4626-a14f-70bcb4e765e2",
    "210cdc2d-ed9b-4760-a84c-21°75c41b677",
    "210cdc2d-ed9b-4760-a84c-21°75c41b677",
    "1d0a4a6c-853e-45ea-802d-cb261b781a6c",
    "1d0a4a6c-853e-45ea-802d-cb261b781a6c",
    "f34b460e-833d-443°-a9ae-c2fc3fe64dcd",
    "f34b460e-833d-443°-a9ae-c2fc3fe64dcd",
    "b70fed8f-3d81-4b5e-8ba5-bbb9b8a6e03f",
    "9d617bab-b438-48cd-add0-ff87f0c0031a",
    "9d617bab-b438-48cd-add0-ff87f0c0031a",
    "b760be9e-90e2-4d59-8°29-6ded60da832b",
    "b760be9e-90e2-4d59-8°29-6ded60da832b",
]
```

As you can see, some of those identifiers are duplicated, meaning they were created for the same context, even though they may be completely different events. To check that, let's use the duplicated identifiers to see what data is presented there:

```
az monitor activity-log list \
   -g <resource-group-name> \
   --end-time "yyyy-mm-dd hh:mm:ss.xxxxx" \
   --offset 1d
   --correlation-id <correlation-id>
   --query [].properties
```

The preceding command will return the properties of each event, which may look like this:

```
{
    "entity": "/subscriptions/.../resourceGroups/.../providers/Microsoft.
Storage/storageAccounts/.../blobServices/default/providers/Microsoft.
Insights/diagnosticSettings/...",
    "eventCategory": "Administrative",
    "hierarchy": "...",
    "message": "Microsoft.Insights/diagnosticSettings/write",
    "serviceRequestId": null,
    "statusCode": "OK"
}
```

Of course, the properties of your event (or rather their values) may be different in your case – it all depends on the kind of event reported to the activity log. However, those properties share some common traits – they describe what kind of event was reported (via category and message properties) and for what entity (resource) that event was generated.

You can play with the command and queries on your own to see what kind of data you can obtain from the activity log. Remember that this log contains items that are reported for ARM-related operations only. This means that they won't contain things such as performance counters or custom logs generated by your infrastructure or application. However, as we're focusing more on the administrative aspect of working in Azure, the activity log will be one of your main tools in day-to-day tasks.

In the final section, we'll describe how we can work with custom alerts.

Implementing custom alerts for Azure infrastructure

Collecting logs is one of the crucial points when it comes to managing Azure infrastructure, but logs alone won't help us when there's an outage or some resources don't work as expected. Of course, logs may help us in finding the root cause, but they're not meant for proactive monitoring of infrastructure. To be notified about anomalies or abnormal behavior of Azure services, we need to implement alerts. Let's see what steps are needed to do that.

Defining an alert

Alerts are part of Azure Monitor and are based on logs reported by services. Each alert consists of three components:

- Scope
- Condition
- Action

Alerts react when a condition is met and perform an action. We'll describe those components in the next few sections.

The scope of an alert

Each alert can be scoped to one of the available scopes:

- Subscription
- Resource group
- Resource

The selected scope will affect the possible conditions that we can define. For example, if you select a subscription or resource group, your condition will be limited to custom log search as those scopes don't provide useful signals that your alert could rely on. However, if you select a specific resource, the condition can be implemented based on the metrics published by a service:

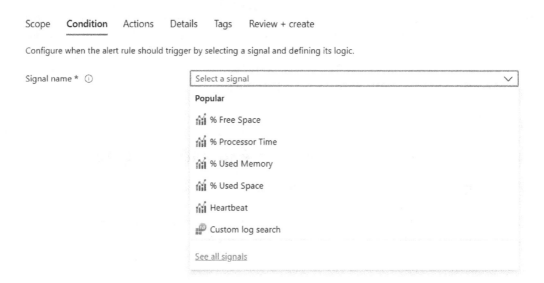

Figure 13.2 – Examples of signals generated by Blob Storage

Let's see how conditions are defined and implemented.

The condition of an alert

A condition is a logical expression that defines when an alert should be triggered. Each condition is based on the alert's selected scope, so which signals you select (metrics that may trigger an alert) will differ. Each condition consists of three factors:

- Logic
- Dimensions
- Evaluation

The logic of an alert tells Azure what kind of threshold needs to be met and how it's compared with the metric's value. For instance, you could create an alert that is triggered if the average utilization of the CPU exceeds a certain value. To make it usable, we need to connect logic with the evaluation factor. Evaluation is based on two parameters:

- How often do we check the metric's value (frequency)?
- What is the lookback period?

If you set the frequency to 1 minute and the lookback to 5 minutes and combine it with some logic that checks the average utilization of the CPU, we'd have an alert rule that raises an alert if the average utilization of the CPU for a resource exceeds the value of X for the last 5 minutes. Such a rule would be evaluated each 1 minute. For reference, check out *Figure 13.3*, which presents the concepts we have just discussed:

Alert logic

ℹ️ We have set the condition configuration automatically based on popular settings for this metric. Please review and make changes as needed.

Threshold ⓘ	◯ Static ⦿ Dynamic
Aggregation type ⓘ	Average ⌄
Operator ⓘ	Greater or Less than ⌄
Threshold Sensitivity ⓘ	Medium ⌄

Split by dimensions

Use dimensions to monitor specific time series and provide context to the fired alert. Dimensions can be either number or string columns. If you select more than one dimension value, each time series that results from the combination will trigger its own alert and will be charged separately. About monitoring multiple time series

Dimension name	Operator	Dimension values	Include all future values	
API name ⌄	= ⌄	GetContainerProperties ⌄	☐	🗑️
		Add custom value		
Select dimension ⌄	= ⌄	0 selected ⌄	☐	
		Add custom value		

When to evaluate

Check every ⓘ	1 minute ⌄
Lookback period ⓘ	5 minutes ⌄

Figure 13.3 – Settings the parameters of an alert's condition in the Azure portal

Additionally, you can split your alert by dimensions. Dimensions introduce an additional level of detail to your alerts (for instance, you could split alerts generated for Azure Storage by adding a dimension of used APIs in the service). Using dimensions is optional but will be helpful if you need additional context for an alert.

Now, let's talk about the last component of an alert – action.

The action of an alert

When an alert is triggered, it will perform an action. To perform an action, the alert needs to have an action group configured. Action groups are additional resources that are deployed in Azure that define what communication channels should be used to communicate with the receiver of an alert. You can either notify members of a certain **RBAC** role or choose a more direct approach, such as an individual email, SMS, Azure mobile app notification, or voice message.

> **Important note**
> Notifying over SMS/voice message may incur additional charges depending on the region you're in.

Besides notifications, action groups define additional actions that may be taken when an alert is triggered. This includes things such as calling Azure Functions, Event Hub, Logic App, or a webhook. The possibilities surrounding customization are extensive, so you'll need to carefully craft your action groups to properly utilize the service.

With that, we learned the basics of the structure of alerts in Azure Monitor. Now, let's see how we can implement a simple alert by ourselves.

Implementing an alert

To create an alert, we need an action group. We can create one with the following command:

```
az monitor action-group create -n <action-group-name> /
  -g <resource-group-name> /
  -l global
  -a email <name> <email-address>
```

The most important part of this command is the action represented by the -a parameter. You will need to pass the email and the name of a user receiving an alert as values. Once an action group has been created, we can create the alert's condition:

```
az monitor metrics alert condition create -t static \
  --aggregation Average \
  --metric "CPU Percentage" \
  --op GreaterThan \
  --threshold 80
```

This command creates a condition that can be used as input for our last command. In my case, I got the following result:

```
"avg 'CPU Percentage' > 80.0"
```

Now, let's perform the last step, which will create an alert:

```
az monitor metrics alert create --name <alert-name> \
  -g <resource-group-name> \
  --scopes <resource-id> \
  --action <action-group-id> \
  --condition "avg 'CPU Percentage' > 80.0"
```

In our case, this alert would be suitable for Azure Virtual Machines as we built a condition related to CPU utilization. Of course, it's possible to build conditions for any resource you're using – to do that, you need to learn about the available metrics. Take a look at the following article to learn about the metrics that are generated by resources in Azure: `https://learn.microsoft.com/en-us/azure/azure-monitor/reference/supported-metrics/metrics-index`.

That's all for *Chapter 13*! Let's wrap up what we've learned and see what awaits in the next chapter.

Summary

Chapter 13 was meant to introduce you to the topic of Azure Monitor and its basic capabilities. We talked about the different kinds of logs that are available, the different types of services that integrate with Azure Monitor, and the methods for triggering an alert. The features that are available in Azure Monitor are not limited to the topics we covered here – it offers much more advanced uses, including methods for visualizing data and AIOps, which can simplify how logs are managed and automate your work.

Understanding how logs are stored and processed in Azure is important from the perspective of the Azure administrator because, eventually, your system will have to generate data, and you will have to analyze it. Having a reliable monitoring solution is critical for production environments where finding a root cause quickly can stop your organization from losing money.

In the next chapter, we'll cover Azure Log Analytics in more detail, which is one of the main components of Azure Monitor.

14

Azure Log Analytics

Azure Log Analytics, being one of the most important components of **Azure Monitor**, allows you to run queries against logs stored in Azure Monitor's datastore. While it's not an independent service, it's still worth diving deeper into, as many services and features allow you to integrate logs with this component. Azure Log Analytics is also one of the key elements of monitoring Azure infrastructure as it centralizes queries, alerts, and data.

In this chapter, we'll extend your knowledge of Log Analytics by discussing details of workspaces, queries, and results visualization. The information contained in the upcoming sections will help you elevate your monitoring solutions in Azure so they provide more detailed, useful information.

In this chapter, we'll cover a couple of different topics, including the following:

- Getting started – an overview of Azure Log Analytics
- Using workspaces
- Querying data
- Visualizing results

Technical requirements

For the exercises in this chapter, you'll need the following:

- The Azure CLI (`https://learn.microsoft.com/en-us/cli/azure/install-azure-cli`)
- A command line of any kind (either the one available in your operating system or your favorite one)

The Code in Action video for this book can be viewed at: `https://packt.link/GTX9F`

Getting started – an overview of Azure Log Analytics

As mentioned at the beginning of this chapter, Azure Log Analytics is a tool that you can use to run queries against data stored in Azure Monitor. While it's not the only thing that it provides, you can consider its ability to query data as its main use case. Log Analytics is a service that you don't deploy personally – however, there are additional components, such as workspaces that may be managed by you (we'll talk about them in the next section of this chapter named *Using workspaces*). Let's start by discussing both basic and more advanced topics related to Log Analytics.

Use cases for Azure Log Analytics

In general, when you collect logs using Azure Monitor, they're saved inside the internal datastore of the Azure Monitor service and can be used when needed. These logs can be leveraged in various scenarios – for instance, when creating an alert rule, you may query the data stored in Azure Monitor to introduce a customized alert based on a non-standard rule. It's possible to craft such rules inside your script (for example, **Azure Bicep** files or **Azure CLI** commands), but in general, it's much easier to test them beforehand. Azure Log Analytics is exactly what you need. You can use it to test and validate your queries before incorporating them into more sophisticated parts of your system.

Keeping in mind what we've just discussed, use cases for Azure Log Analytics could include the following:

- Testing queries
- Validating queries
- Visualizing results of queries
- Debugging
- Statistical analysis

As you can see, all these use cases seem to be related to queries. We'll cover this topic in one of the next sections of this chapter called *Querying data*.

Let's now discuss the structure of Azure Log Analytics to get a better understanding of its infrastructure.

Structure of Azure Log Analytics

Azure Log Analytics is a service that doesn't have a standard structure consisting of instances or nodes. Instead, it's structured based on two main components:

- **Workspaces**
- **Clusters**

Workspaces are standard components used by most Azure users on a daily basis. They provide the capability to integrate with other Azure services to collect logs generated by infrastructure components and native Azure resources. A cluster, however, is an advanced concept that grants you additional capabilities that are unavailable to workspaces.

Workspaces can be linked with a cluster to provide an enhanced user experience and additional features that are typically unavailable. These features may include customer-managed keys, availability zones, encryption, and optimizations.

> **Important note**
> Using clusters requires a 500 GB data ingestion commitment per day.

Clusters are helpful if you face challenges related to the scale of your Azure infrastructure. For example, there are scenarios where you need to query the available data in one Log Analytics workspace from another. When using workspaces only, such queries will be slower when compared with clusters due to technical limitations. To overcome such issues, you could use clusters that would speed up the queries you're using.

Let's talk more about workspaces in the next section of this chapter, where we'll cover lots of details related to day-to-day operations when using Azure Log Analytics.

Using workspaces

Azure Log Analytics can be used as it is without provisioning any additional components. In this scenario, you may even be unaware of its existence as it's incorporated into Azure Monitor in quite a seamless way. However, if you'd like to integrate it with other services (for instance, by deploying diagnostics settings and sending logs from services to a single place), you may be interested in creating a service called Azure Log Analytics Workspace. Let's see how to use it.

Using Azure Log Analytics Workspace

To start using Azure Log Analytics Workspace, we'll need to create it. Use the following command to deploy it inside your resource group:

```
az group create -l <location> -n <resource-group-name>
az monitor log-analytics workspace create -n <workspace-name> \
  -g <resource-group-name>
```

Once created, a workspace can be used as a data sink for logs generated by other services. To send logs from a service to your workspace, you may use the following Azure CLI command:

```
az monitor diagnostic-settings create --resource <resource-id> \
  -n <settings-name> \
  --workspace <log-analytics-workspace-id> \
  --logs <logs-to-send>
  --metrics <metrics-to-send>
```

For more information, see *Chapter 13*, where we discussed diagnostic settings in detail. In the meantime, we'll talk about individual features of workspaces, starting with **capping**.

Workspace capping

Each workspace has a feature called capping. Capping is used to limit data ingested by a workspace and can be leveraged in scenarios where you want to limit charges incurred by Azure on your cloud services.

> **Important note**
> Each workspace deployed has a free 5 GB tier for ingested data. The free tier is refreshed each month.

To set a cap, you may use the `--quota` parameter when creating a workspace. It accepts a value indicating how many gigabytes of data you'd like to store daily. If you don't want to set a cap, just set its value to `-1`.

The same argument can be used when updating a workspace. For example, let's assume we created a workspace the same way as previously:

```
az monitor log-analytics workspace create -n <workspace-name> \
  -g <resource-group-name>
```

The preceding command would indicate that there's no cap for the workspace. Now, to set a cap of 5 GB (so we'd never exceed the free tier), you could use the following command:

```
az monitor log-analytics workspace update -n <workspace-name> \
  -g <resource-group-name>
  --quota 0.1666
```

However, remember that setting a cap will block the ingestion of new data into your workspace. It could cause unexpected side effects in production environments, and that's why it's always better to properly structure the log's schema or refine it before storing it in Log Analytics.

> **Important note**
> The reason why the quota is set as `0.1666` in the preceding command block is to avoid exceeding the 5 GB of monthly data allowed in the free tier. As 30 (days) * 0.1666 will give you 4.998 GB, it provides a safe limit for that scenario.

Let's now talk about data retention available in Log Analytics.

Data retention

Data retention is a process of preserving a certain amount of data for a given period. In other words, it allows you to configure how long data will be stored. In Azure Log Analytics, it's possible to configure this feature using the `--retention-time` parameter. For example, if you'd like to store logs for 90 days, you could update your workspace using the following command:

```
az monitor log-analytics workspace update -n <workspace-name> \
  -g <resource-group-name>
  --retention-time 90
```

Of course, the same parameter can be used when creating a workspace. Regarding the value of the parameter, the allowed values depend on the selected pricing plan. However, the maximum period during which you can store data at no charge is 90 days (assuming you enabled Microsoft Sentinel for a workspace; otherwise, it's 31 days).

Before we go further, let's talk for a moment about the aforementioned Sentinel solution. Microsoft Sentinel is a product offering you both **security information and event management** (**SIEM**) and **security orchestration, automation, and response** (**SOAR**). In short, it's a product that you can integrate with your data sources (such as event logs and audit events) to monitor operations across your ecosystem and detect threats. For instance, you could integrate it with Microsoft Entra ID in order to collect data such as sign-ins to understand the behavior of your users and principals.

You can read more about getting started with Microsoft Sentinel and how it leverages Azure Log Analytics here: `https://learn.microsoft.com/en-us/azure/sentinel/quickstart-onboard`.

If you want to store data for a longer time, it may be worth considering using the archive feature, which allows you to keep data at five times a lower cost per gigabyte per month. The interesting thing with Azure Log Analytics is the possibility to define different retention periods for both the workspace and individual tables. This works by defining a default log retention for the whole workspace (meaning all the tables will share the same value) and then redefining it for an individual table. You can do this using Azure CLI, like in the following:

```
az monitor log-analytics workspace table update \
  --subscription <subscription-id> \
  --resource-group <resource-group-name> \
  --workspace-name <workspace-name> \
  --name AzureMetrics \
  --retention-time 30 \
  --total-retention-time 730
```

There are also data types in Log Analytics that keep data for up to 90 days at no charge. This includes tables from Applications Insights as well. What you need to remember here is the fact that while they have the default retention period of 90 days, when you configure retention for the workspace exceeding that timeframe, the new value will affect those tables as well.

> **Important note**
> Currently, Azure Log Analytics doesn't support retaining data for more than two years. You can prolong that timespan by using the archive feature, which extends it up to seven years.

Let's now talk about network access to workspaces.

Public access to workspaces

As workspaces may contain data that is sensitive to your organization, you should consider disabling public access to them. If public access is disabled, the only way to query data is to leverage a component called **Azure Monitor Private Link Scope (AMPLS)**.

For more information, take a look at the following article: `https://learn.microsoft.com/en-us/azure/azure-monitor/logs/private-link-security`.

In short, when AMPLS is enabled, you no longer access the infrastructure of Azure Monitor with its public IP addresses. Instead, you connect to it securely via your own network (using Express Route or VPN Gateway). As Azure Log Analytics is part of Azure Monitor, you'll automatically obtain access to your workspaces when AMPLS is properly configured.

To disable public access to your workspace, you can use the following command:

```
az monitor log-analytics workspace update -n <workspace-name> \
  -g <resource-group-name>
  --query-access Disabled
```

The same can be configured for data ingestion. For now, we could secure our workspace so it's not possible to query its logs using public endpoints. Public clients, however, could still send data to it. To avoid this, we could disable ingestion from public sources as well:

```
az monitor log-analytics workspace update -n <workspace-name> \
  -g <resource-group-name>
  --ingestion-access Disabled
```

With both of these options, you could enclose your workspaces within a secure environment and have better control over their access.

As we've discussed some of the low-level features of Log Analytics workspaces, let's switch our focus to ways of querying stored data.

Querying data

Being able to query data stored within your monitoring solution is one of the most important scenarios that you could leverage. In Azure Monitor (and specifically in Log Analytics workspaces), queries are written in a language called **Kusto**. This language may look like the syntax of SQL but is crafted specifically to integrate with data volumes and structure supported by Azure Monitor. Let's start learning it by discussing its basic syntax.

The basic syntax of Kusto

Each query written in Kusto requires a data source, which will be used to query data. This data source (table) contains data that is already preprocessed and can be queried without additional actions on your side. Let's cover the following example:

```
VeryImportantTable
| where TimeStamp between (datetime(2022-01-01) ..
datetime(2023-12-31))
| sort by ProjectName asc
```

The preceding query can be read as follows:

1.   Select `VeryImportantTable` as the data source.

2.   Filter the data using the `TimeStamp` column – include records between a certain time range.

3.   Sort the result using the `ProjectName` column.

The query contains one more component that we didn't mention, called *pipe*. A pipe is represented by the | character and allows you to streamline data from one function to another. To understand it better, let's check one more example:

```
VeryImportantTable
| where TimeStamp between (datetime(2022-01-01) ..
datetime(2023-12-31))
| take 10
| project ProjectName, MachineID, EventType
```

This example introduces a slightly different result:

1.   Start by filtering out records outside of the given time range.

2.   Limit the result of filtering to the first `10` records.

3.   Select three columns as a result.

Depending on your use case, you may try out different functions to modify the result.

Let's now talk about common operators that can be used in your queries.

Common operators in Kusto

Kusto allows you to use a variety of common operators that can be used in queries to count, limit, or filter data. In this section, we'll focus on describing all of them as they are the most popular functions used in many queries. We'll start with the operator named **count**.

Count operator

Count allows you to find the number of records that satisfy your query. This operator is used at the end of a query to give you an exact number. You can use it as follows:

```
VeryImportantTable
| count
```

Count can also be used as an aggregation function, like in the following:

```
VeryImportantTable
| summarize Count=count() by ProjectName
```

In the preceding example, you'd get a result where the result data is grouped by a ProjectName column.

The next operator we'll discuss is named **take**.

Take operator

The take operator can be used to take a sample of records to be used as input for your query. As there's no guarantee of which records are returned when take is used, use it with caution and don't expect repeatable results when you apply this operator to your query. take can sometimes be mistakenly used instead of the limit operator, but their behavior is the same if result records are ordered.

You can use take as follows:

```
VeryImportantTable
| take 10
```

The preceding query would return a random 10 records from the selected table. However, we can add sorting, like in the following:

```
VeryImportantTable
| sort by ProjectName asc
| take 10
```

The query will return the first 10 records returned instead of random ones.

Let's now talk about selecting a subset of columns.

Project operator

The **project** operator is useful when you want to limit the columns that are returned by your query. If you don't use it, Kusto will return all the columns available for your records. The use of this operator is straightforward:

```
VeryImportantTable
| project ProjectName, MachineID
```

If you don't like the names of your columns, you can rename them, like in the following snippet:

```
VeryImportantTable
| project InternalProjectName = ProjectName, MachineIdentifier =
MachineID
```

When such a query is run, it'll return your custom names for the renamed columns instead of the ones defined for the table schema.

Let's now see how to list unique values in Kusto.

Distinct operator

To return unique values only in Kusto, you can use an operator called **distinct**. Its syntax looks like the following:

```
VeryImportantTable
| distinct ProjectName
```

When this operator is used, it'll return the values of the `ProjectName` column that are unique. You may treat it as a special-purpose `project` operator, as it also limits which columns are returned. However, the `distinct` operator cannot be used for filtering records. To do so, we need to use another operator that's described in the next section.

Where operator

To filter results, you'll need to use the `where` operator. It allows you to compare columns and values and select records that satisfy your search criteria. Use it as follows:

```
VeryImportantTable
| where ProjectName == "Azure Administrator" and MachineID == "AzAdm"
```

When using the `where` operator, you can combine conditions by using the `and`/`or` operators.

> **Important note**
>
> Like SQL, Kusto will return `false` as a result of the comparison of a non-null value to a null value. There are special functions such as `isnull()` and `isempty()` that are prepared to handle nulls in filtering scenarios.

When writing filters with the `where` operator, it's worth remembering the need for clarity in a query. See the following example:

```
VeryImportantTable
| where ProjectName == "AzureAdministrator"
    and MachineID == "AzAdmin"
    and Timestamp > ago(1d)
    and ResourceType == "Microsoft.Storage"
```

It is much easier to read when compared with the following example:

```
VeryImportantTable
| where ProjectName = "AzureAdministrator" and MachineID ==
"AzAdmin"    and Timestamp > ago(1d) and ResourceType == "Microsoft.
Storage"
```

There's also one special scenario for the `where` operator that allows you to find a word or a string in any column:

```
VeryImportantTable
| where * has "AzAdmin"
```

In this example, we're using `has` as an additional operator, as it allows us to search for a substring in the selected columns. The asterisk used here tells the search engine to look for the value in any column.

Let's now check how we can sort the results in Kusto.

Sort operator

Sorting in Kusto can be performed by specifying a column that will be a reference for sorting. If you don't specify it, by default, Kusto uses ascending order for sorted records:

```
VeryImportantTable
| where * has "AzAdmin"
| sort by ProjectName
```

To sort by more than a single column, just specify it in the same line:

```
VeryImportantTable
| where * has "AzAdmin"
| sort by ProjectName, MachineID desc
```

To specify a sorting order, use asc or desc.

> **Important note**
> Remember that sorting may affect result rows when used in combination with operators that limit the number of rows returned (such as top or take).

Let's now talk about **aggregate functions**, which allow you to combine result data in a summary value.

Aggregate functions

When writing queries in Kusto, sometimes you want to group all the data and present it as a summary. This is what aggregate functions are for – you can use them to group, visualize, or calculate results. We'll briefly explain them, starting with the **summarize** function.

Summarize function

Summarize is the most fundamental aggregate function as it allows you to perform aggregations. In short, it groups data together based on the provided aggregate function. Let's check the following example:

```
VeryImportantTable
| summarize TotalProjects = count() by ProjectName
```

The preceding query would return the number of records grouped by the ProjectName column. However, using count() in this scenario would include duplicates of data; hence, to make the result contain unique values, we could use another function:

```
VeryImportantTable
| summarize TotalProjects = dcount() by ProjectName
```

As there are multiple advanced scenarios when using summarize, it's always a good idea to check its documentation, which is available at https://learn.microsoft.com/en-us/azure/data-explorer/kusto/query/summarizeoperator.

Let's now check how data can be grouped into bins.

bin function

Sometimes, when querying data, you want to understand the distribution of values (for instance, time ranges). To do so in Kusto, you may use the bin function:

```
VeryImportantTable
| summarize RecordCount = count() by bin(Timestamp, 8h)
```

The preceding example would return the number of records divided into eight-hour bins. It would tell you how many records were available for that timeframe.

> **Important note**
> When using `summarize`, you may create an output column in the same way as we did when discussing the `project` operator. The preceding query includes the `RecordCount` column, which would be dynamically created when the query is run.

Let's now check functions that allow you to calculate minimum, maximum, and average values for given records.

Minimum, maximum, and average functions

To understand minimum, maximum, and average values for the records within a selected range, you can use the following functions:

```
VeryImportantTable
| summarize
    MinCpuUtilization = min(CpuUtilization),
    MaxCpuUtilization = max(CpuUtilization),
    AvgCpuUtilization = avg(CpuUtilization)
    by MachineID
```

This example would tell you the values of the minimum, maximum, and average CPU utilization of each machine that is available in the queried data.

A good summary of the discussed functions and operators can be found in Kusto's documentation. Take a look at the following link to read it: https://learn.microsoft.com/en-us/azure/data-explorer/kusto/query/kql-quick-reference.

We'll now proceed to the last part of this chapter, where we'll discuss ways to visualize data returned by Kusto queries. Visualization is helpful when you want to visually understand data distribution or include it in your report.

Visualizing results

Kusto supports a couple of different ways to visualize data stored in data tables. We'll look at multiple examples of available functions that you can leverage in your queries. Let's start with a description of the `render` function.

render function

Most visualization activities in Kusto are done using the `render` function. It supports a variety of different chart types that can be selected depending on the shape of your data. The most basic syntax of this function looks like the following:

```
VeryImportantTable
| render <chart-type>
```

We'll start the description with the default visualization type – **table**.

Visualizing as a table

By default, results returned by Kusto queries are presented as tables. If you want to explicitly define this type, you could use the following query:

```
VeryImportantTable
| render table
```

Results rendered by this visualization type will include all columns unless they're limited by the `project` operator or other functions that redefine the output.

The next visualization type is called **pie chart**.

Visualizing as a pie chart

Pie charts are useful when you want to present the distribution of data as percentages of the sum of all values. In many cases, pie charts consist of two values – label and value. You can visualize the data from your Kusto query as a pie chart with the following syntax:

```
VeryImportantTable
| summarize ProjectCount=count() by ProjectName
| render piechart
```

As a result, you'd get a pie chart that tells you the percentage of the total records that are generated by a given project.

Let's now check how visualizing as a **bar chart** works in Kusto.

Visualizing as a bar chart

Bar charts can be used in scenarios where you want to compare exact values with each other to have a better understanding of their distribution in the context of a selected category (such as the datetime or numeric data type).

The syntax for this type of visualization is slightly different:

```
VeryImportantTable
| summarize ProjectCount=count() by ProjectName
| project ProjectName, ProjectCount
| render barchart
```

In the preceding example, we are using `ProjectName` as the *yaxis* and `ProjectCount` as the *xaxis*. If we want to control the details of the generated chart, we could use additional options:

```
VeryImportantTable
| summarize ProjectCount=count() by ProjectName
| project ProjectName, ProjectCount
| render barchart
  With (
  xaxis="Projects",
  yaxis="Project count"
  )
```

Bar charts can also be rendered as stacked using additional options:

```
VeryImportantTable
| summarize ProjectCount=count() by ProjectName
| project ProjectName, ProjectCount
| render barchart
  With (
  xaxis="Projects",
  yaxis="Project count",
  kind=stacked
  )
```

Use these options depending on your use case. To learn more about the `render` operator, take a look at the documentation available at `https://learn.microsoft.com/en-us/azure/data-explorer/kusto/query/renderoperator?pivots=azuremonitor`. It contains useful information about additional visualization types, advanced scenarios, and gotchas that you may face when working with Kusto.

If you struggle with learning the language, check out this excellent introduction with a couple of exercises: `https://learn.microsoft.com/en-us/training/modules/write-first-query-kusto-query-language/`.

Let's now proceed to the summary of this chapter to see what we've learned.

Summary

In *Chapter 14*, we looked at Azure Log Analytics and its more detailed configuration, deployment, and integration options. We also discussed the fundamentals of the Kusto language, which is one of the most important topics when working with this Azure service. Remember that Kusto is not an easy topic – it requires lots of experience and skill to use it to your benefit. However, it's worth spending some time learning it, as it'll help you find necessary information quickly, especially when your infrastructure is integrated with Log Analytics workspaces using diagnostic settings.

Lessons included in this chapter should provide an additional view of Log Analytics and its place in your architecture. They should also help you gain a better understanding of monitoring in Azure in general, especially having Kusto in mind as your solution to query aggregated data.

In the last chapter of this book, we'll take a look at **Network Watcher** – a native Azure solution that can be used to understand network traffic and data flows in your infrastructure.

15

Exploring Network Watcher

The last chapter of this book will introduce you to the topic of **Network Watcher**. So far, in this book, we have worked with networking components (such as **virtual networks**, **load balancers**, and **network security groups**) by provisioning and configuring them. We also covered **diagnostic settings**, which allow us to export logs from a service to another component (such as Log Analytics, Azure Event Hub, or Azure Storage), which can be of use when investigating issues and auditing resources. However, none of those solutions covered give you the ability to check network traffic and analyze it. To do so, you need to leverage an optional capability of the Azure networking components called Network Watcher.

In this chapter, we'll look at how to enable, configure, and work with Network Watcher. The information contained within this chapter will help you be more confident when working with networks in Azure and will simplify the analysis and debugging of network flows.

In this chapter, we'll cover the following four different topics:

- Getting started – an overview of Network Watcher
- Verifying flows
- Diagnosing next hops
- Visualizing the network topology

Technical requirements

For the exercises from this chapter, you'll need the following:

- The Azure CLI (`https://learn.microsoft.com/en-us/cli/azure/install-azure-cli`)
- A command line of any kind (either the one available in your operating system by default or your personal preference)

The Code in Action video for this book can be viewed at: `https://packt.link/GTX9F`

Getting started – an overview of Network Watcher

As mentioned at the beginning of this chapter, Network Watcher is an additional component that you can leverage when working with networking in Azure. Because networking is an area that is difficult to manage and debug in the cloud (due to the lack of access to the hardware and the use of virtualized network devices), sometimes you may struggle to find the root cause of an issue or track packets being transported over your resources. This is where Network Watcher comes in handy – it covers areas including diagnostics, metrics, and monitoring to help you troubleshoot issues with connectivity, VPNs, and network security groups, and can even capture network packets. Let's see what tools are available when working with Network Watcher.

Network Watcher toolset

As already pointed out, Network Watcher offers a variety of different tools that you can use to work with your network. For our examination, we will divide these Network Watcher tools into different groups of functionality – **monitoring**, **network diagnostics**, **traffic analysis**, and **network usage**. We'll start by describing the monitoring capabilities, which is the most common scenario for using Network Watcher.

Monitoring in Network Watcher

In the context of monitoring, Network Watcher can be used to check the topology of your network and monitor connections. Examining the topology of a network allows you to understand what resources are deployed in your network and how all the elements of the network relate to each other (i.e., what is deployed within the network, where are those resources deployed, which ports are used, and what the health status of a resource is).

Connection monitoring is a slightly more advanced feature of Network Watcher as it may require you to install Network Watcher Agent on a machine so that Network Watcher can recognize and monitor it. This is, of course, only true for **Infrastructure-as-a-Service** (**IaaS**) components of your system; as for PaaS or SaaS resources, there's no need to install anything (Network Watcher can recognize these services on its own).

> **Important note**
> For on-premises setups, Network Watcher requires you to install the Log Analytics agent and then enable **Network Performance Monitor**. You're unable to use Network Watcher Agent with on-premises machines as opposed to Azure VMs hosted within a cloud infrastructure.

Let's check now how we can use Network Watcher for network diagnostics.

Network diagnostics in Network Watcher

Network Watcher offers a variety of features when it comes to network diagnostics in Azure:

- **IP flow verify**
- **NSG diagnostics**
- **Next hop**
- **Effective security rules**
- **Connection troubleshoot**
- **Packet capture**
- **VPN troubleshoot**

It also provides features useful for monitoring and analysis scenarios, including flow logs (for both network security groups and virtual networks) and traffic analysis (which integrates with flow logs and helps in understanding hot spots and general traffic patterns in the network).

As you can see, there is a selection of very different functionalities to cover an array of scenarios. Of course, you're not forced to leverage all of them – some of those capabilities may be more useful to you than others (for instance, if you don't use a VPN, there's no need to use VPN troubleshooting). The benefit of Network Watcher is that its features can be used and enabled anytime; there's no additional charge for using a particular functionality that you're not utilizing right now.

> **Important note**
> Network Watcher is billed separately from other network charges. As of today, it offers a free tier for some of its features, which includes 5 GB of network logs collected per month, 1,000 checks for network diagnostics per month, and 10 tests per month for connection monitoring.

We'll cover some of those features (mainly IP flow verify and next hop) in the following parts of this chapter as they offer the most useful functionalities. Before we move on, let's talk about one more area of Network Watcher, which allows us to analyze usage and quotas in our network.

Usage and quotas in Network Watcher

A useful feature of Network Watcher called *Usage + quotas* allows us to understand the utilization of networking components within our Azure subscriptions. Remember that each subscription has a certain quota in terms of the number and types of deployed resources. When planning bigger deployments, it's always a good idea to look at the status of your quotas to have a better understanding of the current state of your subscription.

> **Important note**
> Remember that Azure has both soft and hard limits for resources. In some scenarios, you can increase a given quota by contacting Azure Support. This is, of course, true only for soft limits; for increases to hard limits, cases must be discussed individually with Azure Support, and there's no guarantee you'll be able to go above the limit.

So far, we have discussed some basics of Network Watcher, including an introduction to its main features. Let's now get to grips with it via an example, leveraging one of its features called IP flow verify.

Verifying flows

Network Watcher can be used to verify traffic flows inside your network using a feature called IP flow verify. It's meant to be used with Azure Virtual Machines, and its main purpose is to validate the network rules applicable to a given machine. Conceptually, it's a simple feature – all you need is to configure the correct machine, IP, and ports you'd like to verify. In the Azure portal, it looks like this:

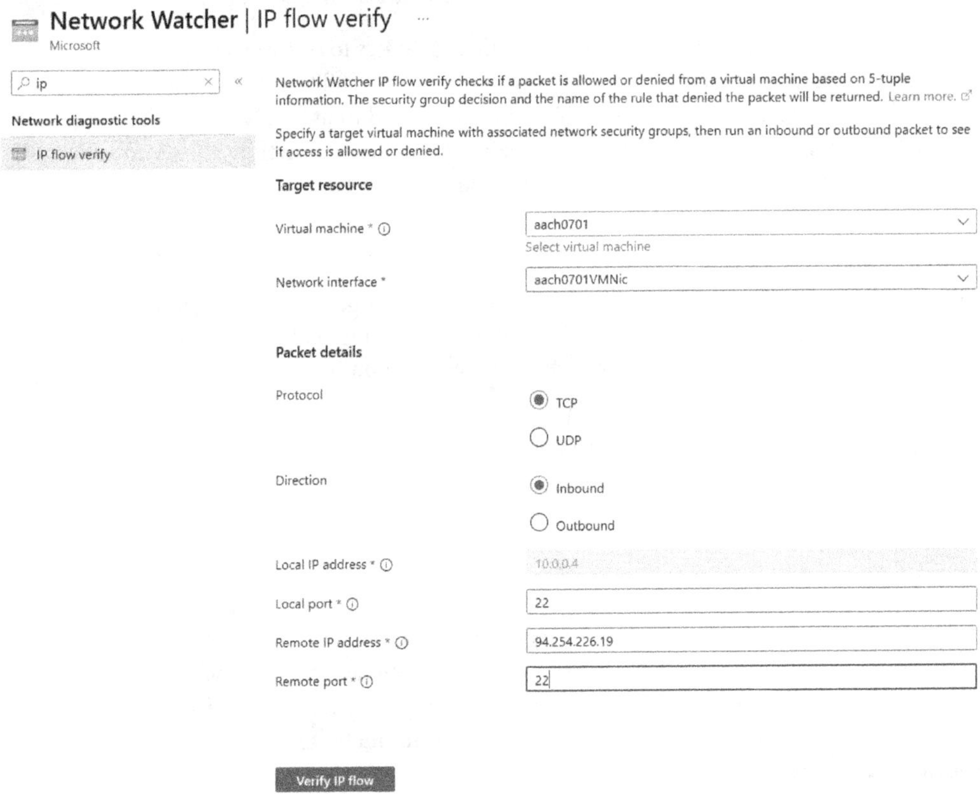

Figure 15.1 – IP flow verify screen in the Azure portal

If the connection is allowed, you'll be notified about it as follows:

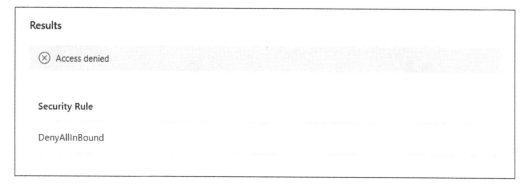

Figure 15.2 – Result of running IP flow verify when a connection is accepted

However, if a connection cannot be established (for instance, because of existing rules in the network security group assigned to the network interface of a machine), you'll get information on what is blocking it (see *Figure 15.3*):

Results

Access denied

Security Rule

DenyAllInBound

Figure 15.3 – Failed verification due to NSG rule

In *Figure 15.3*, the connection is blocked due to the DenyAllInBound rule, which is a default rule on the network security group level. As there's no other information included (which would imply that there's a more specific rule blocking the connection), it means that this is the only security rule related to inbound connections. If you'd like to allow a connection, you'd need to add a single security rule to the network security group to override the default one (DenyAllInBound). In general, IP flow verify is a helpful feature of Network Watcher to quickly check whether you're able to connect to a machine. It's especially useful in scenarios where you have lots of machines with multiple network interfaces and security groups. It saves time when debugging and can quickly point you in the right direction.

Let's check now how Network Watcher can help us diagnose the next hops.

Diagnosing next hops

When running diagnostics on network traffic, sometimes you need to understand what stands between a virtual machine and the traffic destination. To analyze that, Network Watcher offers a feature called *Next hop*. To use it, you need to go to the **Next hop** blade in the Azure portal and configure the machine you'd like to check. In the Azure portal, it looks like this:

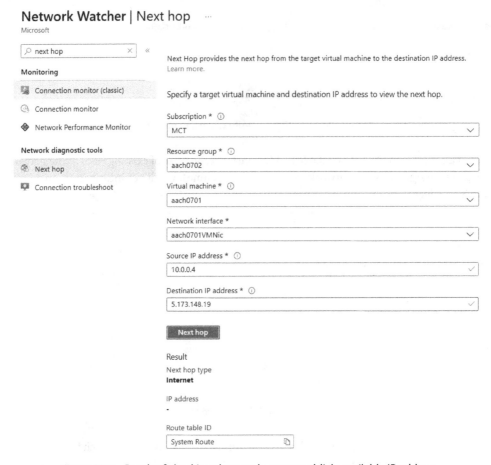

Figure 15.4 – Result of checking the next hop to a publicly available IP address

The hop type presented by the feature depends on your machine's network configuration and the IP address selected as the destination. As of now, the following next hop types are supported:

- **Internet**
- **VirtualNetwork**
- **VirtualNetworkPeering**
- **VirtualNetworkServiceEndpoint**
- **MicrosoftEdge**

- **VirtualAppliance**

- **VirtualNetworkGateway**

- **None**

All of these types come from the route table selected by your machine. The default system routes are **VirtualNetwork**, **Internet**, and **None**. The rest are added depending on the capabilities you enable (such as a service endpoint).

The *Next hop* feature can be used in scenarios where you want to analyze routing issues in a machine and would like to understand which route table and hop are selected for outgoing connections.

Let's now move on to the last topic of this chapter, where we'll learn about visualizing network topologies using Network Watcher.

Visualizing the network topology

When working with a network in Azure, you may want to better understand its structure (or just validate it) by checking the components visually. A visualization feature is available in the **Topology** blade when you access your instance of Network Watcher. In the Azure portal, it looks like this:

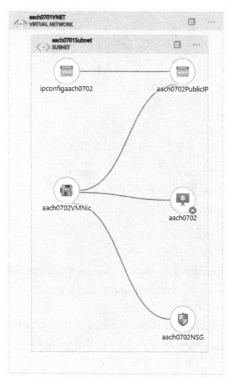

Figure 15.5 – High-level visualization of an Azure VM with its network interface

Visualizing a network topology allows you to understand how different components are connected to each other. Network Watcher enables you to visualize different levels of detail by diving deeper into a given component (see *Figure 15.6*):

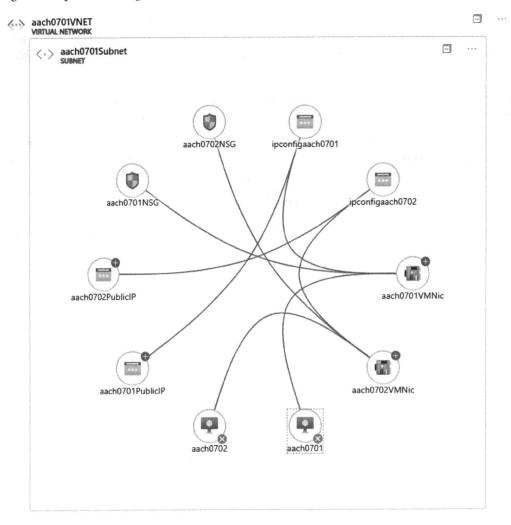

Figure 15.6 – Topology of a network interface integrated with a virtual
machine, network security group, and public IP address

This feature is helpful to quickly validate the state of your network and what exactly is deployed on it. It can also be helpful in some debugging scenarios, as it allows you to check whether a given component is correctly connected (for instance, you may expect network security groups to be assigned to a subnet, but the topology visualization might show that they're assigned to network interfaces).

> **Tip**
>
> Topologies can be exported as SVG files for other uses. To do so, click on the **Download topology** button, as displayed in *Figure 15.5*.

That's all the topics that we'll cover in this chapter. In a moment, we'll wrap up everything we've learned and summarize everything covered in this book.

Summary

Chapter 15 was a short introduction to Network Watcher, which is a useful service for everyone working with networks in Azure. We explained the features it offers and looked at its most interesting capabilities (namely, verifying flows, checking next hops, and visualizing the topology of your networks). I strongly recommend playing around with the service a bit to properly understand everything it offers.

The topics covered in this chapter will help you when you're tasked with debugging or validating network connections in Azure. Not everything can be checked using Network Watcher (it's still a managed service), but it does come in handy when checking resources such as network security groups or troubleshooting VPN connections.

This was the last chapter of this book. Throughout all of the chapters, we covered lots of different topics, starting with an introduction to Azure, its structure, and its main APIs. We learned how to provision resources using the CLI and the Infrastructure-as-Code approach. We also talked about networking, security, and identity in Azure. Even though all those concepts are crucial in the day-to-day work of Azure administrators, they essentially serve as the foundation for more advanced architectures and development tasks, meaning the topics presented in this book are universal in application and can be leveraged in multiple scenarios.

When working with Azure, don't hesitate to consult the documentation if you aren't certain about a setting or a concept. Azure is a dynamic and difficult environment with lots of its services changing constantly. It's impossible to remember everything that this cloud platform has to offer. That's why the best way to learn it is to practice – which, hopefully, this book has helped you with.

Index

`packtpub.com`

Subscribe to our online digital library for full access to over 7,000 books and videos, as well as industry leading tools to help you plan your personal development and advance your career. For more information, please visit our website.

Why subscribe?

- Spend less time learning and more time coding with practical eBooks and Videos from over 4,000 industry professionals
- Improve your learning with Skill Plans built especially for you
- Get a free eBook or video every month
- Fully searchable for easy access to vital information
- Copy and paste, print, and bookmark content

Did you know that Packt offers eBook versions of every book published, with PDF and ePub files available? You can upgrade to the eBook version at `packtpub.com` and as a print book customer, you are entitled to a discount on the eBook copy. Get in touch with us at `customercare@packtpub.com` for more details.

At `www.packtpub.com`, you can also read a collection of free technical articles, sign up for a range of free newsletters, and receive exclusive discounts and offers on Packt books and eBooks.

Other Books You May Enjoy

If you enjoyed this book, you may be interested in these other books by Packt:

Cloud Penetration Testing for Red Teamers

Kim Crawley

ISBN: 978-1-80324-848-6

- Familiarize yourself with the evolution of cloud networks
- Navigate and secure complex environments that use more than one cloud service
- Conduct vulnerability assessments to identify weak points in cloud configurations
- Secure your cloud infrastructure by learning about common cyber attack techniques
- Explore various strategies to successfully counter complex cloud attacks
- Delve into the most common AWS, Azure, and GCP services and their applications for businesses
- Understand the collaboration between red teamers, cloud administrators, and other stakeholders for cloud pentesting

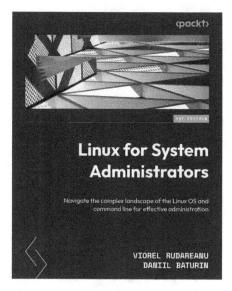

Linux for System Administrators

Viorel Rudareanu, Daniil Baturin

ISBN: 978-1-80324-794-6

- Master the use of the command line and adeptly manage software packages
- Manage users and groups locally or by using centralized authentication
- Set up, diagnose, and troubleshoot Linux networks
- Understand how to choose and manage storage devices and filesystems
- Implement enterprise features such as high availability and automation tools
- Pick up the skills to keep your Linux system secure

Packt is searching for authors like you

If you're interested in becoming an author for Packt, please visit `authors.packtpub.com` and apply today. We have worked with thousands of developers and tech professionals, just like you, to help them share their insight with the global tech community. You can make a general application, apply for a specific hot topic that we are recruiting an author for, or submit your own idea.

Share Your Thoughts

Now you've finished *Learn Azure Administration – Second Edition,* we'd love to hear your thoughts! Scan the QR code below to go straight to the Amazon review page for this book and share your feedback or leave a review on the site that you purchased it from.

https://packt.link/r/1837636117

Your review is important to us and the tech community and will help us make sure we're delivering excellent quality content.

Download a free PDF copy of this book

Thanks for purchasing this book!

Do you like to read on the go but are unable to carry your print books everywhere?

Is your eBook purchase not compatible with the device of your choice?

Don't worry, now with every Packt book you get a DRM-free PDF version of that book at no cost.

Read anywhere, any place, on any device. Search, copy, and paste code from your favorite technical books directly into your application.

The perks don't stop there, you can get exclusive access to discounts, newsletters, and great free content in your inbox daily

Follow these simple steps to get the benefits:

1. Scan the QR code or visit the link below

https://packt.link/free-ebook/9781837636112

2. Submit your proof of purchase
3. That's it! We'll send your free PDF and other benefits to your email directly

www.ingramcontent.com/pod-product-compliance
Lightning Source LLC
Chambersburg PA
CBHW080619060326
40690CB00021B/4752